COME OUT WRITING

Andy Macpherson

COME OUT WRITING
A BOXING ANTHOLOGY

EDITED BY
BILL HUGHES AND PATRICK KING

MAINSTREAM
PUBLISHING

EDINBURGH AND LONDON

Published in Great Britain in 1999 by
MAINSTREAM PUBLISHING COMPANY (EDINBURGH) LTD
7 Albany Street
Edinburgh EH1 3UG

First published in 1991 by Queen Anne Press, a division of
Macdonald & Co (Publishers) Ltd in Great Britain

ISBN 1 84018 206 7

A catalogue record for this book is available from the British Library

Typeset in Berkeley Book
Printed and bound in Finland by WSOY

ACKNOWLEDGEMENTS

The editors wish to extend a very special word of thanks to the following for their invaluable assistance and advice in the compilation of this book.

José Torres, Bert Randolph Sugar (editor, *Boxing Illustrated*), Frank Butler, Harry Mullan (editor, *Boxing News*), George Zeleny (editor, *Boxing Monthly*) and Bob Decker (sports editor, *New York Post*).

CONTENTS

INTRODUCTION

The professional boxer, with a few rare and honourable exceptions, is not generally noted for his cogent and articulate use of language. Perhaps not surprisingly, for like the professional soldier, with whom he has much in common, he is essentially a man of action. Highly trained and motivated, his sole object is to cause as much damage as possible to the enemy at the least possible cost to his own physical well-being. Deeds not words are his stock-in-trade. Fortunately, however, throughout the history of boxing, there has always been a writer on hand to chronicle the passing scene. From the early bare-knuckle days of Pierce Egan's *Boxiana*, through the golden eras of Corbett and FitzSimmons, of Dempsey and Tunney, of Louis and Marciano and the great Muhammad Ali, the tradition continues. Even in this age of worldwide television coverage, instant replays and multi-million-dollar purses, the ringside reporter still sets down his version of that unique 'one-on-one' combat that constitutes the last vestige of the gladiatorial spirit.

For the first time in a single volume this book brings together some of the best that has been written, down the years, on the subject of boxing. Some of these writers are household names. Not all of them are boxing specialists. However, they do have something in common: a love of the 'manly art' and an uncommon ability to convey the essence of that sport which has been called 'the hardest game'.

P.J. King

PROLOGUE

A Matter of Ego

On Boxing

Joyce Carol Oates

> *We fighters understand lies.*
> *What's a feint?*
> *What's a left hook off the jab?*
> *What's an opening? What's thinking one thing*
> *and doing another . . . ?*
>
> > *José Torres,* former light heavyweight champion of the world

One of the primary things boxing is about is lying. It's about systematically cultivating a double personality: the self in society, the self in the ring. As the chess grandmaster channels his powerful aggressive impulses on to the game board, which is the world writ small, so the 'born' boxer channels his strength into the ring, against the opponent. And in the ring, if he is a good boxer and not a mere journeyman, he will cultivate yet another split personality, to thwart the opponent's game plan vis-à-vis *him.* Boxers, like chess players, must think on their feet – must be able to improvise in mid-fight, so to speak. (And surely it is championship chess, and not boxing, that is our most dangerous game – at least so far as psychological risk is concerned. Megalomania and psychosis frequently await the grandmaster when his extraordinary mental powers can no longer be discharged on to the chessboard.)

After his upset victory against WBC junior welterweight Billy Costello in August 1985, the virtually unknown 'Lightning' Lonnie Smith told an interviewer for *The Ring* that his model for boxing was that of a chess game: boxing is a 'game of control, and, as in chess, this control can radiate in circles *from* the centre, or in circles *towards* the centre . . . The entire action of a fight goes in a circle; it can be little circles in the middle of the ring or big circles along the ropes, but always a circle. The man who wins is the man who controls the action of the circle.' Smith's ring style against Costello was so brazenly idiosyncratic – reminiscent at moments of both Muhammad Ali and Jersey Joe Walcott – that the hitherto undefeated Costello, known as a hard puncher, was totally demoralised, outclassed, outboxed. (As he was outfought some months later by a furious Alexis Arguello, who 'retired' Costello from the ring.)

Cassius Clay/Muhammad Ali, that most controversial of champions, was primarily a brilliant ring strategist, a prodigy in his youth whose fast hands and feet made him virtually impossible for opponents to hit. What joy in the young Ali: in the inimitable arrogance of a heavyweight who danced about his puzzled opponents with his gloves at waist level, inviting them to hit him – to try it. (What joy, at any rate, in the Ali of films and tapes, even if in sombre juxtaposition to the Ali of the present time, overweight, even puffy, his speech and reactions slowed by Parkinson's disease.) It was the young boxer's style when confronted with a 'deadly' puncher like Sonny Liston to simply out-think and manoeuvre him: never before, and never since, has a heavyweight performed in the ring with such style – an inimitable combination of intelligence, wit, grace, irreverence, cunning. So dazzlingly talented was Ali in his youth that it wasn't clear whether in fact he had what boxers call 'heart' – the ability to keep fighting when one has been hurt. In later years, when Ali's speed was diminished, a new and more complex, one might say a greater, boxer emerged, as in the trilogy of fights with Joe Frazier, the first of which Ali lost.

Sugar Ray Leonard, the most charismatic of post-Ali boxers, cultivated a ring style that was a quicksilver balance of opposites, with an overlay of streetwise, playful arrogance (reminiscent, indeed, of Ali) and, for all Leonard's talent, it was only in his most arduous matches (with Hearns and Duran) that it became clear how intelligently ferocious a boxer he really was. Losing once to Duran, he could not lose a second time: his pride would not allow it. Just as pride would not allow Leonard to continue boxing when he suspected he had passed his peak. (Though at the time of this writing Leonard has publicly declared that he wants to return for one major match: he is the only man who knows how to beat Marvin Hagler. A matter of ego, Leonard says, as if we needed to be told.)

The self in society, the self in the ring. But there are many selves and there are of course many boxers – ranging from the shy, introverted, painfully inarticulate Johnny Owen (the Welsh bantamweight who died after a bout with Lupe Pintor in 1979) to the frequently manic Muhammad Ali in his prime (Ali whom Norman Mailer compared to a six-foot parrot who keeps screaming at you that he is the centre of the stage: 'Come here and get me, fool. You can't, 'cause you don't know who I am'); from the legendary bluster of John L. Sullivan to the relative modesty of Rocky Marciano and Floyd Patterson. (Patterson, the youngest man to win the heavyweight title, is said to have been a non-violent person who once helped an opponent pick up his mouthpiece from the canvas. 'I don't like to see blood,' Patterson explained. 'It's different when I bleed, that doesn't bother me because I can't see it.' He was no match physically or otherwise for the next heavyweight champion, Sonny Liston.) For every boxer with the reputation of a Roberto Duran there are surely a dozen who are simply 'nice guys' – Ray Mancini, Milton McCory, Mark Breland, Gene Hatcher, among many others. Before he lost decisive matches and began the downward trajectory of his career, the young Chicago middleweight John Collins was frequently promoted as a veritable split personality, a Dr Jekyll and Mr Hyde of the ring: the essential (and surely disingenuous) question being, How can a nice courteous young man like you turn so vicious in the ring? Collins's answer was straightforward enough: 'When I'm in the ring I'm fighting for my life.'

It might be theorised that fighting activates in certain people not only an adrenaline rush of exquisite pleasure but an atavistic self that, coupled with an instinctive sort of tissue-intelligence, a neurological swiftness unknown to 'average' men and women, makes for the born fighter, the potentially great champion, the *unmistakably* gifted boxer. An outlaw or non-law self, given the showy accolade 'killer instinct'. (Though to speak of instinct is always to speak vaguely: for how can 'instinct' be isolated from the confluence of factors – health, economic class, familial relations, sheer good or bad luck – that determine a life?) You know the boxer with the killer instinct when the crowd jumps to its feet in a groundswell of delirium in response to his assault against his opponent, no matter if the opponent is the favourite, a 'nice guy' no one really wants to see seriously injured.

There is an instinct in our species to fight but is there an instinct to *kill*? And would a 'born' killer have the discipline, let alone the moral integrity, to subordinate himself to boxing's rigours in order to exercise it? Surely there are easier ways: we read about them in the daily newspaper. That the fighter, like the crowd he embodies, responds excitedly to the sight of blood – 'first blood' being a term from the days of the English prize ring – goes without saying; but there are often fight fans shouting for a match to be stopped at the very zenith of the action. My sense of the boxing crowd in a large arena like Madison Square Garden is that it resembles a massive wave containing counterwaves, countercurrents, isolated but bold voices that resist the greater motion toward ecstatic violence. These dissenters are severely critical of referees who allow fights to go on too long.

I seem to recall my father urging a fight to be stopped: 'It's over! It's over! What's the point!' Was it Marciano battering an opponent into submission, or Carmen Basilio? 'Kid' Gavilan? A long time ago, and in our home, the bloody match broadcast over television, hence sanitised. One cannot really imagine the impact of blows on another man's head and body by way of the television screen in its eerily flattened dimensions . . .

Granted these points, it is nonetheless true that the boxer who functions as a conduit through which the inchoate aggressions of the crowd are consummated will be a very popular boxer indeed. Not the conscientious 'boxing' matches but the cheek-by-jowl brawls are likely to be warmly recalled in boxing legend: Dempsey–Firpo, Louis–Schmeling II, Zale–Graziano, Robinson–LaMotta, Pep–Saddler, Marciano–Charles, Ali–Frazier, most recently Hagler-Hearns. Sonny Liston occupies a position *sui generis* for the very truculence of his boxing persona – the air of unsmiling menace he presented to the Negro no less than the white world. (Liston was arrested nineteen times and served two prison terms, the second term for armed robbery.) It may be that former champion Larry Holmes saw himself in this role, the black man's black man empowered by sheer bitterness to give hurt where hurt is due. And, for a while, the Rastafarian Livingstone Bramble, whose vendetta with Ray Mancini seems to have sprung from an unmotivated ill will.

The only self-confessed murderer of boxing distinction seems to have been the welterweight champion Don Jordan (1958–60) who claimed to have been a hired assassin as a boy in his native

Dominican Republic. 'What's wrong with killing a human?' Jordan asked rhetorically in an interview. 'The first time you kill someone, you throw up, you get sick as a dog . . . The second time, no feeling.' According to his testimony Jordan killed or helped to kill more than thirty men in the Dominican Republic, without being caught. (He seems in fact to have been in the hire of the government.) After Jordan and his family moved to California he killed a man for 'personal' reasons, for which crime he was sent to reform school, aged fourteen: 'I burned a man like an animal . . . I staked him to the ground. I wired his hands and his arms, and I put paper around him and I burnt him like an animal. They said, "You are mentally sick."' In reform school Jordan was taught how to box: entered the Golden Gloves tournament and won all his matches, and eventually competed in the Olympics, where he did less well. Under the aegis of the Cosa Nostra he turned professional and his career, though meteoric, was short-lived.

In Jake LaMotta's autobiography *Raging Bull* LaMotta attributes his success as a boxer – he was middleweight champion briefly, 1949–51, but a popular fighter for many years – to the fact that he didn't care whether he was killed in the ring. For eleven years he mistakenly believed he had murdered a man in a robbery and, unconfessed, yet guilty, wanting to be punished, LaMotta threw himself into boxing as much to be hurt as to hurt. His background parallels Rocky Graziano's – they were friends, as boys, in reform school – but his desperation was rather more intense than Graziano's (whose autobiography is entitled *Somebody Up There Likes Me*: a most optimistic assumption). LaMotta said in an interview: 'I would fight anybody. I didn't care who they were. I even wanted to fight Joe Louis. I just didn't care . . . But that made me win. It gave me an aggression my opponents never saw before. They would hit me. I didn't care if I got hit.' When LaMotta eventually learned that his victim had not died, however, his zest for boxing waned, and his career began its abrupt decline. By way of LaMotta's confession and the film based fragmentarily on it, *Raging Bull*, LaMotta has entered boxing folklore: he is the flashy gutter fighter whose integrity will allow him to throw only one fight (in an era in which fights were routinely thrown), done with such ironic disdain that the boxing commission suspends his licence.

Traditionally, boxing is credited with changing the lives of ghetto-born or otherwise impoverished youths. It is impossible to gauge how many boxers have in fact risen from such beginnings but one might guess it to be about ninety-nine per cent – even at the present time. (Muhammad Ali is said to have been an exception in that his background was not one of desperate poverty: which helps to account, perhaps, for Ali's early boundless confidence.) Where tennis lessons were offered in some youth centres in the Detroit area, many years ago, boxing lessons were offered in Joe Louis's and Ray Robinson's neighbourhood – of course. To what purpose would poor black boys learn tennis? LaMotta, Graziano, Patterson, Liston, Hector Camacho, Mike Tyson – all learned to box in captivity, so to speak. (Liston, a more advanced criminal than the others, began taking boxing lessons while serving his second term for armed robbery in the Missouri State Penitentiary.) Boxing is the moral equivalent of war of which, in a radically different context, William James spoke, and it has the virtue – how American, this virtue – of making a good deal of money for its practitioners and promoters, not all of whom are white.

Indeed, one of the standard arguments for not abolishing boxing is in fact that it provides an outlet for the rage of disenfranchised youths, mainly black or Hispanic, who can make lives for themselves by way of fighting one another instead of fighting society.

The disputable term 'killer instinct' was coined in reference to Jack Dempsey in his prime: in his famous early matches with Jess Willard, Georges Carpentier, Luis Firpo ('The Wild Bull of the Pampas'), and other lesser-known boxers whom he savagely and conclusively beat. Has there ever been a fighter quite like the young Dempsey – the very embodiment, it seems, of hunger, rage, the will to do hurt; the spirit of the Western frontier come East to win his fortune. The crudest of nightmare figures, Dempsey is gradually refined into an American myth of comforting dimensions. The killer in the ring becomes the New York restaurateur, a business success, 'the gentlest of men'.

Dempsey was the ninth of eleven children born to an impoverished Mormon sharecropper and itinerant railroad worker in Colorado, who soon left home, bummed his way around the mining camps and small towns of the West, began fighting for money when he was hardly more than a boy. It was said in awe of Dempsey that his very sparring partners were in danger of being seriously injured – Dempsey didn't like to share the ring with anyone. If he remains the most spectacular (and most loved) champion in history it is partly because he fought when boxing rules were rather casual by our standards; when, for instance, a boxer was allowed to strike an opponent as he struggled to his feet – as in the bizarre Willard bout, and the yet more bizarre bout with Luis Firpo, set beside which present-day heavyweight matches like those of Holmes and Spinks are minuets. Where aggression has to be cultivated in some champion boxers (Tunney, for example) Dempsey's aggression was direct and natural: in the ring, he seems to have wanted to kill his opponent. The swiftness of his attack, his disdain for strategies of defence, endeared him to greatly aroused crowds who had never seen anything quite like him before.

(Dempsey's first title fight, in 1919, against the ageing champion Jess Willard, was called at the time 'pugilistic murder' and would certainly be stopped in the first round – in the first thirty seconds of the first round – today. Badly out of condition, heavier than the twenty-four-year-old Dempsey by seventy pounds, the thirty-seven-year-old Willard put up virtually no defence against the challenger. Though films of the match show an astonishingly resilient, if not foolhardy, Willard picking himself up off the canvas repeatedly as Dempsey knocks him down, by the end of the fight Willard's jaw was broken, his cheekbone split, nose smashed, six teeth broken off at the gum, an eye was battered shut, much damage done to his lower body. Both boxers were covered in Willard's blood. Years later Dempsey's estranged manager Kearns confessed, perhaps fraudulently, that he had 'loaded' Dempsey's gloves – treated his hand tape with a talcum substance that turned hard as concrete when wet.)

It was Dempsey's ring style – swift, pitiless, always direct and percussive – that changed American boxing forever. Even Jack Johnson appears stately by contrast.

So far as 'killer instinct' is concerned, Joe Louis was an anomaly, which no biography of his life – even the most recent, the meticulously researched *Champion – Joe Louis, Black Hero in White America* by Chris Mead – has ever quite explained. If, indeed, one can explain any of our motives, except in the most sweeping psychological and sociological terms. Louis was a modest and self-effacing man outside the ring, but, in the ring, a machine of sorts for hitting – so (apparently) emotionless that even sparring partners were spooked by him. 'It's the eyes,' one said. 'They're blank and staring, always watching you. That blank look – that's what gets you down.' Unlike his notorious predecessor Jack Johnson and his yet more notorious successor Muhammad Ali, Joe Louis was forced to live his 'blackness' in secret, if at all; to be a *black* hero in *white* America at the time of Louis's coming-of-age cannot have been an easy task. Louis's deadpan expression and his killer's eyes were very likely aspects of the man's strategy rather than reliable gauges of his psyche. And his descent into mental imbalance – paranoia, in particular – in his later years was surely a consequence of the pressures he endured, if not an outsized, but poetically valid, response to the very real scrutiny of others focused upon him for decades.

One of the most controversial of boxing legends has to do with the death of Benny 'Kid' Paret at the hands of Emile Griffith in a welterweight match in Madison Square Garden in 1962. According to the story, Paret provoked Griffith at their weigh-in by calling him '*maricón*' (faggot), and was in effect killed by Griffith in the ring that night. Recalling the event years later Griffith said he was only following his trainer's instructions – to hit Paret, to hurt Paret, to keep punching Paret until the referee made him stop. By which time, as it turned out, Paret was virtually dead. (He died about ten days later.) Though there are other boxing experts, present at the match, who insist that Paret's death was accidental: it 'just happened'.

At the present time boxing matches are usually monitored by referees and ringside physicians with extreme caution: a recent match between welterweights Don Curry and James Green was stopped by the referee because Green, temporarily disabled, had lowered his gloves and *might have been hit;* a match between heavyweights Mike Weaver and Michael Dokes was stopped within two minutes of the first round, before the luckless Weaver had time to begin. With some exceptions – the Sandoval–Canizales and the Bramble–Crawley title fights come most immediately to mind – referees have been assuming ever greater authority in the ring so that it sometimes seems that the drama of boxing has begun to shift: not will X knock out his opponent, but will the referee stop the fight before he can do so. In the most violent fights the predominant image is that of the referee hovering at the periphery of the action, stepping in to embrace a weakened or defenceless man in a gesture of paternal solicitude. This image carries much emotional power – not so sensational as the killing blow but suggestive, perhaps, that the ethics of the ring have evolved to approximate the ethics of everyday life. It is as if, in mythical terms, brothers whose mysterious animosity has brought them to battle are saved – absolved of their warriors' enmity – by the wisdom of their father and protector. One came away from the eight-minute Hagler–Hearns fight with the vision of the dazed Hearns, on his feet but not fully conscious, saved by referee Richard Steele from what would have been serious injury, if not death – considering the extraordinary ferocity of Hagler's fighting that night, and the personal rage he seems to have brought to it. ('This was war,' Hagler said.) The fight ends with Hearns in Steele's embrace: tragedy narrowly averted. Of course there are many who disdain such developments. It's the *feminisation* of the sport, they say.

No American sport or activity has been so consistently and so passionately under attack as boxing, for 'moral' as well as other reasons. And no American sport evokes so ambivalent a response in its defenders: when asked the familiar question 'How can you watch . . .?' the boxing *aficionado* really has no answer. He can talk about boxing only with others like himself.

In December 1984 the American Medical Association passed a resolution calling for the abolition of boxing on the principle that while other sports involve as much, or even more, risk to life and health – the most dangerous sports being football, auto racing, hang gliding, mountain climbing and ice hockey, with boxing in about seventh place – boxing is the only sport in which the objective is to cause injury: the brain is the target, the knockout the goal. In one study it was estimated that eighty-seven per cent of boxers suffer some degree of brain damage in their lifetimes, no matter the relative success of their careers. And there is the risk of serious eye injury as well. Equally disturbing, though less plausible, is sociological evidence that media attention focused on boxing has an immediate effect upon the homicide rate of the country. (According to sociologists David P. Phillips and John E. Hensley, the rate rises by an average of twelve per cent in the days following a highly publicised fight, for the hypothetical reason that the fight 'heavily rewards one person for inflicting violence on another and is at the opposite end of a continuum from a successfully prosecuted murder trial, which heavily punishes one person for inflicting physical violence on another'.) Doubtful as these findings are in a culture in which television and movie violence has become routine fare, even for young children, it does seem likely that boxing as a phenomenon *sui generis* stimulates rather than resolves certain emotions. If boxing is akin to classic tragedy in its imitation of action and of life it cannot provide the catharsis of pity and terror of which Aristotle spoke.

The variegated history of boxing reform is very likely as old as boxing itself. As I mentioned earlier, in the days of Pierce Egan's *Boxiana,* the prize ring was in fact outlawed in England – though the aristocracy, including the Prince Regent, regularly attended matches. Boxing has been intermittently illegal in various parts of the United States and campaigns are frequently launched to ban it altogether. Like abortion it seems to arouse deep and divisive emotions. (Though activists who would outlaw abortion are not necessarily those who would outlaw boxing: puritanical instincts take unpredictable forms.) The relationship between boxing and poverty is acknowledged, but no one suggests that poverty be abolished as the most practical means of abolishing boxing. So frequently do young boxers claim they are in greater danger on the street than in the ring that one has to assume they are not exaggerating for the sake of credulous white reporters.

It is objected too that boxing as a sport is closely bound up with organised crime. Investigations on the federal and state level, over the decades, but most prominently in the 1950s, have made the connection unmistakable, though the situation at any time is problematic. One wonders about 'suspicious' decisions – are they fixed, or simply the consequence of judges' prejudices? As in Michael Spinks's second, highly controversial win over Larry Holmes, for instance; and the Wilfredo Gomez–Rocky Lockridge match of May 1985 (when judges gave a world junior lightweight title to a Puerto Rican home-town favourite). And recent televised performances by former Olympic gold medalists and their handpicked opponents have struck the eye of more than one observer as not entirely convincing . . .

Not long ago I saw a film of a long-forgotten fixed fight of Willie Pep's in which Pep allowed himself to be overcome by an underdog opponent: the great featherweight performed as a boxer-turned-actor might he expected to perform, with no excess of zeal or talent. It occurred to me that boxing is so refined, yet so raw a sport that no match can be successfully thrown; the senses simply pick up on what is not happening, what is being held back, as a sort of ironic subtext to what is actually taking place. You can run but you can't hide.

Not boxing in itself but the money surrounding it, the gambling in Las Vegas, Atlantic City, and elsewhere, is the problem, and a problem not likely to be solved. I have made an attempt to read the 135-page single-spaced document *Organised Crime in Boxing: Final Boxing Report of the State of New Jersey Commission of Investigation* of December 1985 and have come to the conclusion that the Commission, which has moved to abolish boxing in New Jersey, was wrongheaded in its initial approach: it should have been investigating organised crime in New Jersey, in which Atlantic City boxing–gambling figures. That the Commission would vote to abolish boxing altogether because of criminal connections suggests a naïveté shading into sheer vindictiveness: one would then be required to abolish funeral parlours, pizzerias, trucking firms, some labour unions. And if gamblers can't gamble on boxing they will simply gamble on football, basketball, baseball – as they already do.

Since boxing has become a multi-million-dollar business under the aegis of a few canny promoters – the most visible being Don King – it is not likely that it will be abolished, in any case. It would simply be driven underground, like abortion; or exiled to Mexico, Cuba, Canada, England, Ireland, Zaïre . . . Boxing's history is one of such exigencies, fascinating for what they suggest of the compulsion of some men to fight and of others to be witnesses.

The 1896 heavyweight title match between Ruby Robert Fitzsimmons and Peter Maher, for instance, was outlawed everywhere in the States, so promoters staged it on an isolated sandbar in the Rio Grande River, 400 miles from El Paso. (Can one imagine? – 300 men made the arduous journey to witness what was surely one of the most disappointing title bouts in boxing history when Fitzsimmons knocked out Maher in ninety-five seconds.) During Jack Dempsey's prime in the 1920s boxing was outlawed in a number of states, like alcohol, and, like alcohol seems to have aroused a hysterical public enthusiasm. Dempsey's notorious five minutes with the giant Argentinian Firpo was attended by 85,000 people – most of whom could barely have seen the ring, let alone the boxers; both Dempsey's fights with Gene Tunney were attended by over 100,000 people – the first fought in a downpour during which rain fell in 'blinding sheets' for forty minutes on both boxers and onlookers alike. Photographs of these events show jammed arenas with boxing rings like postage-sized altars at their centres, the boxers themselves no more than tiny, heraldic figures. To attend a Dempsey match was not to have seen a Dempsey match, but perhaps that was not the issue.

When Jack Johnson won the heavyweight title in 1908 he had to pursue the white champion Tommy Burns all the way to Australia to confront him. The 'danger' of boxing at that time – and one of the reasons worried citizens wanted to abolish it – was that it might expose and humiliate white men in the ring. After Johnson's decisive victory over the White Hope contender Jim Jeffries there were in fact race riots and lynchings throughout the United States; even films of some of Johnson's fights were outlawed in many states. And because in recent decades boxing has become a sport in which black and Hispanic men have excelled, it is particularly vulnerable to attack by white middle-class reformers (the AMA in particular) who show very little interest in lobbying against equally dangerous Establishment sports like football, auto racing, thoroughbred horse racing.

The late Nat Fleischer, boxing expert and founder of *The Ring* magazine, once estimated that tens of thousands of injuries have occurred in the ring since the start of modern boxing in the 1890s – by 'modern' meaning the introduction of the rules of the Marquis of Queensberry requiring padded gloves, three-minute rounds, one minute's rest between rounds, continuous fighting during rounds. (The bare-knuckle era, despite its popular reputation for brutality, was far less dangerous for fighters – fists break more readily than heads.) Between 1945 and 1985 at least 370 boxers have died in the United States of injuries directly attributed to boxing. In addition to the infamous Griffith–Paret fight there have been a number of others given wide publicity: Sugar Ray Robinson killed a young boxer named Jimmy Doyle in 1947, for instance, while defending his welterweight title; Sugar Ramos won the featherweight title in 1963 by knocking out the champion Davey Moore, who never regained consciousness; Ray Mancini killed the South Korean Duk Koo-Kim in 1982; former featherweight champion Barry McGuigan killed the Nigerian Young Ali in 1983. After the death of Duk Koo-Kim the World Boxing Council shortened title bouts to twelve rounds.

In the era of marathon fights, however – 1892 to 1915 – men often fought as many as 100 rounds; the record is 110, in 1893, over a stupefying seven-hour period. The last scheduled forty-five-round championship fight was between the black titleholder Jack Johnson and his White Hope successor Willard in 1915: the match went twenty-six rounds beneath a blazing sun in Havana, Cuba, before Johnson collapsed.

To say that the rate of death and injury in the ring is not extraordinary set beside the rates of other sports is to misread the nature of the criticism brought to bear against boxing (and not against other sports). Clearly, boxing's very image is repulsive to many people because it cannot be assimilated into what we wish to know about civilised man. In a technological society possessed of incalculably refined methods of mass destruction (consider how many times over both the United States and the Soviet Union have vaporised each other in fantasy) boxing's display of direct and unmitigated and seemingly natural aggression is too explicit to be tolerated.

Which returns us to the paradox of boxing: its obsessive appeal for many who find in it not only a spectacle involving sensational feats of physical skill but an emotional experience impossible to convey in words; an art form, as I've suggested, with no natural analogue in the arts. Of course it is primitive, too, as birth, death, and erotic love might be said to be primitive, and forces our reluctant acknowledgement that the most profound experiences of our lives are physical events – though we believe ourselves to be, and surely are, essentially spiritual beings.

ROUND 1

The Once and Almost King

'Life is the best left hooker I ever saw, although some say it was Charlie White of Chicago.'

– Ernest Hemingway

When world heavyweight champion Larry Holmes successfully defended his title in a points decision over Lucien Rodríguez in Scranton, Pennsylvania, the event marked a turning-point in the history of professional boxing. The date was 27 March 1983, and the fight was the first-ever heavyweight title bout over the twelve-round limit. The classic fifteen-round confrontation which had prevailed throughout the modern era was consigned to the past, and for true boxing aficionados everywhere the sport would never be quite the same again.

Consider this: Had the twelve-round rule applied in past years, the whole history of the fight game would have been radically different. Rocky Marciano might never have been champion, Muhammad Ali might well have beaten Joe Frazier in that memorable first bout in Madison Square Garden, and Billy Conn would have most certainly wrested the heavyweight crown from the head of the great Joe Louis.

There are many such examples, but perhaps none more dramatic than that of the first Louis–Conn battle. Conn was well ahead on points as they ended the twelfth. What ensued in the following round constitutes one of the great 'might have been' stories in the history of the heavyweight division. But, more than that, it emphasises the point that not for nothing were rounds thirteen to fifteen known as 'The Championship Rounds'!

On the Waterfront

Budd Shulberg

When Charley began to talk again, he was groping, almost gasping for words, trying to work his way back toward some relationship with Terry.

'Look, kid. I – look, I . . .' He reached out and tried to squeeze the biceps of Terry's right arm, an old affectionate gesture between them. Terry neither pulled his arm away nor made it easy for Charley to reach him.

'How much you weigh these days, slugger?' Charley suddenly wanted to know.

'Seventy-five, eighty. Who cares?' Terry shrugged off his question in a sullen monotone.

'Gee, when you weighed 168 pounds you were beautiful.' Charley lapsed into the past. 'You could've been another Billy Conn. Only that skunk we got you for a manager brought you along too fast.'

Terry had been slowly shaking his head. Now the past and all the abuses it had stored up in him seemed to cry out. 'It wasn't him, Charley. It was you!'

Terry came out of his corner, leaning toward Charley, incited by the old humiliation that was like the blood from a cut that won't coagulate. 'You remember that night in the Garden? You came down to the dressing-room and said, "Kid, this ain't your night. We're goin' for the price on Wilson." You remember that? This ain't your night. My night! I could've taken Wilson apart that night. So what happens? He gets the title shot, outdoors in the ball park. And what do I get? A one-way ticket to Palookaville. I was never no good after that night. You remember that, Charley. It's like a – peak you reach, and then it's all downhill. It was you, Charley. You my brother. You should've looked out for me a little bit. You should've taken care of me. Just a little bit. Instead of makin' me take them dives for the short-end money.'

Charley wasn't able to look at Terry. 'At least I always had some bets down for you,' he said softly. 'You saw some money.'

'See you don't understand,' Terry raised his voice as if to bridge his failure to communicate.

'I tried to keep you in good with Johnny,' Charley made an effort to explain.

'You don't *understand!*' Terry cried out again. 'I could've had class. I could've been a contender. I could've been somebody. Instead of a bum, which is what I am. Oh, yes, I am. It was you, Charley.'

Black Champion in White America

Chris Mead

Joe Louis had fought six times in six months. He was tired and jaded by constant training. But Mike Jacobs [promoter] had signed Louis for another fight in June, and it was against Billy Conn, the most capable opponent Louis had faced in years. Conn grew up in the East Liberty section of Pittsburgh, an area especially hard hit by the Depression. Conn began to box professionally as a skinny sixteen-year-old. Like Louis, Conn was lucky enough to find a good trainer, Johnny Ray. 'He was drunk all the time, see,' Conn said. 'He was a Jewish guy. He's the only Jewish guy I know that was drunk all the time. But he knew more drunk than the other guys knew sober. In the corner he was always drunk.' Conn learned quickly, and after four years of boxing almost exclusively in western Pennsylvania and West Virginia, Mike Jacobs sent for Conn to fight Fred Apostoli, then the middleweight titleholder. An unknown, and a $2^{1/2}$-to-1 underdog, Conn boxed the ears off Apostoli on 6 January 1939, and won a ten-round decision. Apostoli wanted a rematch, and the two men fought again a month later, with Conn winning another decision in fifteen rounds. In July, Conn won the New York State light heavyweight championship from Melio Bettina, a title he vacated a year later to compete against the heavyweights. Conn knocked out Bob Pastor and decisioned Al McCoy to establish his credentials as a challenger. Conn never gained enough weight to be a full-fledged heavyweight, but he didn't have to. He was a remarkably quick and clever boxer, and his hands were too fast for most of his opponents. Conn was also good box office. He was a handsome Irishman with a boyish grin and just the right mixture of cockiness and youth. Mike Jacobs admitted that he would not mind if Conn beat Louis, since Conn was popular and might inject new interest into the heavyweight division Joe Louis had dominated for three years.

Jacobs and his publicists injected some hostility into the build-up, trying to arouse further public interest in the fight. Conn made appropriately brash predictions of victory. When reporters asked Louis whether he would be able to catch up with Conn's quick feet, Louis supposedly said, 'He can run, but he can't hide.' Shirley Povich insists Louis first used that line before his second fight with Bob Pastor, but the quote became part of the Louis–Conn build-up.

The Louis camp also let word out that Louis was mad at Conn for some things Conn had supposedly said while rooting for fellow Pittsburgher Fritzie Zivic over Henry Armstrong, a black fighter. The Louis entourage supposedly sat behind Conn at the fight and claimed to have heard Conn drop some racist remarks. Forty years later Billy Conn remembered all the publicity and laughed. 'I liked Joe Louis. It's all bullshit to build it up . . . We didn't call each other names. That's for kids, kids' stuff.' On 17 June, the day before the fight, newspapers picked up the story that Conn and his sweetheart, Mary Louise Smith, had applied for a marriage licence, but Miss Smith's father, a former major league baseball player, objected. The story further endeared the underdog Conn to the public.

Louis was aware of the public sentiment for Conn. He worried that if he weighed in over 200 pounds, while Conn weighed in at around 170, he would seem like a bully beating up a smaller man. So Louis, who usually took it easy on his last day of training, worked hard the day before the fight, running and going through his full routine of exercises in the gym. He also dried out, not eating, and drinking as little as possible. Louis weighed in at $199^{1/2}$ the morning of the fight. He felt tired and weak.

Watching Louis and Conn weigh in was Don Dunphy, who would announce the fight over the Mutual Radio Network that night. For years the NBC network and one sponsor, Adams Hats, had broadcast Mike Jacobs's fights. In the spring of 1941, however, Mutual and its sponsor, Gillette, outbid NBC for the broadcasting contract with Jacobs. Mutual held an audition to pick an announcer during the light heavyweight title fight between Anton Christofordis and Gus Lesnevich on 22 May. Dunphy and his competitors took turns calling the rounds. Dunphy said of the audition, 'I tell people later that the other announcers were tripping over those names, and I just called them Tony and Gus.' Dunphy won the audition, and his calm, piercing delivery became the voice of boxing during the sport's golden years.

The Louis–Conn fight was Dunphy's first big match, and as he said forty years later: 'My whole career kind of turned on this one event. . . . I went up to Louis after the weigh-in, and I said, "I want to wish you good luck tonight." He kind of surprised me; he said, "Well, I want to wish you good luck, too." He realised how important this was to me. To him it was another fight. And I thought that was very gracious of him.'

Unlike sportswriters, Dunphy and the major radio announcers of the era – Clem McCarthy, Edwin C. Hill, Ted Husing, Sam Taub, and Bill Stern – rarely identified Louis as a 'Negro' or referred to his race at all. The difference was probably due largely to the difference in the two media. Announcers usually called fighters by their first or last names and stuck with those names throughout. They didn't have the time or the need to think up variations on Louis's name. They had enough trouble trying to keep up with the action. Print journalists, with more time to think about what they were writing and with Louis's name staring at them from the previous sentence, were more likely to vary their references to Louis, and those variations often included references to his colour.

With Dunphy, a kindly man whose voice is as distinctive over the phone today as it was over the radio forty years ago and who is still working as a fight announcer, not identifying Louis as a Negro was also a conscious policy: 'I never referred to colour . . . and now people treat it differently. And yet I still find it hard to do that after not having done it so many years. Now occasionally I will say, "He's the black fellow," or, "He's the white fellow," but in those days you didn't do it. As a matter of fact, our sports announcers' fraternity got some kind of an award from B'nai B'rith for that particular fact . . . I wanted to be colour blind.'

Close to 55,000 people filled the Polo Grounds in New York to see

Conn and Louis fight. Conn, a slow starter throughout his career, was careful to stay away from Louis during the first round. He appeared nervous as he danced away, and once he slipped as he tried to jab and run at the same time. In the second round Conn began to warm up and engaged in a few exchanges with the champion. At one point Louis pinned Conn against the ropes, landed a few punches, and seemed to be in control. But in the third and fourth rounds Conn stood up to some of Louis's shots and began to beat the champion to the punch. Sensing that his fighter was letting Conn get his rhythm, Jack Blackburn told Louis to pick up the pace. Louis clearly won the fifth and sixth rounds, opening a cut on Conn's nose. But Conn used his speed to weather the storm and was unhurt when he came out for the seventh round. Louis was tired. The fight began to slip away from the champion.

Conn was making Louis walk around the ring after him, and he easily avoided Louis's long leads. When he danced into range, Conn could throw three punches in succession before Louis had a chance to retaliate. Conn's hands were too quick for Louis, and even though the smaller Conn was not hurting Louis badly, he was taking the lead on points. During the fighting, Conn said, 'You've got a fight on your hands tonight, Joe,' and Louis replied, 'I know it.'

During the tenth round, with his title at risk, Joe Louis did a rather remarkable thing. He was walking after Conn, and the challenger was backing towards the ropes. Suddenly, Conn's right leg slipped out from under him, and Conn had to grab the ropes to avoid falling. Conn was momentarily helpless, and by the rules of boxing Louis was entitled to take advantage of the situation and hit Conn. Instead, he backed away and waited for Conn to regain his balance. Louis reacted from habit; he never hit his opponents when they slipped, and he didn't hit on the break or use other underhanded tactics. Louis's gesture towards Conn revealed his ingrained sportsmanship, but it was also a measure of his deep confidence. Even while he was losing control of the fight, Louis never lost his calm and did not feel desperate enough to take advantage of Conn's slip.

In the eleventh round Conn continued his dominance, landing good flurries in close as the champion covered up. After the round ended, one of Conn's handlers rushed out to meet Conn, almost hugging him. Conn put his right hand in the air, exultant. By the end of the twelfth round Conn was in complete control. Coming out of a clinch, he threw a left hook to Louis's body. Louis covered up, and Conn followed with a lightning-quick hook to the head and a right cross-left hook combination to the face that staggered Louis. Another left made Louis step sideways and fall back into the ropes.

Conn went in to get Louis. He threw a left to the body, then drew the left back and barely missed a hook to Louis's head. Louis grabbed Conn with both hands, smothering a Conn right. Conn tried to throw Louis around his left side and hit him with a left at the same time, but Louis held on and dragged Conn with him, and for a moment the fight looked like a comical wrestling match. The referee broke the two fighters, and Conn came in throwing a left hook. Louis ducked and held again, and again the referee had to break them. Conn hurt Louis with a left, but Louis backed away from another left just in time. Conn tried another left that missed. Louis smothered a left-right combination and clinched again. Conn wrapped his left around Louis's head, and they broke. Louis jabbed, then backed away from a big left hook and countered with a left to the face and hit Conn with a short right as the challenger came in, and the bell rang.

Conn had had Louis in trouble and was well ahead on points. His handlers and his trainer, Johnny Ray, told Conn to box cautiously the rest of the way, because he would surely win the decision and the title that way. But Conn thought he could knock Louis out, and a knockout would bring greater glory.

Three rounds to go. In the champion's corner Jack Blackburn and assistant trainer Mannie Seamon told Louis that to win, he would have to knock Conn out. When the bell rang for the thirteenth round, the two fighters came out of their corners and circled each other. Conn threw a left-right combination. Louis covered up and clinched, and the referee broke them. Louis landed a solid jab and blocked a Conn left. Conn feinted, and Louis jabbed again. Conn landed a right to the body, and the fighters clinched. Conn was no longer thinking about dancing away from Louis. He wanted to stay on the offensive, hoping for a knockout. In tight, Conn threw a left to the body and missed a left aimed at Louis's face, and Louis jabbed and threw a right cross that Conn slipped. Louis missed a jab and missed another as Conn ducked and moved in, but Louis landed a right cross in tight that knocked Conn off balance, and Louis put his left out and held Conn's right glove and threw a right uppercut that snapped Conn's head back and followed with a left hook, Conn clinching and leaning in. Louis backed away and landed a right uppercut and left hook. Tired as he was, Joe Louis could still punch. Conn's head was bouncing like a yo-yo. Louis missed a right, and both fighters threw lefts and got their arms hooked together. Conn landed a left hook on the top of Louis's head, but Louis crossed with a right and grazed Conn's face with a left hook. Conn tried a left and a right to Louis's body, but Louis smothered the punches in close. Conn wrapped his left around Louis's head, landed a right hook to the side of Louis's face, tried a left hook that Louis blocked, then landed a solid right to the head and left to the body, and once again Louis covered up. Conn missed a left around Louis's head that pushed Louis's shoulders down, landed a right uppercut, and missed a left and landed a right cross and a solid left hook to Louis's head. Conn missed a right uppercut but landed another left to the head, and Louis put both arms around Conn and held on. The referee broke them.

Louis came out of the clinch unhurt, even after all the punches Conn had landed, and Billy Conn stayed in range. Louis jabbed, blocked a Conn left hook, and clinched again. Conn came out of the clinch with a left to the body, a solid right cross, and missed a left as Louis jumped at him with his own wild left. The fighters clinched, and the referee broke them. Louis ducked a Conn left hook, and as Conn came in to clinch, Louis missed a right to the head. Louis pushed Conn away into the ropes and jabbed, and Billy Conn dodged and leaned in to avoid a Louis right. The referee broke the clinch.

Conn backed away, then started a left jab–overhand right combination, but Joe Louis stepped aside to slip the jab and beat Conn to the punch with his own overhand right. It was the one solid punch Louis needed, and it slowed Conn just enough. Conn bent at the waist with the effects of the punch, and Louis backed away and circled for punching room. Conn tried to lean in, but Louis swung a right hook that Conn had to dodge by backing towards the ropes. Louis jabbed, Conn covered up, and Louis landed a right to the body and left to the body. Conn tried to lean in again, but Louis stepped to the side, and Conn came out of his crouch with a left that landed on Louis's face but had no sting. Louis threw an overhand right that hurt Conn. As Conn tried to clinch, Louis stepped back and hit him with a solid right uppercut. Conn's hair flew up. Conn fell into Louis, and Louis tried another uppercut, but he was backed into the ropes and didn't have room. Louis pushed Conn around so that Conn's back was to the ropes and threw another right. Conn, still hanging on, managed to smother the punch and even tried a weak left of his own, but Louis countered with a short, sharp right that gave him punching room. Louis put his left out to the side of Conn's face, measuring, and took it back and threw a right to the top of Conn's head and pushed Conn out towards the centre of the ring as Conn tried to clinch. Louis held the dazed Conn at arm's length and threw a right uppercut that jarred Conn, and Conn fell into Louis again.

Louis backed away, and then so did Conn, but Conn suddenly lunged into another clinch, trying to hold on to Louis. Louis hit him with a right uppercut, and Conn blocked another one as Louis backed away from Conn. Conn landed a left hook and tried to clinch, but Louis hardly noticed the punch and easily pushed Conn away. Conn backed away, his hands low. Louis followed and threw a jab, then a murderous overhand right, getting his full weight into the punch. Conn, now completely unconscious though somehow still standing, leaned into Louis, but Louis stepped back and landed a left hook and a right to the body that spun Conn around him. As Conn went by on Louis's left side, Louis followed him with a right that cuffed Conn on the back of the head and then a right hook and left jab and right uppercut, and still Conn leaned in. Louis landed a left hook and a right cross with everything on it, and Conn spun slightly around and still clinched.

Louis threw a left to the body, stepped back and threw a right uppercut, a left hook, and a right cross, and readied another right as Conn took a small step with his left foot, leaning forward. Conn just fell that way, his body bent at the waist. Conn fell on to his right side, and his head hit the canvas and bounced up before coming to rest.

Louis looked at Conn and then turned and walked away, his shoulders rising as he took one deep breath. Louis turned around in his neutral corner in his usual pose, one arm draped on either side of the corner post. Conn sat up and looked at Louis, and Louis stepped forward with his left foot and kind of leant forward, arms still holding the ropes and supporting his weight as they spread-eagled behind him. Conn got one knee up at the count of ten, and as he started to get to his feet, the referee waved his hands. Two seconds remained in the round.

Louis came off the ropes with his arms at his sides, his hips swinging. Louis walked towards Conn, and Conn was looking at Louis, but the referee turned Conn's head and patted Conn on the back. Louis walked by as if to pat Conn on the back as well, but the referee got in his way, so Louis just walked past with his head down.

Conn's handlers came into the ring, took out Conn's mouthpiece, and splashed him with water from a sponge before wiping his face with it. Forty years later Billy Conn, who lives in a beautiful home in Pittsburgh and still has an easy smile and the restless energy of an athlete, remembered the punishment he took before falling that night and just laughed. 'I had a strong neck.'

Ethnic-conscious sportswriters found an easy explanation for Conn's defeat. They wrote that Conn's Irish blood got him caught up in the fighting and made him go for the knockout instead of boxing cautiously and going for the decision. Conn's manager, Johnny Ray, agreed. Ray said of his fighter, 'If he hadda Jewish head instead of an Irish one, he'd be the champ.'

Mike Jacobs was delighted with the Conn–Louis fight. It had revived interest in the heavyweight division, drawn $451,743 in gate receipts, and ensured that a rematch between the two fighters would draw much more. But Jacobs faced a dilemma. To give Billy Conn a title shot, Jacobs had passed over Lou Nova, a good-sized, tough fighter who had clearly established himself as the number one contender by twice knocking out Max Baer. Nova was ahead of his time, or maybe it was just that he came from California. He claimed to have studied yoga and to possess a 'cosmic punch'. Nova and his cosmic punch had received a lot of publicity, and there was considerable pressure from the press to give Nova a title shot. A Louis–Nova fight would draw a big crowd, and doubtless Jacobs reasoned that a Conn–Louis rematch would be even more popular if boxing fans had a while to think about it. Jacobs signed Louis and Nova to fight on 29 September 1941 in the Polo Grounds and planned to match Louis and Conn the following year. Some 56,000 fans watched Louis spar cautiously with Nova for five rounds, then demolish the Californian in the sixth. The number one heavyweight contender was just one more easy knockout victim for the champion. The 'cosmic punch' turned out to be an ordinary right cross that Nova could not land to any great effect against Louis.

From June 1938, when he knocked out Max Schmeling, to September 1941, when he knocked out Lou Nova, Joe Louis's public image became slightly more favourable. By then Louis was a universally familiar figure, and during that period reporters and the American public acquired a fixed idea of what Joe Louis was like.

The central part of Louis's image was his reputation as a fighter. His convincing victory over Schmeling had erased all doubts as to his ability, and in the next three years Louis defended his title fifteen times, winning thirteen of those fights by knockouts. (The Buddy Baer fight was officially recorded as a 'disqualification'.) No champion had ever fought so often or so completely dominated the heavyweight division. By January 1939 Ed Van Every of the *New York Sun* wrote that Louis was generally believed to be the best fighter of all time. Richards Vidmer and Bill Corum expressed the same conclusion in columns they wrote in 1939, and Grantland Rice wrote that Louis was holding up as an athlete after becoming rich and famous better than anyone he had ever seen. Lester Scott of the *New York World Telegram* wrote a column in early 1939 with the headline 'There Should Be a Law Against Putting Men in Ring with Louis'. Journalistic respect for Louis's ability probably reached its height on the day Louis fought Gus Dorazio, 17 February 1941. A *Washington Post* headline read '15,000 to See Champ "Risk" Heavy Title'.

Louis was so good that no one took his opponents seriously. This depressed attendance at Louis's fights and also made his opponents the butt of jokes, 'Bum-of-the-Month Club' being just one example. On a National Urban League Programme aired over the ABC radio network on 30 March 1941, two actors did a skit, a dialogue between Louis's fictional next opponent, Eddie One-Round Green, and Green's manager. The manager asked his fighter to imagine his fight with Louis – he began the skit as follows:

'It's the first round. Joe Louis climbs into the ring like a tiger. What do you do?'
'I climbs out of the ring like another tiger.'
'Any other man would run. But you don't.'

'What's the matter? Am I glued to the floor?'

'It's the fifteenth round, and you're crawling around the ring on your hands and knees. What are you doing on your hands and knees?'

'Looking for a trap door.'

'Joe Louis is covered with blood. Your nose is broken. Both your eyes are black, and your jaw is cracked. Now is the time to see what you're made of.'

'What's he gonna do? Turn me inside out?'

'The crowd is yelling to the referee, "Stop it. Stop it." And what do you say?'

'Okay with me.'

'I can't stand to see you take any more punishment, so what do I do?'

'You close your eyes?'

'No, I throw in the towel, and they give the fight to Louis.'

'Let him have it; I don't want it.'

'But you fought so well that they give you a reward.'

'Oh yeah? What do they give me?'

'They give you a return fight with Joe Louis.'

'Oh no they don't.'

'Oh yes they do.'

'Oh no they don't.'

While Louis's dominance brought him attention and respect from the American public, it often made him seem impersonal and distant. Boxing crowds always applauded him, but they tended to root for his underdog opponents. The white press often noted and shared the public's sentiment for Louis's opponents, though white reporters were careful to say the sentiment was not racially motivated. In December 1938 *Newsweek* magazine said:

> Another White Hope search – less hysterical but the same sort of movement that bestirred fight fans when Jack Johnson, Negro, held the championship (1910–1915) – is on to unearth a replacement for Joe Louis. In the current quest race plays but a minor role, however, for the second Negro ever to hold the heavyweight title is a respected and popular fighter.

Rather, the hunt is prompted by the realisation that none of the present-day well-known heavyweights has a good chance to beat the Brown Bomber, and a longing on the part of boxing experts to be the first to discover the unsung hero who must inevitably come from obscurity to knock Louis's block off.

Tom Meany of *PM*, a New York afternoon paper, wrote before the Conn fight that most boxing fans were rooting for Conn. 'This isn't because the public dislikes the Bomber, who has been an exemplary champion; it's merely because the public likes a change.' After the fight John Kieran of the *New York Times* noted:

> Most of the onlookers wanted to see Conn win. It had to be that way. Not because of any difference in colour in the warriors. If there were any present who felt that way, they were an insignificant minority. But the shuffler was the champion. He had been the champion for four years. The crowd usually goes for the newcomer, the challenger, the younger man trying to scale the heights against known odds and heavy odds.

Because Louis remained far and away the most famous and salient black personality in America, many sportswriters again suggested that Louis had a symbolic importance beyond the prize ring. After Louis almost lost his title to Billy Conn, Ed Sullivan wrote in his 'Little Old New York' column:

> The fists of Joe Louis are the megaphones and microphones of his race on the nights that he defends his championship . . . He is, to all intents and purposes, never an individual – he is all the sorrows and joys, and fears and hopes and the melody of an entire race . . . He is a compound of every little cabin in the Southland, every tenement or apartment in the Harlems of the North; he is the memory of every injustice practised upon his people and the memory of every triumph . . .
> In eighteen victories, Louis has done more to influence better relations between two races than any single individual . . .

Remembrance of Things Past

❛I beat the main fellows, the contenders, so I figured we'll try Joe Louis, he's just another guy. You don't fight guys like Joe Louis unless you beat all those guys that really knew how to fight and then you learn how to fight. You're not just some mug coming in off the street corner to fight Joe Louis, because he'd knock you through the middle of next week. It's a business and it takes a long time. It's the toughest business in the world. But when you're good, you automatically know all the fine points of the game and what you're supposed to do. And the main thing is they're not supposed to hit you. That's the game. Get out of the way. I knew that you had to keep moving from side to side and keep him off balance and never let him get a good shot at you because he was a real dangerous man. Keep away from him. Just move in and out. Feint him out of position and whack him and just keep going. Left hook and a right cross, a left hook to the body and a left hook to the chin – all in the same combination, bing, bang, boom! Real fast; like a machine-gun, then get the hell out of the way. There's a set that comes natural to you if you know how to fight. You look straight at the fellow and you just take the lead away from him. You try to mix him up, to befuddle him. Then you take the whole combination of shots at the same time – one, two, three, four, bing, bang, bing and you get the hell out of there real fast. Then when he goes back you get him to drop his hands, feint him out of position, then you can hit him. But every time that you lead with one hand you have to know to keep the other one up so you don't get hit. You can't let him get set to get a clear, good shot.

I hurt him in the twelfth round so I figured I'll try and knock him out. I made a mistake. He was waiting for me. He'd have never hit me in the ass if I didn't make a mistake and try to knock him out. They told me to stay away from him, that I was beating him all the way. But when I hurt him in the twelfth round he started to hold on.

I said, "I'm going to knock this son-of-a-bitch out. Don't worry about it." Don't worry about it, and I made one mistake! I liked Joe and I knew he was a real good man. I used to be a wiseguy with some of those fellows. When I hit him in the thirteenth round I said to him, "You've got a fight tonight, Joe." He said, "I knows it," and he kept on going. And that was the end of the line. He hit me about twenty-five real good shots. I tried to outpunch him, but I only weighed $169^{1/2}$ and he was a big fellow. He weighed $199^{1/2}$, a big man, and he could box, too. *

Billy Conn (from *In this Corner* by Peter Heller)

*Billy Conn gave me my toughest fight. He was an excellent boxer. He was one of the best American boxers. One thing about that fight. The end of the twelfth round, which was Billy's best round, he really hit me. Of course, he wasn't hitting me that hard, but he hit me with a lot of punches. So beginning of the thirteenth round he walked out and said, "Well, Joe, you're in for a tough fight tonight." I'll never forget it, about four or five seconds after he said it he was on the floor. I looked at him and said, "You're right." He was a great light heavyweight champion. *

Joe Louis

ROUND 2

The Mauler and the Egghead

Paul Gallico was one of America's most outstanding sportswriters. In the thirteen years of his best reportage, 1923 to 1936, he covered all the great sporting events, including the Berlin Olympics. A prolific writer, Gallico went on to complete some twenty-seven books, including such international bestsellers as The Snow Goose *and* The Poseidon Adventure.

In the classic compendium A Farewell to Sport, *first published in 1937, he recalled some of the great moments of his early career. In this chapter are two excerpts from that book, two wonderful vignettes of two well-remembered heavyweight champions. Jack Dempsey, the Manassa Mauler, one of the all-time greats; and Gene Tunney, the thinking man's champ, who twice beat Dempsey and retired undefeated.*

Who do you think you are – Dempsey?

Paul Gallico

The most popular prizefighter that ever lived was Jack Dempsey, born William Harrison Dempsey, 24 June 1896, at Manassa, Colorado, and heavyweight champion of the world from 4 July 1919 to 3 September 1926. It has been generally forgotten that for a long time he was also one of the most unpopular and despised champions that ever climbed into a ring.

And, curiously, it is possible to place one's finger upon the exact time and place, almost, when the switch occurred and the cult of Dempsey-worshippers was born – a public love and idolatry that have transcended anything ever known in the ring and perhaps, for that matter, in any sport.

It was, I suspect, some time between the hours of one and two o'clock in the morning of 4 September, in 1926, in a room at the Ritz-Carlton Hotel in Philadelphia. It was about then that he returned there minus the heavyweight championship of the world, which he had left with Gene Tunney at the Sesquicentennial Stadium a short while before. They had fought for half an hour in a torrential rain and Tunney had battered the supposed invincible champion almost beyond recognition.

He was not alone. Seconds, hangers-on, reporters crowded into the room behind him. A lovely woman came to him with pity and tenderness and took him into her arms and held him for a moment. Lightly she touched his face with her fingertips. One side of that face was completely shapeless, red, blue, purple in colour, wealed, welted and bruised, the eye barely visible behind ridges of swollen flesh.

She said: 'What happened, Ginsberg?' Ginsberg was Estelle Taylor's pet name for her husband.

Dempsey grinned out of the good corner of his mouth, held her off for a second, and then said: 'Honey, I forgot to duck.'

From that moment on, everybody loved him.

John L. Sullivan, the Boston Strong Boy, was reputedly the most popular heavyweight champion of all times, but this is not so, because in Sullivan's day (his last fight was in 1892) prizefighting was neither respectable nor widespread in its appeal. It was long before the days of Tex Rickard, million-dollar gates, new-laid millionaires with an itch for publicity, and the freedom of post-war manners and morals which made it possible for a prizefighter to aspire to and eventually marry a society girl and be accepted in her class as a human being. It was before the days of high-pressure newspaper publicity and prizefight ballyhoo and also before the time when Sweet Charity learned, to borrow one of boxing's own expressive terms, how to put the bite on prizefighting as a quick and at first infallible money-getter. In the old days the sport was socially outlawed. Women – that is to say, ladies – did not go to the boxing pits and therefore Sullivan's popularity was limited strictly to the class then known as 'sports'.

But nearly everyone in every walk of life seemed to love and admire Jack Dempsey. There was hardly any class to whose imagination he did not appeal. He was and still remains today in the minds of millions of people the perfect type of fighting man.

He was, as fighters go, a pretty good performer, though not nearly so good as legend and kindled imaginations pictured him. He had great truculence, pugnacity and aggressiveness, a valuable and unlimited fund of natural cruelty, tremendous courage, speed and determination, and good, though actually not extraordinary, hitting powers. He was never a good boxer and had little or no defence. His protection was aggression. He was not, for instance, ever as good a fighter and boxer as the Negro Joe Louis is today, notwithstanding Louis's defeat by Schmeling. Dempsey's entire reputation was based, actually, on two fights, the one in which he knocked out gigantic Jess Willard at Toledo to win his championship, and the thrilling, atavistic brawl with Luis Angel Firpo, the big Argentine, at the Polo Grounds in New York, 23 September 1923. But they were sufficient, for they marked Dempsey as a giantkiller, a slayer of ogres. He became one with David, Siegfried and Roland. And it is interesting to note in connection with this that Dempsey's period of unpopularity, even though he was branded a slacker during the war, really dates from the day in 1921 – 2 July, to be exact – when he knocked out the Frenchman Georges Carpentier, at Boyle's Thirty Acres in Jersey

City, in four rounds. Carpentier was hardly more than a heavy middleweight. He probably didn't weigh more than 168 pounds for the fight. He was a little man, much smaller than Dempsey. And he was a war hero. This fight also marked the first of the million-dollar gates.

But Dempsey was a picture-book fighter. By all the sons of Mars, he looked the part. He had dark eyes, blue-black hair, and the most beautifully proportioned body ever seen in any ring. He had the wide but sharply sloping shoulders of the puncher, a slim waist and fine, symmetrical legs. His weaving, shuffling style of approach was drama in itself and suggested the stalking of a jungle animal. He had a smouldering truculence on his face and hatred in his eyes. His gorge lay close to the surface. He was utterly without mercy or pity, asked no quarter, gave none. He would do anything he could get away with, fair or foul, to win. This was definitely a part of the man, but was also a result of his early life and schooling in the hobo jungles, bar-rooms and mining camps of the West. Where Dempsey learned to fight, there were no rounds, rest intervals, gloves, referees, or attending seconds. There are no draws and no decisions in rough and tumble fighting. You had to win. If you lost you went to the hospital or to the undertaking parlour. Dempsey, more often than not, in his early days as hobo, saloon bouncer or roustabout, fought to survive. I always had the feeling that he carried that into the ring with him, that he was impatient of rules and restrictions and niceties of conduct, impatient even of the leather that bound his knuckles.

But all of these characteristics added to the picture of a man who could swing his fists and slug bigger, heavier, stronger men into unconsciousness. It crystallised something that all of us at one time or another long for – to be able to 'up' to someone, a giant, a bully, a tough guy, without qualm or tremor, and let him have it.

All the great legends of the ring are built upon the picture that the average man has of himself as he would like to be, a combination of D'Artagnan, Scaramouche, the Scarlet Pimpernel and – Jack Dempsey. If we could, we would all be gentle, soft-spoken creatures, tender with women, cool and even-tempered, but once aroused – 'Whap!' A lightning-like left or right to the jaw. Down goes truck driver or footpad or hoodlum. We mentally dust our hands, readjust our cravat, smile pleasantly, step over the body of the prostrate victim, and carry on. Just like that. The most popular thing a sportswriter can say about a prizefighter, the good old standby, is that outside the ring you would never take him for a pug. No, sir, more like a bank clerk or a businessman. Just as quiet and gentle – loves birds and flowers, and you ought to see him with his kiddies on his knee. Look back into the files. Sharkey cultivated petunias. Schmeling would lie for hours in the grass and watch a mother bird feed its young. Tunney retired in a rowboat to some secluded portion of a mountain lake and read a good book. Joe Louis studied the Bible (or at least he was trying to learn how to read so that he could study the Bible if he wanted to) and was good to his mother . . . But what killers when aroused! Could that soft-spoken fellow with the well-cut clothes, the rather queer, high-pitched voice and the perfect manners be the Jack Dempsey who clouted Jess Willard until he resembled nothing at all human, and floored Luis Firpo eleven times before he knocked him out? How wonderful to be so quiet, so gentlemanly – and yet so terrible!

Actually, for many years, Dempsey was inclined to be as cruel outside the ring as he was in action within. I have seen him in a playful wrestling match in a training camp with one Joe Benjamin, a lightweight who used to be kept around as a sort of a camp stooge and jester (every big fighter always has a camp butt or jester), bring up his knee into Benjamin's groin and leave him squirming with pain. Gus Wilson, who came over from France with Carpentier as trainer and remained here, became one of Dempsey's good friends and even trained him. But in friendly roughing, Dempsey once hit him what he thought was a playful tap on the side and Gus went to the hospital and the damaged kidney was removed. Estelle Taylor loved Dempsey, but all through their married life she lived in constant terror of him. It must have been a good deal like being married to a catamount.

To me this always added to the picture rather than detracted from it, because I like my prizefighters mean. Cruelty and absolute lack of mercy are an essential quality in every successful prizefighter. I have never known one who wasn't ruthless and amoral. It is childish to believe that this can be put on and off like a mantle. The gentle lambs outside the ropes are never much good within, and vice versa. The managers and press agents for prizefighters were not long in discovering what the public wished to think about the comportment of their tigers in street clothes. For the most part, the stories about their sweet and lovely natures are untrue. Much later, when they are older and retire from the ring, the mean streak may become more deeply submerged, as it has in the case of Dempsey. But the life that a prizefighter lives while in daily training is hardly conducive to softening his character. His brutality and viciousness are carefully cultivated, fed and watered like a plant, because they are a valuable business commodity. He practises daily cruelties upon spar boys who are paid to accept them uncomplainingly. There never was a meaner man than Dempsey with his sparring partners unless it be the cold and emotionless Joseph Louis Barrow.

Dempsey used to have such big, inept hulks as Farmer Lodge in his training camps. He slugged them and slogged them. If he knocked them down, he waited until they got up and then knocked them down again. If it looked as though they were about to collapse from the effects of the punching he was giving them, he would hold his hand just long enough to let them come back a little – and then slug them again.

The average boxing fan or person familiar with the beauties of the game will inquire at this point: 'Well, what are sparring partners for?' This is unanswerable, but there are degrees of permissible brutality, especially with injured men. But wounds or no wounds, taped ribs or none, fresh cuts, bad eyes, bruised lips or no, when they went in to spar against Dempsey they expected no mercy and got none. When his trainer called 'Time', he set out to beat them into insensibility, and generally did. Most fighters, in training, will let up when they have hurt a rehearsal mate with a punch to the extent that he begins to come undone at the seams and wobbles a little. There is nothing to be gained by knocking him out unless a bunch of the boys from the press have arrived from town, when it makes good copy for them and will sometimes affect the betting odds. They have even trained Joe Louis to hold back a little when he gets a spar boy going, but Dempsey never eased up in all his life, so far as I ever saw or knew. The first signs of their eyes glazing a trifle or that sudden little leaning forward of the body and shaking of the knees that telltales a lethal punch, and he would leap forward, his lips drawn back over his teeth, and rain his hooks upon them until they collapsed slowly and slid to the floor. He treated each and every one of them as his personal enemy as soon as he entered the ring. He seemed to have a constant bottomless well of cold fury somewhere close to his throat.

Dempsey is accused by many of having been a foul fighter, and the same is fervently denied by the Dempseymaniacs. Dempsey himself never denied it, to my knowledge. In point of fact, under the strict interpretation of the modern rules of ring combat, he was a foul fighter, rough, anxious to hurt and careless of his punches. But psychically Dempsey actually never was a foul battler, because in his simple way he recognised no deadlines on the body of his opponent and certainly asked for none to be enforced upon his. He also knew that such smug and arbitrary divisions as 'fair' and 'foul' cannot be made of the word 'fight', nor are they properly applicable as adjectives. The word stands all by itself and complete in its meaning, not to be tampered with, increased or diminished, like 'love' or 'red'. You either do or you don't. It either is or it isn't. And either it was a fight or it wasn't. He had no advantage of protective armour that was denied his opponent. He was equally vulnerable. He was not a deliberately low puncher, though sometimes, with a touch of macabre humour, he liked to test out the courage and disposition of his opponent with a few low ones, but he was simply unconcerned with such niceties and obvious decadencies as a belt line. After all, wasn't it sufficient that when he got his man down he refrained from putting the boots to him?

In a way these probings of Dempsey's were frequently interesting tests and two men reacted quite differently to them. He hit Sharkey low. Sharkey immediately looked to the referee for help and made the error, during the rendering of his complaint to authority, of turning his head for a moment and taking his eyes from his opponent. Dempsey immediately hit him on the chin with a left hook while his head was turned and knocked him out. In Dempsey's school if you didn't keep your eye on your opponent you paid for it. He hit Gene Tunney low in both of their fights and Tunney took it without a murmur.

In that round and that fight, incidentally, occurred an incident that to me will always be the complete characterisation of Dempsey. About a minute of the round had passed when Dempsey caught Tunney with a right hook that knocked him towards the ropes and numbed him so that he couldn't get his guard up. Immediately Dempsey slugged him to the floor with rights and lefts, the last of which caught Tunney on the jaw even as he was collapsing slowly to the canvas. Then happened the historic long count, for which only Dempsey was to blame, and Tunney finally got up, glassy-eyed and still badly stricken, but recuperating quickly because he was in magnificent condition, and retaining sufficient of his stunned and badly scrambled intelligence to tell him what to do – which was to retreat.

Those were dramatic seconds. Tunney retreated. Dempsey pursued with his precious title (it hurt his pride terribly to lose it) almost in his hands. Round and round the ring they went, Tunney backwards with that peculiar limping gait of a back-pedalling fighter, Dempsey forwards after him with lust on his face. But Dempsey was then pugilistically an old man. He was then thirty-two and his tired legs could not stand the strain of that pursuit. He was not a smart enough boxer to sidestep and change his direction and herd Tunney into a corner or to the ropes where he could slug him again. He was a fighter with his kill in front of him. He could feel it slipping away from him and he knew but one direction in pursuit – forward.

Finally his legs failed him altogether. He stopped. And over his swarthy, bluejowled fighter's face there spread a look the memory of which will never leave me as long as I live. First it was the expression of self-realisation of one who knows that his race is run, that he is old and that he is finished. And then through it and replacing it there appeared such a glance of bitter, biting contempt for his opponent that for the moment I felt ashamed for the man who was running away. With his gloves Dempsey made little coaxing pawing motions to Tunney to come in and fight. That was it. Don't run. Come in and fight. This is a fight.

For that is what Dempsey would have done. Staggering blind, punch-drunk, head swimming, sick and reeling as he was when he was pushed back into the ring after Firpo knocked him out of it, and again after his terrible first-round beating at the hands of Sharkey, his instincts were yet to move forward, close with the enemy, and fight.

It would have been foolhardy had Tunney accepted this desperate battle gage, but as our hearts and not our heads reckon those things, it would have been glorious. In his place Dempsey would have done it and would have been knocked out as Tunney would have been. Tunney continued to run backwards, recovered, won the fight and retained his championship. And from his second losing encounter with the ex-Marine Dempsey emerged the greatest and most beloved popular sports hero the country has ever known – a title that, curiously, his greatest victories never won for him.

And after all, who can say that it was not deserved, because at least, unlike many other heroes, he had for those ringing, dramatic fourteen seconds justified the legends that had grown up around him, satisfied the picture of him that so many people had in their minds? He did hit Tunney, and hit him hard enough to keep him on the canvas for the officially required ten seconds and four more for good measure. That fate was against him and robbed him of his victory and his title was something that we could all understand. That made him human and one of us. And that he never once railed or complained against the luck of that fate or claimed the victory or sulked or was bitter brought him closer to divinity than many of us may come. Ah yes, there we were again, looking at ourselves in that satisfying hero's mould, smiling calmly and saying as Dempsey did: 'It was just one of the breaks. Tunney fought a smart fight.'

The old Dempsey training camps were probably the most colourful, exciting, picturesque gatherings ever. I was too young in the sportswriting game to see the one outside of Shelby, Montana, where he was preparing to meet Tom Gibbons, or the earlier one at Toledo when he was a tough young challenger training for the task (then thought impossible) of beating the enormous Willard.

But I remember the grand, exciting, bawdy atmosphere of the camp at Saratoga Springs at Uncle Crying Tom Luther's Hotel on the shore of the lake. There were sparring partners with bent noses and twisted ears, Negroes and white fighters, boxing writers, handsome state troopers in their grey and purple uniforms; doubtful blondes who wandered in and out of the lay-out of wooden hotel and lake-front bungalows and blondes about whom there was no doubt at all; a lady prizefighter; old semi-bald Uncle Tom, always crying and complaining over the Gargantuan pranks of the sports writers; and Jack Kearns, smart, breezy, wisecracking, scented, who virtually tore the hotel apart. The old, tough Dempsey was there, slim, dark-haired, still crinkle-nosed (you have probably forgotten that

Dempsey once had a typical pug's bashed-in nose and had it lifted), dressed in trousers and an old grey sweater, playing checkers on the porch of his bungalow with a sparring partner. And wandering about the grounds was all the rag, tag and bobtail of the fight game, broken-down pugilists looking for a hand-out, visiting managers, the always dirty and down-at-the-heels One-Eye Connolly and a fine assortment of bums and dames. There was nothing either high-hat or sinister about the plant. It was gay, low, vulgar, Rabelaisian and rather marvellous.

This was of course before the days when clusters of millionaires and socialites of one kind or another patronised fighters and fight camps and, too, just shortly before the time when the dangerous hot-eyed gangsters took over the fight business and brazenly visited the training camps to look over their properties, mingling with the élite, or sat in smouldering groups in corners and weighed and speculated upon every arrival and talked out of the sides of their mouths.

But times were changing and so was Dempsey. This was the last of those merry, carefree, colourful camps. The next one was at Atlantic City at the dogtrack, where the champion prepared for his first encounter with Gene Tunney. By that time Dempsey was rich. Kearns was a mortal enemy – they had quarrelled over the girl who was then his wife, the darkly glamorous Estelle Taylor, who had one trait which marred her chances for success as a prizefighter's wife, a devastating sense of humour. Detectives were already guarding Dempsey night and day, and one Tommy Loughran, a fast, brilliant, cream-puff-punching light heavyweight got a job with Dempsey as a sparring partner and wrote Dempsey's finish in letters large enough for all of us to see, except that we, too, were blinded by our own ballyhoo and the great Dempsey legend that we had helped to create. We refused to believe what we saw, a Dempsey unable to land a solid punch on Loughran, and Tommy stabbing and jabbing Dempsey as he pleased.

I remember that we made apologies for him. He was going easy on Tommy, because, after all, Tommy was of championship calibre in his own class and no ordinary sparring partner, and Dempsey didn't want to hurt him. That was a laugh; Dempsey, who never went easy on anybody, who would have broken Loughran in two if he could have caught him. Here again was an example of the strange grip that this man had even on the minds of the hardboiled and unbelieving sportswriters trained to look for and detect weaknesses in a fighter.

His last camp for his final fight against Tunney, in Chicago, at the Lincoln Park racetrack, was probably the quietest and dullest of all. He had engaged old Leo Flynn to act as his manager, and Joe Benjamin was the camp jester, but he missed Kearns and the old life. His marriage with Estelle Taylor was beginning to break up. He was still too much the prizefighter for any sensitive woman. He lived alone near the track. But he was then no longer the ignorant, hungry, inarticulate, half-savage fighter. He had grown into a man.

I am not attempting in this short chapter to write either a life or a history of Jack Dempsey, but rather to give an impression of him as I remember him. But somehow I feel as though I could go on and on, writing about him, and never exhaust the colourful, incredibly fascinating story of a strange man and a full life.

Because he began as a rough, tough nobody, a hard, mean, life-battered hobo, a kid with little or no education, truculent, bitter, disillusioned, restless and vicious, digging food and living out of an equally hard rough world in which there was never any softness or any decency, a tramp, a bum and a misfit at heart. I can see him as a surly, dangerous inhabitant of that spiteful nether world, just on the borderline of the criminal, a world of steely toughness, foul language, greasy food, dirty linen, grey clapboard shacks and unpainted frame houses, smells and stinks and curses, and nowhere any peace, comfort or beauty.

And yet this boy who must have escaped only narrowly from being sucked into the underworld became a champion who eventually married a Hollywood moving-picture star who actually for a time caged him in a silken boudoir with stuffed taffeta and lace pillows and big, simpering painted dolls with bisque heads and nothing but voluminous satin skirts for bodies, squatting on his bed – Dempsey's bed. He learned to wear silk next to his skin and to eat with proper manners. He moved in those days through those absurd frills like a tiger in the circus, dressed up for the show in strange and humiliating clothes.

He had his nose remodelled, made a motion picture, took a triumphant tour through Europe, talked to the Prince of Wales in England. His lovely wife left him. He loved her terribly, too. Too terribly. Can you picture the old, hard Dempsey in a jealous rage? Had he met and married Estelle in his last phase, after he had quit the ring, when his restless, rising gorge was crushed deeper and deeper within him through experience, through living and, above all, through disuse, this love-match might have lasted. But in those days he was still too close to the disgusting things that every prizefighter needs in his trade.

Curiously, I have never seen it written or commented upon that nothing ever went to Dempsey's head – not his money, not his title, and not the amazing change in his social position. He is one of the three famous international sports characters and celebrities to remain unspoiled, natural and himself. The others are Bob Jones and Babe Ruth. The same bums, now a little older and frowsier, who used to put the bee or the arm, as the fight slang goes, on their more successful pal see him today and get the same handouts. His touch list must be staggering. Probably a fifth of the money he has made he has given away in touches, handouts and loans that were never repaid.

The Dempsey of today is still a fascinating figure. As part owner and host at the loud, blatant, garish chophouse that bears his name on the corner of Eighth Avenue and Fiftieth Street, opposite Madison Square Garden, he has slipped into the Broadway post-crash scene and become one of the landmarks of the city.

His restaurant is always jammed to the doors. You will see very few of the Broadway regulars there except on fight nights at the Garden after the show is over, when the fight writers and some of the Broadway mob drop across the street for a glass of beer and to find out what Jack thought of the outcome of the match. The clientele consists mostly of out-of-towners who have come to see in the flesh the man whose breathtaking and fiction-like career they have been living for the past eighteen years. They are calling, in short, upon a beloved alter ego. They shake his hand, pat his broad back, and take home one of the red and gold menus with his picture and his autograph on it.

That restaurant, too, somehow seems indelibly imprinted upon my memory. You enter from a little door on Fiftieth Street and come into the foyer, where three skinny blondes, dressed in riding costumes, tan, ill-fitting jodhpurs, red coats and white stocks, snatch your hat and topcoat. To the right is the entrance to the long public bar. Remember, old John L. Sullivan once kept a saloon too. There is a green rope stretched across that entrance to the bar. The bums, the thugs, the panhandlers and the drunks do not cross that deadline.

Off from the centre of the foyer is a little glass and silver cocktail bar. Nobody ever seems to be in it. And to the left is a high desk with an enormous guestbook reposing on it and then the entrance to the restaurant is hard by. The restaurant proper is a huge, barn-like, cheerless place in red and gold, jammed and noisy, with a head waiter or two standing guard at the rope that bars ingress. There too, if he is not in the main room, you will find Dempsey. He will be dressed in a dark blue suit. He is not fat, but heavier, and his face is older and more settled. His hair is still blue-black, his chin faintly blue, and his movements still quick, restless, catlike.

If he knows you it will be: 'Hello, pally' (in that high-pitched voice). 'Glad to see you. Glad to see you. How's my old pardner? Sure, I can find room for you.'

He sweeps the rope aside, taking you by the arm. He grips the shoulder of the head waiter. No matter how crowded it is, he will say: 'Find a nice table for my friend from Portland, Oregon, here, and see that he gets taken care of. I'll be over later and have a chat with you, pardner. Hope you enjoy yourself.'

And you march in, proudly, under escort. It feels like being presented at court. Or if he knows you very well he might take you down to a table himself and sit down with you for a moment. But only for a moment. He still cannot remain sitting in one spot for more than two or three minutes at a time. Like all men who have knocked about and been knocked about, he has a miraculous memory for names and faces. I have stood and listened to him rattle off greetings to one group after another: 'Sure, sure, hello. How are you? Sure, sure, I remember you. Met you in Cleveland at the Athletic Club about five years ago . . . Well, well, well, how's my old pardner from Toledo? How's the missus? She come with you? Remember me to her and the little girl – guess she's a big girl now . . . Shake, pally. Sure, I remember your name. It's Bill Slotwell. How long's it been since I've seen you? Eleven years. Kansas City, wasn't it?' This can go on indefinitely.

Probably sitting in the first booth, just inside the door, you will see Hannah Williams, the 'Cheerful Little Earful' of the pre-crash days, his present wife, and mother of his two children, whom he adores as only hard, primitive men seem to love children. From six o'clock in the evening until closing time he works at his job, greeting, autographing, glad-handing, answering stale questions about his fights, suave, smooth, cordial, even-tempered, tactful.

This, then, is the haven in which this storm-driven ship is resting. I often wonder how deeply the old, cruel, snarling Dempsey is buried, and *does* character change? He wheels his daughter Joan, his first-born, in her carriage, and this is genuine because now that his ring days are long over, there is no longer any need for the pretence of being a kindly soul and a 'perfect gentleman' outside the ring. He is actually more the gentleman than most that come into his dining-hall. And it must be true that as men age, the lust for fighting grows less, and that if there is no need or use for truculence and cruelty, these traits can become submerged. He loves his pert, bright little wife who has borne him children, and if the old, wild rages that tore his marriage to Estelle Taylor to bitter shreds ever boil and bubble over any more, no one knows of it, because there has been no hint or no sign of this lately.

It has been many years since he fought for his championship for the last time. There have been new heroes and new fighters and new champions, supermen, superchampions. But the name of Dempsey is still synonymous with the ability to lay a man low with a punch. The kids on the street still scuffle together and brawl and hit, and say: 'Aw, who do you think you are – Jack Dempsey?'

By Horatio Alger, Jr

Paul Gallico

James Joseph Tunney was once an unknown, no-account clerk in a Greenwich Village office in New York City, a quiet, undistinguished, good-looking Irish boy who might barely be listed as living on the fringe of the white-collar class. He belonged to the great unidentified mass, and his importance except to himself was nil.

James Joseph became Gene Tunney, heavyweight boxing champion of the world, who was paid $1 million for a single performance, married a wealthy society girl and retired from the ring as undefeated heavyweight champion. No fictional story ever based on the beloved from-rags-to-riches theme was ever more unbelievably fantastic or more characteristic of the cock-eyed post-war sports period that made it possible. Twenty-five years ago it could not have happened. It took war, post-war inflation, an unprecedented sports mania, the weirdest assortment of characters ever gathered beneath one tent – and Gene Tunney, himself probably the most remarkable of all the people who were featured in the success story to end all success stories.

The *dramatis personae* of this goofy comedy are themselves sufficiently astonishing, but they all figured in the final happy ending and contributed in one way or another to it. First there was the hero, Gene Tunney, one of the handsomest men who ever laced on a boxing glove, the Leyendecker Arrow Collar man of the advertisements come to life. The heroine was Polly Lauder, Greenwich, Connecticut, society girl, social registerite, allied to the Carnegie millions. The heavy was Jack Dempsey, heavyweight champion of the world, the most feared and colourful character of the modern prize ring. The *deus ex machina* was Tex Rickard, former faro dealer and far-West gambling-house proprietor become the world's greatest promoter of prizefights, and included in the cast were the United States Marines; Georges Carpentier, boulevardier, manufacturer of boxes designed to hold Camembert cheese, ex-soldier of France and light heavyweight prizefighter; Maxie Boo-Boo Hoff, Philadelphia underworld boss, dabbler in prizefight promotions, and alleged proprietor of an imposing string of *maisons de joie;* William L. Muldoon, a reformed wrestler turned anti-tobacco crusader, health-farm proprietor and member of the New York State Athletic Commission; James J. Farley, a small-time state politician from Haverstraw, New York, a whistle stop along the Hudson, a member of the Boxing Commission and eventually Postmaster General of the United States of America; Al Capone, America's greatest gangster and robber baron, now a guest in the nation's most impregnable cooler, Alcatraz; Estelle Taylor, a glamorous motion-picture queen; Sam Pryor, a hero-worshipping semi-social American businessman from Greenwich, Connecticut, who went abroad with the AEF; Bill McCabe, a connoisseur of prizefighters, likewise a soldier; Billy Gibson, an old-time fight manager, once manager of Benny Leonard, lightweight champion of the world; Dave Barry, a referee with a poor sense of time; Italian Jack Herman, a mediocre prizefighter with a spotty record; Harry Wills, a Negro prizefighter and perpetual heavyweight championship contender; and a chorus and assortment of walk-ons consisting of millionaires, socialites, bums, gangsters, promoters, fighters and fight managers, not ever forgetting John Q. Public, who paid the freight.

The plot in itself was simple. Young American boy, who has done a little boxing with no particular success, enlists in the Marine Corps when war comes, and goes to France, where he wins the light heavyweight championship of the American Expeditionary Force and makes admiring friends who upon his return continue acquaintance. One of them, a wealthy businessman, introduces him to a fine girl with whom he falls in love, but who is out of his reach because of position and wealth. Decides he can hurdle the social barrier, but must be a millionaire in his own right before he can ask her to marry him. Self-educates himself, wins heavyweight championship of the world, makes a million dollars, weds the girl.

But the incredible feature of the tale is that where the amassing of a million dollars for a man who starts with nothing may be considered a lifetime job, Gene Tunney did it in forty minutes by the clock. The times, the age, the situation, the strange characters who wandered in and out of his story, made it possible for him to earn that amount in a single ten-round contest, win the contest, and retire from the ring undefeated and wealthy.

There are those who believe that the time, the place, the era and the accidental components of any situation are unimportant, that it is the man that counts and that he would triumph or gain his end under any set of circumstances. The story of Tunney makes out a hard case for this philosophy. There were disquiet, ambition and courage in his soul, but he needed the war, Tex Rickard, Jack Dempsey, the million-dollar gates and the wildest spendingest era in the history of the country to help him. Without them he might still be totting up columns of figures on his high stool, or at best have become one of the many minor pugilists who clutter up the record books for a time and then vanish into the limbo from where they came.

So many extraneous events influenced his plot. It was Muldoon and Farley, the New York boxing commissioners, who first insisted that Dempsey fight Harry Wills, the Negro, before any other contender, and then outlawed the match in New York State. This gave rise to the circumstances that made Rickard sign Tunney as challenger, giving him his chance, and taking the match to Philadelphia, where it was fought in pouring rain, a circumstance that certainly was no aid to Dempsey or his style. Or suppose that Dempsey had not met and married Estelle Taylor, with the result that he became estranged from his manager, Jack Kearns. There are many who believe that had Kearns trained Dempsey and been in his corner that soaking night in Philadelphia, events might have turned out differently. But would they, at that? There is documentary evidence that Tunney signed a pact with Maxie Hoff, boss of the Philadelphia nether regions, in which Hoff was to give Tunney what is known as 'protection'.

Had Tunney not fought in the AEF, he never would have made the contacts that eventually led him to his love affair and his bride. And had Dempsey not allied himself with Al Capone in Chicago at the time of their second fight, Dave Barry, who gave Tunney the long count, never would have been in the ring that night. Davey Miller was the number one referee around Chicago in those days. But Davey was Capone's man, and too blatantly so. The situation outraged the Chicago Boxing Commission sufficiently to give it courage to buck Capone, keep Miller out of the ring, and substitute Barry, with the results that are history. Miller would have counted Tunney out.

Scandal fogged Tunney at every turn on his way to the top, because boxing is a scandalous game, but somehow it never managed to hurt him and he always stepped clear of it. Hoff sued him and produced the agreement bearing Tunney's signature. After Tunney knocked out Italian Jack Herman, a newspaper charged that Herman had succumbed to the good old push to the shoulder-blade, a libellous statement if untrue, especially since it was intimated that the Tunney management had engineered the deal. Nothing ever came of that, and nobody ever knew whether it was true or false. I once asked Tunney point-blank about it and he replied with considerable logic: 'Why bother to fix that one? If I can't knock out all the Italian

Jack Hermans there are, one after the other, I'd never put on another glove.'

Just what 'Protection' Hoff was to have given him, or did give him, never developed because when the bell rang for the first fight with Dempsey to begin, it turned out that it was Dempsey and not Tunney who needed protection. There was nothing particularly remarkable about the fact that a prizefighter should have made a deal for assistance in a strange town. The help that gangsters could give to prizefighters was always problematical, but most fighters preferred not to take chances. The remarkable thing is that the same young man could contract two alliances separated by a distance greater than that between the two poles – Boo-Boo Hoff and the Lauder family – and get away with both. The qualities of Gene Tunney I suspect have never been fully appreciated. Coming from the middle stratum, he was neither gangster nor hoodlum nor blue-blood, but apparently he was able to use the one connection as a stepping-stone to the other. Only an Irishman could try that. And only an exceptionally strong character could get away with it. There was never any weakness in Tunney. He always knew what he wanted and how to play the game to get it. But it takes an unusual man to play a dirty game to attain clean ends and not suffer damage from it. Not that Tunney played a deliberately dirty game during his fighting career, but no one ever got to the top of a game as essentially foul and unprincipled as prizefighting with absolutely clean hands. Tunney was always very badly misjudged, and by those of us who were closest to him and to boxing. From where we sat, it looked as though he were a prizefighter, a common pug with a decidedly snobbish and unpuglike desire to mingle with his betters. The truth was that Tunney was far from common. He was in many ways an idealist. He was always ambitious and preferred the company of pleasant people to toughs. But he had the great strength of character to take that little stroll through the sewer when there was no other way. His end always justified the means, to him. His curious associations were made not from choice, but from necessity.

The story-book hero goes through life resisting every temptation and preferring to sacrifice himself rather than abandon his ideals, and we like to read about him because it is such a pretty picture; but we know that in life it doesn't work that way and that all strong men and great men, with few exceptions, have had, at one time or another in their careers, the strength to do something to attain an end that they would prefer to forget once the end is reached. And it is only when they fail to attain that end that they are not forgiven. I maintain that it takes extraordinary strength for a man constitutionally decent and essentially idealistic temporarily to abandon those ideals for eventual better service to them. It is more Machiavellian than Christian, but disciples of Messer Niccolò's recipe rule the earth today. We may not admire it, but we recognise it. Tunney apparently had that strength when he needed it. When it was possible to ply his trade decently, he did.

Probably no athlete ever has had to take the public beating that fell to Tunney on his way to realising his ambitions. He was caught groping for light, serenity and education and ridiculed for it. He probably never knew it, but he was paying the penalty for violating a popular concept – that of the pugilist. The only serious mistake he ever made in his career was when he let his managers, for publicity, trade on his genuine appetite for education and beauty. Again we all mistook the real Tunney for the false, and the false for the real. We kidded him nearly to oblivion about Shakespeare and books because we thought it was a phoney pose. But that wasn't the part that was phoney. That was real. It was the pugilist that was false. Tunney was always an artificial fighter. He never in all his career in the ring made a natural movement. For that very reason he was one of the most correct fighters the ring has ever known and one of the best boxers. He only lost one fight in his entire career, and that, properly enough, to unorthodoxy. He was soundly thrashed by the wholly unpredictable Harry Greb. But it is an indication of Tunney's mental capacity and powers of study that he demanded a return fight with Greb and reversed the decision.

Certainly Tunney overplayed his rapidly acquired learning, but no more than any college sophomore. He was so avid for education that he never bothered with selection. He took it all in, in great gulps. He took so much in that some of it had to spill over. This phase would have been unnoticed had he been on a campus. But he was by choice and profession a prizefighter, and the effect against that background was comic and sometimes even a little pathetic, had any of us been attuned to pathos.

When the typical denizen of the fight world said bitterly: 'That Tunney! Thinks we're not good enough for him . . .' he was quite right. It was exactly what Tunney thought. And they weren't good enough, either, but I don't believe Tunney ever lost much time brooding over it, because it doesn't take much to be better than the average citizen of Cauliflower Alley. He was accused of base ingratitude to the fine game that had made him, because he had the intelligence and strength of character to escape from it before boxing had a chance to exhibit its usual form of gratitude to the men who participate in it – jiggly legs, stuttering tongue, failing sight and an empty purse.

Tunney was thoroughly unspectacular in the ring, but he was workman-like and efficient. Boxing actually is a science, and Tunney studied it from that angle. If there was any truth in the scientific angle, it could, with study, application and practice, be made to serve his purpose. Fighters like Dempsey and Joe Louis and others too numerous to list are natural battlers. Their styles are developed from within themselves and suited to their physical abilities and temperaments, and all of them have weaknesses which eventually prove their undoing. It is safe to say that in the ring Tunney had no weaknesses. He made occasional mistakes – vide the time Dempsey put him down in that historical eighth round in Chicago; but no one is ever perfect. His style was correct by the book. When he knocked men out as he did Carpentier and Tom Gibbons and Tom Heeney, it was because he hit them so often compared to the number of times they were able to hit him that eventually they collapsed from the accumulative and numbing effect of steady punishment. He would have knocked Dempsey out both times, in Philadelphia as well as Chicago, had the fights gone fifteen rounds instead of ten. Dempsey was on the verge of collapse at the end of each fight.

Before he was ever matched with Dempsey for the title, Tunney once said to Ned Brown, a newspaperman: 'I've seen Dempsey fight and I was impressed with his lack of knowledge of boxing. He knows so little about the science of boxing that I'll surely knock him out if I ever get the opportunity to fight him. I'm not saying that Dempsey is not a great fighter. He is just that, a great natural fighter, but I'm certain that I can outbox him. He's got to hit you to beat you, and he won't hit me – that is, not with any of the pile-driver punches that he has landed on the others. He couldn't do much with Tom Gibbons. I knocked out Gibbons, and Dempsey couldn't. I know I'm a faster and straighter hitter than Dempsey. Jack never was much of a stayer. By that I mean he fights so fast in the early part of the bout that he tires quickly. Generally by the time he tires he has the other fellow all-in too. Witness the Willard and Dempsey fight. Jack was almost as all-in at the finish as Willard was. When he fights me he'll not be hitting me, and I will be hitting him – and hitting him hard, too. That is, of course, if I'm ever lucky enough to meet him in the ring.'

That sort of talk drew loud and raucous laughter from the cognoscenti and experts, most of whom were as far off in their predictions of the outcome of the first Dempsey–Tunney fight as they were when they prophesied that Joe Louis, a natural fighter, would annihilate Max Schmeling, another chap who knew more than a little about boxing. But the interview was an exact description of what actually happened when Tunney and Dempsey *did* meet – barring the knockout. And the bout was too short for that. Dempsey could not have gone two more rounds in Philadelphia.

Tunney left nothing to chance. His style was orthodox and correct, straight left-hand leads and straight right-hand crosses delivered from the shoulder, the fastest punch there is and one that will always beat a hooker. Schmeling used it to beat hooker Louis. Tunney worked for years hardening his hands, chopping trees, doing manual labour, strengthening the bones, pickling them in brine to harden the skin, because they were the weapons of his trade. Three-fourths of the fighters in the business know nothing about taking care of their hands and as a result lose thousands of dollars annually through being laid up with injuries to their knuckles, thumbs or wrists. Tunney was the only fighter I ever knew who spent hours on the road, practising running *backwards*, because when a fighter goes into retreat in the ring, he moves in that direction and that direction only. His famous retreat from Dempsey and a certain knockout after he got up off the floor in Chicago may have been unromantic, but it was effective and masterly. He was prepared for it.

His care of his body was as efficient as his study of the art of self-defence. He knew that without condition and perfect training he could not carry out the manoeuvres demanded by the science for survival and victory. He also knew that he must always be in shape to withstand punishment, as the boxer has not yet been born who can go into a fifteen-round fight, carry any kind of an attack, and not have to take a certain amount of punches. Tunney took as few as was humanly possible.

The night before he broke his camp at Stroudsburg, Pennsylvania, in the Pocono Mountains, where he trained for his first fight with Dempsey, he did a thing that was characteristic. And he did it practically in privacy. Only one or two of the boxing-writers were there. What was the use of too much coverage? He was going to be knocked out by Dempsey anyway. Tunney in his final workout took on three of his best sparring partners for a round each and never let a punch go the entire time, but contented himself merely with blocking, slipping and ducking punches. I had a little boxing-writer on the job down there by the name of Jackie Farrell. Farrell reported to me that it was the most marvellous exhibition he had ever seen anywhere, any time. Tunney boxed the entire nine minutes, consecutively and without a rest, one man after the other, each spar mate attacking him for three minutes, and in that time not one solid punch was landed on him. It didn't seem possible, but it happened. I wish I had listened to Farrell. I picked Dempsey.

Tunney's faults were all those of youth, tactlessness, a devastating frankness and inability to conceal his dislikes. If he was a social climber as he was always accused of being, at least he was consistent at it, and he got there. I have thought lately that Tunney was always smart enough to know that many of the crew of socially prominent and wealthy millionaires, as they were called in the fight racket, were patronising him because he was a famous personage and the heavyweight champion of the world, and it was at the time fashionable to consort with prizefighters, but he was also smart enough to get his back out of them. He used them as much as they used him. Someone had told him or he found out for himself that if you can manage to consort with money long enough some of it will eventually rub off on to you. But many fine people genuinely liked Gene because he was a likeable personality.

Eventually the public that once despised him caught on to the fact that by and large, as men are in this far from perfect world, he was a pretty good specimen. Two years ago I got him to make one of his rare public appearances. We had invited a team of English amateur boxers to come to the United States and meet our Golden Gloves team in an international match at the Yankee Stadium. I wanted a referee who understood boxing and who could be trusted to be scrupulously impartial to a guest as well as home boy, who would know what he was looking at and call them as he saw them. I went to Gene Tunney and asked him to take on the job. He was a little diffident as to what his reception might be. But I had a hunch, and it was the right one. When Tunney was announced as the referee and climbed through the ropes, the 50,000-odd people in the stadium rose and cheered him for ten minutes. He had never received an ovation like that before. It came a little late, but must have been a great satisfaction nevertheless.

ROUND 3
Fight of the Century

8 March 1971: an evening etched in the memory forever. I was here to see Muhammad Ali meet Joe Frazier for the heavyweight championship of the world. There would be other occasions when I would watch the great Ali in action, but nothing would ever surpass the tension and excitement of that unforgettable night in a packed Madison Square Garden. My companion on that night was a casual acquaintance. A man who was not really a fight fan, or even a sports fan per se, but a man who, nevertheless, wanted to see a good fight. He was hoping for a Frazier victory. Not because he held Smokin' Joe in particularly high regard but because, like many people at that time, taken in by the Ali rhetoric and not realising that it was a superb bit of showbiz hype, he wanted to see the loudmouth humbled. How could you tell such a man that this wasn't just another fight? That Muhammad Ali wasn't just another boxer, that this contest transcended mere pugilism, and that what was about to unfold before his eyes, and mine, was nothing less than history in the making? It couldn't be done, so I didn't try.

One memory stands out. A small thing, in its way, but indelibly imprinted. Ali, warming up, swings his right arm in a huge windmilling motion. The crowd, adrenaline pumping, respond with a roar of pent-up emotion, the kind of sound you hear in only one other place: the bullring. A mighty Olé of anticipation. Olé – and, the fight had not yet begun! It was an appropriate overture for the fifteen-act mano a mano to come. The consummate matador that was Ali would indeed confront Frazier's raging bull.

Probably more has been written about this contest than any bout in ring history. However, one man present that night was in a unique position to convey the essence of this titanic struggle, from an equally unique angle:

the boxer's point of view. Former world light heavyweight champion, former chairman of the New York State Athletic Commission, and that rare combination, a boxer with a writer's talent, José Torres. This protégé of Norman Mailer and Budd Shulberg here recounts the story of that 'Fight of the Century'.

Sting Like a Bee

José Torres and *Bert Randolph Sugar*

In thirty seconds we are going to see the first second of the Fight of the Century. I'm just thinking about what Yancey Durham said before the fight. He had sounded cool. 'The first round is going to be Ali moving away with my man chasing. Clay is going to look good,' Durham said. 'In the second, Clay is going to be like in the first, moving fast and Joe missing. In the third, Clay is going to start getting hit in the body. By the sixth he might start picking the place where he's going to fall. He shouldn't be able to take Joe's punishment for more than seven rounds.' Durham is not a man who is known to brag about his fighter, but this prediction sounded accurate enough for me. My idea of the fight was more or less the same.

Dundee put it this way: 'It's a very dangerous fight. Tough fight. This will be a great fight. Muhammad's toughest fight. But he'll beat Frazier! Frazier is made-to-order for him. I love that kind of style for him. I feel Joe Frazier's fighting a fighter he won't be able to contend with. This guy's got the speed, the agility. He's going to make him fall short with punches. Frazier's never missed people with punches before 'cause guys were there to be hit. This guy is not gonna be there to he hit and he, Frazier, is gonna catch punches. And if Joe walks into a shot – leaping at Ali or trying to catch him – he's gonna get nailed. It could be the end of the fight. If Ali plays with him I'll not be surprised. I won't be surprised at anything this guy does.'

Dundee had told me that about three weeks ago. But in Miami about a week before this night, I asked Dundee, Cassius Clay, Sr, and Bundini the same question: 'Why do you think Ali is going to win?'

'This man is destined to be the greatest,' was Dundee's response.

'Champions are born, they are not made,' Clay, Sr answered proudly. Could any father say the opposite?

'God is his trainer, his manager, his companion. God and only Him, will win this fight,' Bundini said with conviction – he was part of the Trinity.

You can't go to a boxing man like myself and offer that kind of explanation. They knew it. If they were expecting Ali to win by something based on those answers, then it would be proper to think that they were whistling scared.

That afternoon Ali had not been too good. In fact, he had been hit with some good shots from three of his sparring mates.

I, myself, had boxed that day with Ali. In the one round I sparred he took it easy. He knew this was my first time with boxing gloves in two years. It was only after the first two minutes that Ali began to use a little pressure on me. He threw a few combinations and I made him miss. At one point he lay against the ropes and I hit him with a couple of hard shots to the body. There was a moment when I used a double right hand – uppercut to the body and short right to the head – and both punches made contact with the spots I had chosen. But I had to admit Ali was fantastically fast with both his hands and legs.

Yet, again, what really worried me was his head. Physically speaking, I couldn't make any judgement on the one round we boxed. I made other judgements after I saw him finishing his training with the other sparring partners. I came to the conclusion that Ali's reclining back against the ropes was no theatre, no tactic, no laziness. It was a habit. A habit created by the sensibility he developed in the three and a half years he was off.

It took three and a half years to develop that habit, and he's not going to break it in one night. One consolation I have and it is what Cus told me a few minutes ago: 'I think both of them [Ali and Frazier] lost some interest in boxing. They are saying that they are going to quit after this one. If they are telling the truth then it means that they have lost some desire to fight. So we might be seeing a lousy fight tonight.'

But it has been established. A fighter lies a lot. When Ali and Frazier said that they might quit, they could very well be lying. One thing is sure: Ali is going to lie back against the ropes and he might run into damaging hooks.

The assumptions are over. The crowd is silent. The fighters are ready to charge at each other. In the corner, Ali just ended his prayer. It seems as if the man with the bell can't start this damn fight.

The echo just reached me. The bell.

Frazier walks straight in, Ali comes in a circle. They both meet almost in the centre of the ring with Ali feinting. Frazier charges, slower than a tank, faster than the fastest turtle. He is like a special machine, a computerised machine which has been fed only with a truth chart. A machine which will reject lies automatically. You can't lie to this machine. You can't fool him with your feints. The first thing Ali does is to try.

Ali jabs. He jabs again. Frazier bobs and weaves as he comes in to Ali. Now Frazier falls short with his own jab. Ali steps back and counters with a jab. Frazier still walks in. Ali stops and throws a jab, another jab. A lot of his punches are missing. Steps back. Frazier keeps coming. Ali stops again, he throws a jab, steps back, feints, throws a fast jab and follows with a right cross, comes back with a fast left hook–right cross combination. A lot of his punches are still missing. Frazier still charges.

Joe is moving his head as he comes in. His body moves from side to side, his strong legs push him in, his hands move up and down, his chin close to his chest. He jabs and hits Ali on the gloves. Ali moves back. Frazier connects for the first time in the fight. It is a right to Ali's chest. Ali keeps moving. He moves straight back and Frazier follows. It is a relentless pressure. Ali looks cool as he moves back with class, looks like the old Ali, the young Cassius Clay. Ali hits Frazier with a jab, steps back and throws a slow chop of a right which goes over Frazier's head.

Frazier keeps the same pace. They are inside now and Ali pushes Joe to the side and hits him with a jab. Ali smiles. Frazier throws a left that falls short again. The bell. Ali's round.

Ali is good tonight. Pete agrees. The first round was not what you call a one-sided round for Ali, but undoubtedly he won it.

As the crowd sits quietly waiting for the second round, I see Ali standing in his corner. He didn't sit down after the bell. He's still trying to lie. He hasn't understood yet that you can't lie to a machine. But Ali looks confident. He looks as if he is going to be a hard man to knock out tonight. If he keeps up that confidence I see in his eyes, he'll play with Frazier. He seems to he listening to what Dundee is telling him. The bell.

Again Ali comes in a circle. Again, he feints. Frazier jumps back and jumps back in. Frazier seems to be in the path of Ali's punches while at the same time he doesn't seem to he able to reach Ali. It's understandable. Ali's reach is eighty-two inches to Frazier's seventy-three and a half. Besides, Frazier has been trained to use his shoulders and body with his punches. He has to come close to you to land solid blows. In turn Ali taught himself to use only the snap of the arms. So he doesn't have to be too close when punching.

Ali stops now. He throws a barrage of punches. Pushes Frazier back beautifully and then jabs at him again. Ali smiles again. He had Frazier on defence a second ago. Now Ali moves with Frazier chasing, maintaining the same exact pace. Ali's eyes seem to be fixed on Frazier's forehead, Frazier's on Ali's chest. Fighters have sub-conscious habits. Some believe that the opponent's eyes send them a message before a punch comes. Others feel that looking at the opponent's gloves gives them the clue. I always looked at my rival's chest. Nobody taught me, but I felt that something moved around the other man's chest muscles before the punch came out.

Ali circles around Frazier and looks like he has never been away from a ring. Jabs come out like old times. He jabs again, moves to his right, now to his left. Frazier follows. His face seems like a wild animal. He looks like he's grunting as he keeps up his chase. Like Bonavena, Frazier is waiting.

Ali jabs and Frazier falls short again. The truth is that Ali is not moving voluntarily, he's being forced to move. It reminds me of what Joe said yesterday: 'It is not the same when a fighter moves because he wants to move, and when he moves because he has to.' But again, Frazier is not cutting the ring short, he is following Ali.

Frazier connects this time with a jab to Ali's head. Another jab by Frazier falls short. Ali comes back with a jab of his own that passes over Frazier's moving head. Another jab by Ali that misses. Frazier seems to put a little more speed to his charges. Twenty seconds to go and Ali throws a left-right combination, both over a moving target. They get close, and there is the bell.

This round could be considered one-sided. But what caught my eye here is that Ali won the first two minutes and forty seconds handily, but for the last twenty seconds he did nothing while Frazier seemed to increase the pressure.

Again, Ali stands up in his corner. Frazier sits down to listen to Durham who speaks calmly to Joe. Dundee is doing the talking in the opposite corner. Once in a while Bundini says something. But when

Dundee opens his mouth, Bundini remains quiet. Another corner-man with Frazier washes his mouthpiece. Durham wipes some of Joe's sweat from his forehead.

Ali remains with his mouthpiece in his mouth. I don't know why. It is a relief – or it was for me – to have that bulk out of my mouth. But Ali might have his own reasons. After all, who has his mouth?

Third round. Frazier gets up as usual. He walks straight to Ali who has to meet him in his own corner. Ali doesn't circle around as he did in the first two rounds. Ali moves one, two, three steps back into the ropes. There he is! Against the ropes! *Is* he tired already? Frazier begins to work. A wild left by Frazier. Ali pulls back and the hook sends waves of hot air to ringsiders. It went so fast you couldn't see the glove. It was a hard, very hard left hook. Ali remains on the ropes. Joe looks for openings. Joe connects with a right to the body, comes back with another long left hook, it misses again. Ali still against the ropes. Joe hits with a vicious left hook to Ali's elbow. A right that hits Ali's face as it moves away. A fast hook grazes Ali on the right side of his face. Now Ali tries to move, Frazier won't let him. Joe pushes Ali back to the ropes. Ali smiles. Now Frazier smiles.

Another hook by Frazier lands on Ali's face, but without any power. Ali saw it coming and rolled with the punch. Ali gets out. Frazier pursues with anger. He chews his mouthpiece. Ali flicks a jab. Another one. Joe is walking now like a German tank. Yes, it is a machine with brains. Frazier only stops when he has Ali against the ropes. His legs cease to move. The switch that turns the movement of the legs off, automatically puts the hands on. And that's happening now.

Frazier throws vicious punches. Ali looks at the crowd and shakes his head no. He is not hurt. His constituents laugh. Ali now smiles at the crowd. Again, his crowd laughs and applauds. Meanwhile, Joe is punching. Joe punches now to Ali's stomach. Joe furiously throws a left hook, a right, another hook. Only the right made contact. Frazier is making the fight.

Ali throws a flurry of punches which wouldn't budge my sister. Now Frazier is the one who laughs. The 'other crowd' laughs with him. He has his constituency here too. Frazier comes back. A mean left hook misses Ali by accident. Ali never saw that punch. He was moving at the time Joe happened to throw it. Somehow Ali has not been hit with a real damaging blow. He seems to hold some control over his thinking. His head is clear. He knows what's going on. Is he testing Joe's punching power? Is he trying to get Joe to punch himself out? Is he being stupid? Is he trying to discourage Joe? These questions seem to be in everybody's minds. But the question to ask is: Can he do otherwise? Is this a put-on, or real?

My question is: Is he lying again?

Muhammad Ali is too smart to stay against the ropes using that as a tactic. He's getting killed. Not in the literal sense, because Joe hasn't been hitting accurately, but Ali is losing this round big.

Ali doesn't even try to get off the ropes. He is in bad trouble if he keeps this up. You can't do that against a powerful man like Frazier. He has the power and the head that goes with it. Frazier is going to find an opening sooner or later. He isn't Bonavena who just throws punches at you. Frazier knows when to throw them.

Like now, he just hit Ali with a left to the body. Ali rolls with a left hook and a right cross. The bell. This is a big round for Frazier. Perhaps, the worst round of the 204 rounds Ali has boxed in his whole pro career, including the times when he was knocked down by Sonny Banks and Henry Cooper. In those fights he got up to finish the round on his feet. And lost those rounds in which he got knocked down only because of the punch that put him down. But here tonight, Ali was punished thoroughly and miserably for three full minutes. Sure, he didn't get hurt, but not one soul could say that *maybe* he won this round. And only a few here knew what effect those body blows might have later on. He just managed to lose this round big. I don't know what this might do to his confidence.

The bell just sounded for the start of the fourth round.

Frazier comes out fast towards Ali who tries to move but can't. Ali is caged again against the ropes. What is he doing? Ali laughs with the crowd. He's lying. He's been too obvious.

The pattern of the fight changed in the third round and it seems as if this new pattern will prevail for the next couple of rounds. Of course, this transition is being forced by Frazier on Muhammad, who tried to establish a pattern in the first two rounds. And couldn't. Usually, the model of a fight is 'mutually' agreed upon by both fighters. One of them chases, the other moves back. If the one in continuous motion and retreat, stops and finds out that by moving less he can hit his opponent and at the same time doesn't get hit *more* than he was when he was moving, then it would be *convenient* for him to slow his footwork. It would, because he won't be 'wasting' energy. If the pursuer feels that he's also now more comfortable hitting the other man, then the shift in pattern has been agreeable to both.

So here, Muhammad is installed against the ropes and Frazier is banging away with murderous punches. Naturally, he's not landing with half of them. This transition was chosen by Ali but it has been happily accepted by Frazier too. After all, wasn't he looking for this change? The trouble with Muhammad is that he is not sure of what he's doing. So in between he shakes his head, woos the audience, sticks his tongue out at Frazier, smiles and throws slaps at Joe.

If what he's doing in the ring is not giving him much pain now, you can bet it will when he sees the score cards of the fight judges after the fight. He is alienating them. Ali is contributing to their natural prejudices. Don't forget, in the Ali–Bonavena fight the money man was Ali. Now he is not the future money man. He's not as far as Madison Square Garden is concerned. Frazier, we should remember, became champion in this town. And of his seven title defences, including this one, four have been in New York. He is the clubhouse boy. Ali is the independent, the uncontrollable one. Ali has to win his fight. He knows that. Or at least he should know that if he fights a doubtful fight, the benefit of the doubt will probably go to his opponent.

In the ring he's still in the new pattern. He's 'resting' in corners. The bell catches him for the second consecutive time on the ropes.

Ali walks slowly to the corner and for the first time in the fight, there is the stool waiting for him. He sits down. In the opposite corner Frazier sees Ali on the stool. Dundee is literally yelling at Ali. Dundee is talking and working on Ali's legs. He massages Ali's legs and Ali is saying something to him. If Ali once criticised football players, skiers, hockey players and even wrestlers for working in sports which were too dangerous, I don't know what he is thinking now. He once said: 'I became a fighter because I didn't want to be hurt like in those other sports.'

I hear the bell for the fifth.

Frazier flies towards Ali, who again chooses to stay in his own corner. Referee Mercante is letting the fighters stay inside. Mercante is doing a fine job. A referee should step in between the fighters only when one of them is holding with one hand and hitting with the other, when one fighter doesn't have the free movement of both hands or when they are both inside doing nothing for a reasonable period of time. So Mercante does not make them quit the ropes. And Ali doesn't grab, he simply lies back on the ropes and evades some punches, takes some on his arms, some on the belly, a few on the face. He is not countering.

Patterns have to do with this matter. Muhammad changed his pattern from moving fast to seeking the ropes for more than one reason, the most important being that Frazier set up the change. Joe tried from the beginning to stop Ali from moving, to make him change his first pattern. Ali didn't for the first two rounds because he was fresh enough to move around without jeopardising his future energy this night. He was hoping his speed would force Frazier to decrease his pressure. That way Ali could control the pace for the entire fight, and so run it on his best estimate of his own energy.

When the opposite occurred, and Ali was forced to take up Frazier's preference for a slower fight along the ropes, his professionalism panicked. You didn't see it. I saw it. He was not lying back against the ropes thinking that he was going to remain there all night because it was best for him. He was instead going to look for spots to let go punches like the one that toppled Bonavena.

In fact, he just tried to do that. Now, quickly, he moves out of the ropes and throws a stiff left jab. Feints. Goes back to the ropes and Frazier hasn't shifted tempo. So Ali connects, moves out, and comes back with a very fast left hook–right uppercut combination. The bell sounds with Ali's right on Frazier's nose. But Ali started too late. I think he lost this round too.

When pressure makes a fighter think ahead of time which precautions he should take, he is in trouble. Boxing is not a sport in which you can take an hour, a minute or a second to think. In boxing your sense of anticipation turns on only one-thousandth of a second before the actual action.

When a man is losing a match and then tries to change the pattern, he could be doing one of two things: searching to turn the tide – desperately – or looking for his excuse to lose a fight. However, when a winning fighter changes his pattern, the reasoning becomes more interesting.

For example, when I fought Pastrano, I knew that his best offensive weapon was the jab – he had a beautiful jab which came out of a deceptive movement – it was hard to anticipate; his best defensive weapon was his legs – they were very nimble. So, in the first round I outjabbed him, looking to beat him at his own game. In the second, I cut the ring short. It was some of the best fighting I had ever done, and it meant I had succeeded in lifting his best tools. In the third, I changed the pattern. After destroying his blueprint, I began using mine. I began to walk in and use my combinations to his body.

Ali, himself, did this when he boxed Cleveland Williams. After moving like lightning in the first couple of rounds in his own style, Ali came out in the third and outpunched Williams, and beat him at his own game – punching out murder. So he kept his body close to Williams in the third until his punches split the senses of the big man from Houston.

There are about thirty seconds left in this round, and for the last minute, Ali has been moving a little more than he did in the last few rounds. He hits Frazier coming in. Frazier misses a hook and a right cross, while Ali moves backwards towards the ropes. Frazier smiles. The bell. Not too good, but not that bad. I can just about give this round to Ali. I am prejudiced in his favour but no more prejudiced than any judge who is subconsciously for or against him.

Ali sits on the stool and from here I can see how hard he's breathing. Both Bundini and Dundee are talking to him. In the other corner Frazier is also breathing hard. I think that Frazier has never been hit so much in his pro career. Both fighters are working under tremendous pressure.

In the sixth, Ali seems to move more. Jabs and moves. Jabs again. Frazier hasn't changed. He's still coming in. He wants to maintain himself like a mirror in front of Ali. Frazier wants Ali to think that his forceful body is Ali's double. Ali throws an uppercut. Misses. Ali is trying more. This is his third pattern. He begins to throw uppercuts to a head that doesn't stop moving.

No one can argue about these two men's class. Both have their own special class. Ali and Frazier both have learned every punch there is in boxing. Yet Ali seems to have a more likeable style. He seems to throw punches with a special elegance. Frazier throws punches like the word 'boxing' sounds.

Could it be that Ali, with this elegance, is working a premeditated plan in which he will show Frazier that he is not going to collapse in the later rounds under Joe's body attack, but can take it and to some degree give it back, and take it, and – here comes the doubt for Frazier – still be in there fighting about the time Frazier wears down? If this is true, he is indoctrinating Joe. Yes, Ali could be showing Joe that he can take anything Joe has to offer and come back later to give it back.

Ali is not doing too bad now. I look at the clock on the Garden's wall and see that there are only ten seconds left in this round. Ali remains against the ropes, but Joe doesn't have the same drive. Joe misses a left hook. Ali jabs from the ropes. Ali smiles at Frazier. Frazier smiles at Ali. Joe attacks and misses two wild left hooks, both to Ali's face. The bell. I'm trying to be as objective as I can, but I saw Ali winning this round. On my score card I have Ali ahead at the end of seven rounds, four rounds to three.

Still, it is not a great performance by either of the fighters. Ali and Frazier are giving us their best, but their best tonight is not the best of them. They are both better fighters than they are showing.

Frazier, the more impersonal of the two, is showing the effect of pre-fight pressure. Of course, the build-up of this fight had no parallel. Frazier, as objective as he looks, as impersonal and unemotional as he has shown himself to be, seems, all the same, trying to overdo it. He is forcing himself to do his best. He is not fighting his natural fight. Although he won rounds three and four handily, he doesn't have the zip he did in those two rounds.

Ali, at times, seems to believe what reporters have said about him: that his three and a half years of inactivity have affected his performance, that he has lost speed of hands and legs, that he is pulling away from punches too slowly and that he's going to get caught with one of Frazier's powerful left hooks. It has to be a clash in his mind. I think he has come to believe reporters since the Quarry fight. So now his mind seems to be receiving no respect from his physical mechanism. The mind commands him to do this and the body is not answering. I only hope he can wake up. As long as the body can't believe what the mind says it can do, Ali will have trouble winning this match.

Round eight began thirty seconds ago. Ali walked out very slowly. Frazier goes straight to him, daring Ali, inviting him to try. 'C'mon, phoney, hit me if you can,' Frazier seems to say. Ali has no expression on his unmarked face. Frazier is the first one to punch; a left hook to Ali who turns his body as the hook lands right above his right hip.

Both fighters, because of the special circumstances, might be worried about going the full fifteen rounds at this speed. Right at this moment the fight is halfway through. The punches that are making contact on Ali's body and head are not too damaging, or hard enough to produce a knockout. In return, Ali's punches, although they have brought a little blood to Frazier's nose and mouth, are not of any knockout calibre either.

My confusion here is that this fight is so close that I can't predict at this moment who I think is going to win. Ali is now against the ropes on the south side of the Garden and Frazier is throwing punches while people are screaming with excitement. Yet Ali is laughing.

I counted seven punches thrown by Frazier; seven punches missed the target. Ali drops his hands at times, daring Joe to hit him. Now, again, as in the fifth, Frazier drops his hands and Ali throws a one–two combination that hits Frazier flush on the face, above the jaw. Now Frazier is the one laughing. He laughs in Ali's face, and Ali is not laughing. Frazier's legs push him towards Ali and Ali goes back to his favourite spot tonight: the ropes. Frazier lashes out another of his attacks. They seem ineffective and, in fact, they are now, but they might have their effect later.

Ali should know by now that Joe is not being indoctrinated yet. At times he seems to forget and his legs carry him to the ropes, as if still tempting Joe. But Frazier always appears delighted by the invitation. Round eight ends. Frazier made this round.

Ali is welcomed in his corner by two open mouths. They are telling him off. He deserves it. He's fooling around. At this point if Ali thinks he's fooling Frazier, he has the cards upside down. He is fooling himself. My notes tell me that the fight is even, four to four, but believe me, the third, fourth, and this last round, were giveaways by Ali. In each of these rounds he invited Joe to come and punch, Joe did, and Ali did nothing in return. Joe is obviously still strong enough to *take* some of the remaining rounds on his own, if not all of them. It looks as if Ali's choice of patterns has failed.

Of course, every time Ali comes back with quick moves, jabs and combinations, he shows his physical superiority. What bothers me is that Frazier is showing the confidence *and* the will.

The bell announces round nine.

Ali circles Frazier. Frazier misses a left hook and a right. Ali is moving beautifully again. He looks like he believes he has found his 'second wind'.

A jab by Ali, another one. Ali follows with a jab, a right and a snappy left hook. Every jab hits Frazier who still laughs. Joe trails Ali closely. Ali snaps a left jab, turns to a left-handed stance and jabs with his right. Ali comes right back with a one–two combination. Now steps back calmly.

I don't know what to make of Ali now. He seems like the old Ali. He connects again with his left. Then Ali pushes Frazier back. What? Yes, that's right: he just pushed the Machine back. Ali hits Frazier with a right. Frazier comes back with a jab and a right cross. They are now in the middle of the ring and they exchange blows. Man-to-man. Ali is the first one to step out of the short exchange. Frazier waves with his gloves at Ali to come back in close. Ali answers with a jab. Frazier comes running to Ali, and Ali stops him coming in with a stiff left jab, a perfect punch which can hurt as much as a good right cross. There is the bell. The fight is completely turned around. Ali won this round big, his best since the second.

One thing is clear to me now. I can't see how Frazier can win this fight. Ali just proved that when he wants, he can out-manoeuvre Joe. When they both are looking good, one can see Ali is the better man. But, one other thing is conclusively clear: Ali doesn't have full confidence. For if he does, why doesn't he force himself to try what he did in round nine more consistently? He is inconsistent, because he has no confidence. Either he is afraid of getting tired or afraid that if he takes more chances, he could get nailed by Frazier's left hook.

Meanwhile, Frazier seems to maintain the same type of pressure he's been putting on since the first second of fighting. When Ali was fresh, Joe was fresh. But now, the pace has slowed them a little. That's why when Ali stops fooling around in the ropes and throws punches, Frazier seems uneasy. At times, when Ali punches and moves, he makes Joe look like an amateur.

The gong says round ten.

Ali comes out and moves to his left. Joe throws a wild right that misses Ali. Now Ali moves to the centre of the ring. Joe meets him. Ali moves back towards that spot, to his cursed spot. Joe begins his work again. He is throwing fewer punches than before, but he's making more contact. A wicked left hook lands on Ali's body. A right takes Ali on his forehead. He is still there as if nothing is happening. He seems to be resting, which means he's thinking of giving this round away too. That's the beginning of corruption in a champ. My notes say that Ali is ahead by one round. If he presents Frazier with this round, it will be an even fight. At least, in my notes.

Ali has his own plan worked out. It has to be. He's not the same fighter he was in the ninth round. This man is using, in my opinion, wrong tactics, wrong patterns. Every change he makes is detrimental to him. When he tries to change, he loses his quality.

Undoubtedly, Ali's actions are encouraging to Joe. Every time Ali changes his pattern, Frazier's confidence builds. It's simple to understand. Ali is giving Frazier credit for too much complexity. He thinks if he shifts his pattern, Frazier will be confused. But Frazier just thinks Ali is getting dumb under the pressure. Joe just gets faster and stronger while Ali provides the ingredients.

Twenty seconds to go in this round and Ali has moved from one corner to the other, he has been on each set of ropes. Now he is to my far left, near his corner, north-east side of the Garden. He bobs and weaves under every single punch Frazier throws. He pulls away, Frazier misses again.

Frazier stops. He thinks, extends his left hand until it touches Ali, feints with his right and comes back with a vicious left hook. Misses. Goes back. Ali bends, Joe throws an uppercut. Misses. Ali throws one . . . two . . . three jabs. Hits. Comes back with a left-right combination of his own. Misses. Frazier throws a chopping right, comes back with a wicked left hook. Misses. The bell. This action by Ali took place in the last twenty to twenty-five seconds. But for two and a half minutes Frazier was chasing and Ali was going back doing nothing. Frazier missed a lot, but he was doing something. So my notes tell me that if the fight had been a ten-rounder, I would have scored it a draw.

However, I think that Ali turned the fight around in those last twenty seconds. When he stopped in his corner and concentrated on the defence, he made Joe miss ninety per cent of his punches. When he decided to punch, he landed ninety per cent of the time.

Of course by now, nothing is going to discourage Joe, but it might give Ali some support for his otherwise dubious performance.

Since the beginning, the fight has been in Ali's hands. He can win it or lose it himself. No matter what Frazier does, Ali has command. So far we have seen Frazier's consistent pattern and Ali's various ones. With the different transformations this fight has gone through, with Ali's performance averaging perhaps a poor forty per cent, with some of the shots that have landed on Ali's face, the fight is close.

The buzzer disturbs my thoughts. Now the bell. It is round eleven. The next five rounds are the most important ones. If Ali continues to do what he did at the end of round ten, he can even knock Frazier out. But, his damn legs are leading him to the ropes again. Again! Frazier doesn't mind. He walks comfortably towards Ali.

I'm mad. What is he doing? Is he punchy? He had the fight won again in the final seconds of the tenth, and now he's spoiling it once more, staying up against the ropes with his back, shifting his face from one side to the other.

A left hook hits Ali!

Ali's legs shake. He was tagged! That was to the button. Ali can't control his weak legs. Frazier goes to the attack. He's hitting Ali's body with some vicious punches. A right to the body, a left to the body, now Frazier pushes Ali against the ropes.

Another sinful left hook!

Ali's legs buckle. He's at the edge of going to the canvas. His eyes are glassy. He has never been hurt this bad before in his entire career. He looks tired, disgusted, surprised, almost defeated. I don't know what's keeping him on his feet. Friends, Ali has guts. He has as much balls as Frazier. Believe me. I have never seen Frazier hurt this much. When Bonavena hurt him in their first fight, it was not as bad as the condition Ali is now in.

Ali's legs seem to be protesting. They can't carry the weight of his body too much longer. Ali's will is struggling to keep him on his feet. Frazier is punching. Frazier's muscles are forcing the arms to move faster, stronger. I can see it on his face.

Ali gets off the ropes and we can all see that his legs are still weak. Strength keeps them from total collapse. Frazier has become a ferocious animal, a bear sending his claws in for the kill.

Yet Ali still plays games. He is a magician who will not let go of the cards. He pretends to be worse than he really is. He makes believe that he's going to fall. Frazier keeps coming. The bell. Bundini is up, outside the ring throwing water at Ali who walks slowly to his corner. Water splashes some of the newsmen at ringside. Bundini's man is hurt.

Ali slumps on the stool. Dundee works on his weak legs. Bundini pours water over Ali's head and back. Dundee and Bundini are both hurt. Bundini, surely, got hit with the same punches Ali got hit with.

A betrayal occurred when Ali got hit with those wicked shots. Ali's physical mechanism double-crossed his mind. I'm very much inclined to believe that the three and a half year inactivity did in fact affect Ali's body performance. Ali's eyes saw both of Frazier's deadly hooks start, saw them from the beginning. Both hooks were extremely hard. Both slow, wild, telegraphed. Ali's mind said to his body: 'Move'. The body answered: 'I can't.' With that answer, his quick mind provided an alternative; it resisted the impact. Ali's courage kept the body from crumbling away. That was why he didn't go down. Could that courage which *kept* him on his feet be consistent enough to help his will win the fight?

My notes say that Ali is behind technically and my mind tells me that he is far behind psychologically. Ali might come back in the next round to try to vindicate himself. I hope not. He could get flattened. No emotion please. Be cool.

Round twelve just began.

Round twelve finds Ali searching for answers. He had a minute to recover from the beating he got in the previous round. On the stool he saw better what had happened to him. I think he's testing his legs. He moves to his left, now to his right. Frazier resumes the attack. Frazier pins Ali against the ropes once again. Ali keeps his right hand close to his cheek. He doesn't want to catch any more of those savage hooks on his chin. He is not showing it, but I know he is worried. He is even afraid to throw punches. He doesn't want to expose his chin to Joe's hooks.

Seems to me that Ali has chosen defeat as a reality tonight. He is doing it with class; he is making the choice Ché Guevara made; the Kennedys made; Martin Luther King; Malcolm X; Benny 'Kid' Paret. These men didn't purposely go to be killed in the particular place or day that they died; they just got killed. And each of these men had a distinct way of dying. Each of them died being a man. Paret and Bobby Kennedy smiled; King and Malcolm and John Kennedy had ironic looks. It was as if they'd fooled that part of the world which is rotten.

Ali has that sign. He's going to get beat, but with class. It'll be his choice, not Frazier's. Of course, that's his confidence talking. Yet sometimes when confidence lies positively it can convince the will. With Ali, of course, this could be a complicated situation.

Ali's confidence could believe it is the boss. It might have conversations with his will. 'Mister Will,' confidence could say, 'I'm going to lie about us, I want those lies to be true.'

So Mr Will begins to work, to fight. Many times they come out victorious.

Round twelve dies. It took a little of Ali with it.

Let me remind you, Ali has the physical ability to beat this man. He is like the 155-mm cannon loaded with shells, but with no one to pull the string. D'Amato used to tell me when I committed a stupid mistake inside the ring: 'José, a stupid man could be forgiven for his stupidity; a smart man who doesn't use his intelligence shouldn't.'

The bell. For those of you who are superstitious; for those builders who raise towers and jump from the twelfth to the fourteenth floor, this is round thirteen. It is for poor Ali too.

After his big ninth round, Ali has lost three consecutive rounds. If he wants to impress the three officials who will decide this fight, if both fighters are still walking straight after the fifteenth round, he better start doing something now.

And I don't mean that! He is on the ropes again. Frazier now looks like a man who began pushing a loaded truck uphill a long thirty-six minutes ago and his energy is threatening to give out. At the top of the hill is $2^{1/2}$ million in loot. Thirty-one real tough men have tried before and each one has failed. It is not a game, it's serious business.

His arms are tired, his legs weigh 200 pounds each, his lungs want everyone to stop breathing so he can get all the oxygen. Joe Frazier doesn't even stop now to look how far he is from the loot. He is going to find the strength someplace. It could be in a place beyond all his past capacities.

That's the way Frazier is punching now. His body burns with fire, his blood boils. Every organ of his body works for Joe. He might retire after this match. It could be his last fight and Joe is not going to let the 'phoney' in front of him tarnish his unblemished record. He is fighting with ego, with selfishness, with sadism. He's going to push the truck all the way up there. Even if he has to die to do it. Ladies and gentlemen, you can't ask for more. This is the will to win at its maximum posture.

Not once did I look at the clock. So the bell catches me listening to the murmur of Ali's constituency, the noise of Frazier's crowd.

This is the fourth round in a row that Ali has failed to win. I see no reason why he should come out and try harder in the next two. His ego, his machismo is not working for him. I think he's going to concentrate on going the limit. That's right. Ali is going to be a hard man to hit clean from now on. Every little energy he has is going to be put into one place: defence.

Sometimes, when I was in a tough spot with regard to my boxing training, I used to sleep. That was my way of escaping the real world. I feel that way now. I'm sleepy.

The fucking bell awakens me. It's, for those who are still counting, the fourteenth.

Ali is pulled again by the magnet of the ropes. The power of the magnet seems to increase on his body which in turn pulls in Frazier. And Frazier swings. Misses. Frazier swings again. Misses. Wait a minute! What's going on? Ali moves out and now he is the one doing the swinging. Connects. Swings again with a vicious left hook to Frazier's head. A right. He pushes Joe back and hits him with a one-two combination. Wow!

It seems as if this supreme effort is his alternative. He is using those mysterious forces. I can't explain it any other way. Ali is moving again.

He slides to his left and shoots a left jab. He changes to southpaw and jabs with his right. Comes back with a long left hook that passes over Frazier's moving head. I don't know if Joe is surprised, but I am. I think there is only one explanation for what's happening in the ring now. Ali, thinking that the pace was too fast, laid on the ropes for the last four rounds to see if Joe could punch himself out. At the same time he was saving energy for the last two rounds.

He explodes now. He looks like a new man. But he could be faking. The punches could be empty. I hope not. He throws a jab, another one, follows them with a right. He's not smiling. He knows that his psychology inside the ring has not been working against Joe. So he is all business now.

Joe still tries to connect but in vain. Ali has become a moving target once more. Of course, he's not moving fast, but Frazier is not charging fast either.

That was the bell and Ali *could* have a chance to pull through this fight. I have it eight rounds to six with Joe ahead, but I found myself cursing at Ali and in my pad I have round ten circled with a question mark. Any one of the three officials could have given it to Ali. With that possibility in mind, the fight could be seven to seven, with round fifteen the decisive one. If that's a fact, this is a very interesting fight. A great fight.

Expectation is still the word to use to describe the excited crowd. No one is sure who is ahead. Some say Ali, some say Frazier, but nobody is yelling one-sided.

Last round!

They are tired. Mercante is tired. The crowd is tired. I am tired. How much can the crowd do for their favourite? How much can I do for Ali? Maybe no waves can penetrate the root of the fighters. They have to stop outside waves. Their forces can't permit any outside interference.

Friends, Frazier is ready. He's walking a little faster, with more conviction in his steps. Frazier is getting ready to go beyond the tiredness of human flesh, beyond the function of the muscles. Joe Frazier has the attitude of a Trujillo, Duvalier, Franco. Yes, Joe is a dictator who tells his subordinates what to do. He is telling his hands, his legs, his heart and his lungs, that they must respect his mandate; that they are going to withstand every imposition he might coerce on them. That's that.

And Ali, what is Ali? Some kind of crazy democrat? I have to think about that. Into the fifteenth!

Ali is moving towards his corner with Joe almost on top of him. Ali moves to his left. He moves now to the centre of the ring. He moves straight back to the south side of the ring between his corner and the north-west corner. He moves his left foot back. Joe starts a left hook. He leaps with it. Ali is moving his head back slowly and not looking at Frazier. The left hook is reaching Ali's jaw. Too late. Ali sees it at contact. Ali's neck snaps to his left. Explosion. One million ants enter his body! As soon as they get in, they get out. Ali is not aware that his legs are folding under him. His eyes are closed momentarily. His body is falling fast. He's flat on his back. His joints are being moved by the nerves, without any message from the consciousness.

One second has passed and Ali's eyes are trying to focus desperately.

If he stays down every patriotic sportswriter will have a word to describe Ali: coward.

The referee says three and Ali is up. He is going to fight back. He walks towards Joe with a swollen jaw, the right side of his face distorted with the power of Joe's malevolent left hook. Frazier attacks. He just won the fight. The damage has been irreparable. The impact of that blow took everything Ali had left. He is there strictly to finish the fight on his own two feet.

Ali's magic didn't work. Ali's magic is honest. Ali's magic now works detached from Ali's other ingredients. Ali's magic is the only ingredient in Ali's boxing qualities that tells the truth. And Ali's magic says that when two great black fighters have a serious conflict, the one to win is he who deserves to win.

Tonight, in fact now, as Johnny Addie announces the decision of the two judges and the referee – all voted for Joe – Mr Frazier deserved to win. Long live Ali's magic conviction.

ROUND 4
Ring Quartet

Throughout the long history of professional boxing, the British Isles have produced some very worthy ring warriors. From England, Ireland, Scotland and Wales have come some great fighting men, to make their mark in the annals of fistic fame. Only that most glittering of all prizes, the heavyweight crown, has consistently eluded them, and looks like continuing to do so for the foreseeable future.

To do full justice to the many home-produced ring maestros would require a whole book in itself. We will therefore confine ourselves to just four such worthy examples.

Tommy Farr, the Welsh heavyweight who, against all the odds, took the legendary Joe Louis (then in his prime) to a fifteen-round decision. Tommy epitomised the tenacity, courage and sheer guts of the underdog, and gave the Brown Bomber a good run for his money.

Barry McGuigan who has done more to unite the people of his divided land than any politician, of any stripe. He won the world featherweight title in 1985.

Ken Buchanan was piped to the ringside to win the world lightweight title in a ferocious battle with Ismael Laguna.

Benny Lynch, last, but by no means least. The tough little Scot who gave his country its first-ever world boxing title. Rated by many as the greatest flyweight ever.

Four great fighters. Four great stories.

Tommy Farr

Frank Butler

No proud holder of a British passport did more to erase the phrase 'British horizontal heavyweight champion' from the American boxing lexicon than Tommy Farr. The snide phrase had come from the pen of a New York boxing writer following a series of unhappy endings to Phil Scott's battles in America. Scott's predecessors, Bombardier Billy Wells and Joe Beckett, suffered one-round annihilations at the hands of Georges Carpentier, which did not boost the export trade in British heavyweights. When Tommy Farr, an angry, hungry Welshman from Tonypandy, arrived in New York to challenge the newest sensation Joe Louis, the American writers scoffed at him, making him a 10-to-1 underdog. One New York columnist declared Farr had less chance against Louis than Shirley Temple. But the American writers and most British scribes were made to eat their words; they had not taken account of the toughness and guts of the man who had already won his fight against poverty. In his finest hour on 30 August 1937, Tommy Farr took on the Brown Bomber for fifteen punishing rounds and, though he did not win the title, he won the admiration of America as well as the hearts of every man and woman in Britain.

Farr did not emerge as an overnight hero. He had sweated down the mine as a boy. At the age of twelve he was fighting in the valleys to earn a few shillings. He served the hardest apprenticeship of any British heavyweight champion, taking on all comers in the booths. His ambition was to fight in London but his early visits as a teenager brought defeats against Eddie Steele, Eddie Phillips and Dave Carstens. He had tremendous faith in himself and was determined, despite the lack of enthusiasm from fans, not only to survive but to succeed. He moved to London, even though promoters showed no desire to give him fights or the sort of cash he felt he was entitled to. He took on Ted Broadribb as his manager. As Ted was also matchmaker for Jeff Dickson at the Albert Hall, opportunity began to knock for Farr in 1936. The ambitious Welshman received controversial decisions against the Americans Tommy Loughran and Bob Olin, both former world light heavyweight champions, but he won little praise from British critics. This only made Farr more determined to succeed and he went on to stop Jim Wilde to become Welsh heavyweight champion. This allowed him to qualify for a crack at the British title, which was in the hands of the South African-born Ben Foord, who had beaten Jack Petersen.

1937 was a vintage year for Tommy Farr. He took the championship from Foord in a dull fight and, though he still received little credit from the boxing writers, the title was his gateway to the stars. Sydney Hulls, then the top promoter, induced Max Baer, the former world heavyweight champion and a tremendous personality, to come to London to face the Welshman. The critics ridiculed the match and forecast a quick knockout for the hard-punching American playboy. They underestimated Tommy's determination and ability. Becoming British champion had boosted his already ample ego and his pride. He gave Baer a lesson in the left jab as he moved in and out, punishing the American, who in the early rounds clowned and scowled, obviously believing he had time to put the cheeky Welshman away with one big right. It never happened. That left jab split Maxie's left eye, and as the blood trickled down his face he began to show respect for Farr, who was moving with more rhythm than he had shown before. Baer, like everybody else, had underrated Farr's ring know-how, gathered the hard way in the booths for nearly a decade.

Always a little truculent, Tommy allowed earlier resentment and bitterness to thaw and be replaced with a philosophy and wit he had picked up from old Jobey Churchill, his mentor from the hungry days in the valleys. He also revealed a new charm which made him many friends apart from the usual hangers-on who dedicate themselves exclusively to life's winners. To Farr's credit, he could recognise the spurious and thrived on the embarrassment of those who had knocked him beyond fair criticism and who were now rushing to shake his hand.

Farr's victory over Baer provided the most exciting night since Harringay was built in 1934. Never had a British heavyweight handled a top American so easily. Sydney Hulls, who in his heart had not given Farr a chance, had a new box-office king. Previously he had had to work hard at selling tickets when Tommy was fighting. But that night, as a few hundred Welsh miners who had made the journey to London nearly lifted the roof with a rendering of *Land of My Fathers,* we all realised a new Tommy Farr had been born. Hulls immediately negotiated for Walter Neusel to meet Farr. The Welshman was again in scintillating form as, moving with the speed of a middleweight, he jabbed Neusel into confusion and put him down and out in three rounds. The German had entered the ring wearing a knee support and when he failed to beat the count some accused him of quitting, but the facts are that Farr had so demoralised him that he had no stomach to fight on.

This was the period when the Nazis were preparing to take over Europe. We had seen the Olympic Games in Berlin in 1936 turned into a political jamboree for Hitler and in the same year the German leader had sent his personal congratulations to Max Schmeling who had inflicted the first defeat on Joe Louis. This night von Ribbentrop, the German Ambassador to Britain, sat at ringside. After Neusel's defeat he immediately made for the exit.

The delighted Hulls now wanted Farr to meet Schmeling at White City. The German accepted £15,000 and Broadribb and Farr agreed to £7,500, but the fight never came off because Broadribb did a better deal with Mike Jacobs for Tommy to meet Louis, who had won the world title from Braddock exactly a week before Farr knocked out Neusel. Jacobs offered Tommy £10,000. Though Broadribb had signed with Hulls, the Welshman sailed for New York in August to the annoyance of both Hulls and Schmeling.

The New York writers wrote Tommy off from the day he arrived. It was only a question of how many rounds he could last with the Brown Bomber. One? Two? Three? Or perhaps six? The fact that they rated him so cheaply without even seeing his fight acted as a stimulus to Tommy, who was determined to make the Yankees rue their own sarcasm. And what a show the Tonypandy kid put on!

Farr was probably the only man in the Polo Grounds, New York, who believed he had any chance of beating the mighty Louis. Had he not picked up a cut eye in training a few days before, he would have stood an even better chance. His confidence was unbelievable as he walked into the champion from the first bell, despite the fact he had been called to enter the ring twenty minutes before the fight was due. Yet he had calmly sat watching a preliminary bout, an ordeal that would have unnerved most men about to face Louis. The world champion was surprised by Farr's confident aggression and still more puzzled by the Welshman's crouch. Tommy jabbed so well with his left that he soon raised a swelling under Joe's right eye and freely hit Louis about the body. All the Welshman lacked to become a world beater was a lethal right-hand punch. Louis began to settle down to hand out some pretty fierce punishment with his famed combination punches. Tommy's damaged right eye was made worse and Joe smashed some of his hardest rights against the Welshman's jaw. But the more punches Louis threw, the more Farr came back, ducking and weaving inside, always busy with his left jab and two-fisted attacks to the body. The Brown Bomber seemed determined to put a stop to the Welshman's bold bid in the seventh round when he released three smashing left hooks to Farr's chin and crossed as many times with his right, but the Welshman spat blood from his mouth, brushed aside more blood from his eye with the thumb of his glove and went back into the attack.

So it went on and on to the fifteenth and last round. The New York crowd were now cheering the brave underdog whom nobody expected to see still standing after six rounds. Tommy took a great deal of stick from the great champion. His face was badly marked yet never did he resort to a defensive role. The big difference was in their punching power and while Tommy's courage and toughness matched that of any fighter in the world, he did not have the dynamite with which to blast Joe Louis. After a magnificent stand by the challenger, Joe Louis was declared the winner and still champion. But no British fighter received more hosannas from an American fight crowd than Tommy Farr.

With hindsight, I believe Tommy made a mistake in hitching his waggon to the Mike Jacobs star. He got on well with Uncle Mike, far better than with his manager Ted Broadribb, with whom he had quarrelled after the Louis battle. Jacobs wanted to rematch Farr with Louis, but said Tommy needed a win first and thought he could easily beat Jim Braddock, whom Mike had persuaded to come out of retirement. But Braddock was a cagey boxer and as Tommy did not possess a big knockout punch, the fight was disappointing, with

Braddock taking the decision and Tommy's stock slumping. It would have been wiser for Farr to have gone back to Britain, defended his British title and had a few easy fights; he could then have gone back to Louis. But he stayed with Jacobs and took a return fight with Max Baer. This time Maxie gained revenge over fifteen rounds, dropping Tommy twice with tremendous rights. Jacobs still stuck by Farr and matched him with Lou Nova, but the Welshman lost another decision. His last appearance in America was against Red Burman, a moderate protégé of Jack Dempsey, but Farr dropped yet another verdict.

It was 1939 and Tommy had no option other than to return to London. He had lost all five fights in America but had finished on his feet every time. His moment of glory had been against Louis.

Though he beat Burman in a return in London and Larry Gains at Cardiff, Tommy's best days were over and he retired in 1940. He was discharged from the RAF in 1942 and for some years was a successful property dealer. Things later went wrong and Tommy, who had made and lost a fortune, returned to the ring after ten years' absence. It was a tremendous tribute to his ability that after living softly for a decade he was, at thirty-seven, able to win eleven of sixteen comeback fights. It was a pity that in this spell he suffered the only knockout defeat in his long career at the hands of Frank Bell, who would not have been able to shake the Farr of ten years earlier. Tommy showed tremendous guts in his comeback. It enabled him to straighten himself out financially. He retained the same courage he showed against Louis until his death in 1986.

'Leave the Fighting to McGuigan'

Jim Sheridan

'Let's go,' McGuigan says with all the cool of a commando. He's ready. In that moment a burden is lifted. It's too late to stop now. We are sucked down the long corridor by a tremendous noise. Desire made manifest in the shape of one long inexhaustible howl that would be a continuous scream except for the fact that it breaks like waves, each succeeding one crashing into the slipstream of its predecessor. What depth of passion created this roar?

The long corridor to the ring has a life of its own, opening and closing like a demented accordion. Ahead, the peace flag mast-head of this crazy caravan dances on the edge of a whirlpool that constantly threatens to pull us down. Eddie Shaw is a boxer, he fights his way through the crowd. There is no etiquette in hell. Tonight the roar is McGuigan's theme song and the score from *Rocky* plays a muted second fiddle, like a crazy violinist reading from the wrong stand. For 25,000 people at a football stadium in London, McGuigan is not the Great White Hope, he's the only hope.

The swell ends at the no-man's-land where the paying public meet the ringside commentators. Viewed from outer space, McGuigan is the centre of a sparkling necklace as a hundred photographers try to pull reality down to earth in a flash. Reality tonight is a dream come true. McGuigan is getting into the ring to fight for the world title. Ireland is good news for once, and 25,000 people erupt as He Who Never Steps Backwards comes through the ropes. He dances forward. 'Buy land,' said W. C. Fields, 'they don't make any more of it.' McGuigan dances across the ring, each hook and jab a down-payment on this piece of real estate. For fifteen rounds tonight this space is up for grabs. A boo stifled at birth warns us that the other bidder is on the way, and then the boo turns into the sustained applause worthy of this world champion.

Now all the forces are assembled and it's time for the national anthems. The British national anthem doesn't sit easy on the shoulders of 25,000 Irishmen, but eventually everybody behaves with the decorum invented in the heart of that other great empire . . . for a couple of minutes we are all in Rome. Suddenly from nowhere comes a sound as remote as the theme from *Rocky* was. It's impossible to make it out in the din. Pat McGuigan, microphone in hand, answers this musical quiz with the deadly ear of the born crooner:

But come you back when Summer's in the meadow
and when the Valley's hushed and white with snow.

Now everybody knows what it is and Pedroza looks around in belligerent defiance as the whole crowd joins the chorus:

'Tis I'll be there in sunshine or in sorrow
Oh Danny Boy, oh Danny Boy, I love you so.

These are 'the men that God made mad, For all their wars are merry and all their songs are sad'. If Pedroza is pulled in by the deceptively beautiful air then he's lost a psychological round. *Danny Boy* is a recruiting song for war. It's a brilliant ploy from the Eastwood camp, uniting the crowd in a lull before the storm.

Now each corner has one last trick to play from its psychological armoury. True to form and with a little nod to Carl Jung, Eastwood produces his from a subterranean level. Paddy Byrne lifts the skirts of the ring and the dwarf emerges. They wait till Pedroza turns away and then the little man jumps into the ring. The crowd shouts. Pedroza turns and the look in his eyes is astonishing. It's as if for a moment he allowed his subconscious to think that this was McGuigan. If only it were so . . . Reality returns and the cheekiness of the gesture demands a smile which Pedroza gives with a cool mastery. The MC's announcement of 'My Lords, Ladies and Gentlemen' is drowned out, presumably by the gentlemen. It's time for the seconds to get out of the ring. Eastwood feels something tugging at his sleeve. McGuigan looks around. '£5,000, my man at even money,' says Lyonel Hoyte. Eastwood looks into his eyes. '£5,000, my man will take him out,' repeats Hoyte. Eastwood looks for the green which is nowhere in sight and so he pulls away. Money talks, bullshit walks. There are no more ploys to play.

The opening round is marked by a combination of speed and phenomenal concentration. Pedroza's concentration is remarkable, given the fact that he is fighting on foreign territory – but then he has already performed in front of the grass-skirted warriors of Papua New Guinea. He has an amazing mind. He goes on his bicycle, shooting out long left jabs and keeping well out of McGuigan's way. The first solid blows are landed in the neutral corner where Dermot McGuigan has parked himself. They came from Barry. Dermot claps. McGuigan pursues the champion for the whole three minutes, but Pedroza wins the round with the effectiveness of his counter-punching.

Round two is much the same as round one, with one small exception. McGuigan, instead of following Pedroza around the ring, starts to cut off his territory. It's like the snake and mongoose, but

Pedroza is not hypnotised. He leans down in the middle of the round, staring into McGuigan's headlamps. Fighting inside, Pedroza can use his famed bolo punch which comes from below like an upwardly mobile piston. In this round he also lets loose a strong left hook, but the inescapable fact is that he is not overwhelmingly superior inside. McGuigan has neutralised his greatest asset.

From his commentary position Harry Carpenter is shouting, 'This can never go fifteen at this pace.' The third is the start of thirteen rounds that will make a liar of him. At the opening of the third round Pedroza fights brilliantly, whipping in a punch that is a combination of an uppercut and a bolo. Pedroza is such a craftsman he invents punches. This one lands under the heart. It should have slowed McGuigan down. It didn't. McGuigan keeps coming forward, and now he begins to slip Pedroza's jabs and counters with his own hooks to the body. The champion is acting as if these are having no effect on him. McGuigan's cheeks are rouged from Pedroza's left jab, but he never looks in trouble. This is not just a physical contest, this is going to be a battle of minds. That both men are in perfect physical condition is obvious from the first nine minutes. At the end of three rounds, nobody is ahead in either the psychological or the physical battle.

At the start of round four, Pedroza hesitates. The bell goes to call them to the centre of the ring and the champion turns back to get his gumshield. It is the first lull in the action. It lasts only five seconds but it's like a blemish on perfection. Is it a conscious ploy of Pedroza's or his unconscious asking for respite? Pedroza has trained himself to go fifteen rounds. He has trained to go three minutes a round – but not like this, this is inhuman. Not since the legendary Henry Armstrong has a fighter thrown as many punches per round as relentlessly as McGuigan. Each one of them is intended to take Pedroza's head off. He knows he is in with somebody desperate to win, fearless and strong. Pedroza is the master tactician looking for time to work out his strategy. He isn't getting any. Immediately the round opens, McGuigan catches him with a hard right. Pedroza shoots back a left hook and right uppercut. Most people at the ring think they see Barry smile as if the punches had no effect on him. He was in fact grabbing his gumshield in his mouth. McGuigan has two reactions when he has been stung: he grabs his gumshield tighter and he wipes off the gloves on his trunks as if to obliterate all that's gone before.

After that it's as if he's moving the contest on to a higher, more demanding level. It's this ability constantly to bring his performance up to the required level that reminds people of Sugar Ray Robinson. During the fourth and fifth rounds he wipes off his gloves on his trunks several times. Pedroza has only one answer: he must stand his ground. Somehow he has to stop this Niagara pouring over him. In the middle of the fifth, he tries to move Barry back. They stand toe to toe, exchanging orthodox and unorthodox blows. The kid is brilliant inside. And strong. Too strong. Pedroza decides to get on his bike again. This time he has a slow puncture.

Boxers are so alert physically in the ring that they sense what will later be revealed only by slow motion. At the end of the fifth round McGuigan sensed that Pedroza was slowing: he moved against the ropes in McGuigan's corner, looking for a breather. McGuigan didn't give him an inch. He loaded up to land the big one. When he threw out his long left jab he felt a tear at the elbow. The psychological advantage had been countered by a physical problem. McGuigan told his corner that his arm was acting up. Eastwood said he could beat Pedroza with one arm. He didn't get a chance to throw that arm until the seventh round.

Towards the end of the sixth round, a strong right to the body catches Pedroza. His knees buckle momentarily. Pedroza is hit with a strong overhand right. He stumbles and then looks to the ground as if he missed his footing and slipped. This man never gives out hurt signals. This is the technique Ali used against George Foreman until the champion ran out of heart. McGuigan's heart is as big as Loftus Road.

There's no faking the reaction to the right McGuigan hits Pedroza with at the end of round seven. His legs give out from under him and, before he can bring up his instinctive right arm in defence, McGuigan's left glances off it and sends him to the canvas. The champion has been humiliated. He recovers as best he can, getting up at three and acting as if an unruly banana-skin had just entered his life. McGuigan comes scything his way across the ring, a figure of death. Pedroza escapes the harvest. He is the coolest man in Loftus Road. In McGuigan's corner Gerald Hayes is banging the canvas, screaming, 'Feint and throw the right hand.' McGuigan's feint at the end of the seventh was worthy of catching a world champion. He feinted with his head as if he was going to throw a left to the body and then followed up with the big overhand right. Before Pedroza hit the canvas the crowd was on its feet.

The eighth round is Pedroza's best of the fight. He keeps McGuigan at bay with long left jabs and extraordinary counterpunching. Towards the end of the round he exchanges short sharp punches with McGuigan. This man is not going out without a fight.

At the start of the ninth round Pedroza catches McGuigan with a good right. He punches and boxes the same cool round as he did in the eighth, but then lightning strikes again. In almost the identical spot in the ring, McGuigan hits him with another right. McGuigan follows this up with a right to the temple and suddenly Pedroza looks like a Rip Van Winkle who has just woken up with his legs full of pins and needles. He stumbles across the ring. He lurches and tosses, miraculously avoiding the raging torrent that is McGuigan. Somewhere in his head, bells are ringing and blows are falling from all angles. At the end of the round Santiago del Rio is in the ring protesting to Mr Christodoulous that Pedroza has been hit after the bell. He holds up three fingers. Pedroza stands in the centre of the ring and then arches his back like one of the Scots Guards outside Buckingham Palace and heads back to his corner. This proud man is still featherweight champion of the world.

Pedroza slips at the start of the tenth round. He looks at the floor where the dwarf had sprinkled his gold dust as if to say, 'So that's why I've been falling in the same spot.' He has his mind trained so that it is impossible to lose, but his body will not obey. The tenth to thirteenth rounds are purgatorial. In each of them the champion boxes with the fervour of redemption, only to have his potential salvation snatched away at the end.

Pedroza tries his best shots in the thirteenth, hitting McGuigan with a long left and then a strong right hand. McGuigan hits him with another powerful right. By now Pedroza knows the reaction to that particular weapon: grab tight and hold on for dear life. He reaches out and grabs McGuigan with both hands. With pure animal strength McGuigan shrugs him off like a sack of potatoes and hits him with left hooks for his trouble. The referee raises his hands to stop the fight and puts them down as quickly again. Hope is deferred and Pedroza survives the round. At the end of the round Pedroza's corner gives him something that looks like ammonia to revive him.

At the start of the fourteenth Pedroza blesses himself as though it is the last, and then spends most of the round hanging on, determined to go out on his feet. Late in the round Pedroza is crouched low, trying to avoid McGuigan, when suddenly he sees his chance. He shoots a long straight right through McGuigan's guard to the chin. It is the hardest punch he has thrown all night. It is too late. When Pedroza goes back to his corner he sees Eastwood raise three fingers. He is three minutes away from losing his world title. In his corner, McGuigan is asking Eastwood, 'Are you sure I'm ahead?' Eastwood answers, 'You're as far ahead as from here to Belfast.'

Both men touch gloves at the beginning of the fifteenth round. Pedroza behaves with decorum and nobility. He is making his final exit with style. McGuigan ducks and weaves in close to Pedroza. This is what a normal fight looks like in round one.

The three minutes go by on a wave of euphoria. McGuigan is on his way to the world title, but somewhere deep down in him is the fear the verdict might be given against him. Close to the end of the fight he lunges at Pedroza with a Saturday-night special. The distance he misses by is a measure of Pedroza's class as world champion. The bell goes and Pedroza hugs McGuigan. The Eastwood camp are in the ring. Daniel McGuigan watches as Sean McGivern and Ross Mealiff in the company of the whole Eastwood entourage lift McGuigan shoulder-high. Pedroza is acknowledging McGuigan as champion, but when his team get into the ring they quickly raise his hand in a last, empty, professional gesture.

Like the Ali–Frazier epics, this fight defies mere professionalism. It's as if the divorce proceedings are over and McGuigan and Pedroza can become friends. There is no doubt that the old champion respects the pretender to his title. The announcement that officially confirms McGuigan as world champion is lost in a huge roar. Possessed young men hurl themselves at the ring as if they could levitate over the hunched journalists. They rise on the substantial backs of the penmen and engulf the ring, searching for McGuigan in an entranced fit.

As McGuigan realises that the title is officially his, he looks to his brother Dermot as if seeking proof that he won't wake up from this dream. Back home in Clones, Irish Television are asking Katie McGuigan if she is proud of her son. 'I'm happy,' she says. 'Pride is not a word I like. Just say I'm happy.'

Amidst the milling crowds McGuigan is led back to his dressing-room. Davey Irvine congratulates him. All the rest of the boxers on the bill congratulate him. When he has gone into his own dressing-room I ask Davey Irvine how it went. 'Beaten,' he says, 'in the third round.' He pauses. 'Or was it the fourth? That will just tell you how it went. That's it. That's me finished. I'm retired. I'm not tough enough. I hurt too easy.' The amazing thing about Davey Irvine is that there is not an ounce of self-pity or jealousy in his words. He appears as happy as a man can be who has finally resolved some inner truth about himself.

Paddy Byrne comes in and goes straight to Peppy Muir. 'There's your money,' says Paddy. 'I don't know if there's any point in fighting out there, but there's your money anyway. It's bedlam.' Peppy Muir looks at Paddy and then says, 'I want to fight. I want to be able to say that I fought on the McGuigan bill.' As McGuigan goes upstairs to meet the world's press, Peppy Muir goes out to fight a lonely fight with Simon Eubanks.

I have been with these boxers for two months now and the amazing thing is I have never felt any aggression from any of them. I don't mean aggression towards me, I mean aggression as part of their personality. It's as if they leave all their aggression in the ring. The world of the boxers themselves is a closed silent order where they can communicate with each other with a simple nod of the head.

Upstairs, at the heel of an enormous press throng, one of Gerry Cooney's people keeps asking rhetorically, 'Who trains this guy? I want to meet the man that gets this kid into that condition.'

Brian Eastwood tells him, 'You'll never meet him. We only stop McGuigan getting fit. That's our job – to stop him training too much.'

Cooney's man keeps shaking his head and saying, 'I wish I had fighters like that.'

Ferdie Pacheco, Muhammad Ali's fight doctor, is there. Long ago he recognised the special qualities in McGuigan. He presented McGuigan with his paintings of all the world champions. Ferdie knows talent when he sees it.

McGuigan can never redefine boxing in the way Muhammad Ali did, but he could redefine the definition of sport in this bloody business. He has the talent to be one of the major sportsmen of the second half of the twentieth century.

At another table Barry Cluskey is telling tales. He is an old family friend. 'I think they even called Barry after me. I was there the day he was born. After the fight people went mad. One fellow was jumping up and down with a towel in his hands. "I got the towel," he says. "I got the towel. Look," says he, and he holds the towel up in my face. "Look," says he, "it's the towel. The blood and all." Don't be showing me that, says I. I've got his fucking nappy.'

Cluskey, in the company of about 25,000 others, had a few jars after the fight . . . This had the effect of dislodging his memory somewhat and he ended up in the Grosvenor House Hotel, insisting that he was staying there. He turned round and saw the former champion come through the door. 'I turned round and there was the head and his entourage. I got a surprise, so kind of spontaneously I started to clap and all the people in the lobby started clapping too. Pedroza just froze on the spot and then tears started to come out of his eyes. Down his cheeks. He saw the cross around me neck and he came over and bent down to kiss it. With that his hat fell off. I stood back in surprise like and there was a momentary pause and I didn't know what to do. I got the feeling like that it might be an insult to him to pick it up for him. He bent down to pick it up and he couldn't make it. He couldn't bend down.' Barry's eyes start to mist over. 'What a champ. One of his people came over and picked it up for him. He couldn't bend down with his ribs. That's how much punishment he had taken. Then he put the baseball hat on and just walked away.'

Buchanan and Partner

Hugh McIlvanney

It will he a healthy irony if the damage done to Ken Buchanan's eyes at Madison Square Garden in the week helps him to see the way ahead more clearly. In the past Buchanan's view of himself and of the relationships crucial to his boxing career has been distorted by factors even more basic than bumps on the cheekbone and lacerations on the eyebrow. The fierce independence of his nature – a solitary strength nourished early in his life by what he saw as the implacable hostility of the world outside his family – has sometimes encouraged an excessive emphasis on self-sufficiency. He has seemed to feel that, with his powerful talent and the loyal support of his father and a few close friends, he could go on dominating the lightweights of the world without the need of professional advice or assistance. Specifically, his utterances and his actions have occasionally suggested that the presence of Eddie Thomas, the Welshman who has managed him since he began fighting for money, is now expensively incidental to his success. Monday night at the Garden may have changed all that.

The outcome of the championship war with Ismael Laguna was, above all else, a tribute to Buchanan's heart and the depth of his reserves as a fighting man. With his jab almost invalidated by the swelling that rose swiftly under his left eye in the third round, severely restricting his vision and multiplying the difficulties of measuring an opponent whose head movement had been a big problem from the start, he had to compromise by coming round into a square, slugger's stance and winning his points with sustained, two-handed pressure. Most boxers, faced with the demand for such an adjustment, would make a respectable lunge at it for a few minutes, then sag into resignation. The Scottish world champion, whose blindingly sudden and confusingly flexible left jab is not only his most telling weapon but the triggering mechanism for all his best combinations, might have been forgiven if he had gone out that way.

Yet, far from wilting, he gained in assurance and authority as they moved into the decisive final third of the contest. Time and again he turned back the spidery aggression of Laguna and drove his own flurries of hooks and crosses through the flailing black arms, reducing the Panamanian to an impotence which made it hard to remember that he had twice been a distinguished holder of this lightweight title. Any remaining doubts about the verdict dissolved in the one-sided turmoil of the fourteenth round, when Laguna was all but overwhelmed. If his head had not fortuitously slipped under the top rope, he would have been a lolling helpless target for the furious assault aimed at him. As it was, the rope protected him during the fifteen or twenty seconds in which Buchanan, whose magnificent physical condition was at last giving way to tiredness, could maintain maximum ferocity.

'That was a hard one,' Buchanan said as he stepped wearily out of the shower in his dressing-room. 'Man, it was hard. Still, we beat them at their own game.' As he bent over the wash-hand basin to bathe the abused left eye, no one was inclined to question his assertion. The classical boxer had been forced to desert the principles that have taken him where he is, to charge where he would rather have ambushed, to bludgeon when he would rather have pierced. Nevertheless, he had found the strength and the persistent courage and the adaptability to do whatever was necessary to keep his championship. Those who had come to the Garden to see a kind of artist had stayed to cheer a reluctant rough-houser. And Laguna, who precipitated the battle, lived to regret it. An equally significant fact about the fight, however, was that someone else did a job to match Buchanan's. For years the men who work in the corners with American fighters have been presented to us as possessors of almost mystical powers. They are seen, and certainly see themselves, as guardians of potent secrets passed down through generations of the craft in bleak gyms. Of all the legends that surround these men, arguing their superiority over their counterparts anywhere else in the world, the most vivid concerns their ability to cope with injuries and especially to stop the bleeding from cuts about the eyes. The best of them are credited with being able to make the blood clot around a gunshot wound before the smoke is cleared from the barrel.

It was a shock to some of these gentlemen when Eddie Thomas

announced in Los Angeles not long ago that, as a corner-man, he would not take his hat off to any of them. It was perhaps a greater shock to any who were within earshot when Harold Conrad, a far from naive New Yorker who has seen thousands of important fights and always known what he was watching, declared categorically on Monday night that Thomas is the best corner-man operating in the world today. 'That was a helluva job Thomas did in Buchanan's corner,' said Conrad. 'I watch corners and I've never seen one work better. Thomas was like an icicle. No matter what was happening in the ring, how much damage was being done to his guy, he never got flustered. He watched every move in there and he seemed to hand out the right advice, for he turned his guy over to fighting just when he had to. But during the rounds he went on getting ready for what he would have to do in the rest period. That minute really flies by when you've got problems. But Thomas always had all his stuff ready to use and never once looked panicky. Buchanan's a terrific fighter, one of the real ones but I wouldn't bet that he would have won the fight without Eddie Thomas. That man gives the impression of knowing more about all aspects of working a corner than anyone around right now. Even Angelo Dundee has to bring someone in to do the intricate stuff on the cuts. Thomas and Buchanan make quite a partnership.'

That eulogy, and the extent to which it was merited, encourage the thought that Monday's experience may have persuaded Ken Buchanan that while he would still be a tremendous champion without Thomas, he will always be a better one with him. Tom Buchanan is a vital influence on his son's life, a solid base of affection and trust, but it would be unrealistic to expect the father or any of his friends to cope with the sort of situation that developed in the Garden. That was a crisis only a pair of professionals could have survived. One would not have been enough. Controlling the bleeding from the gash along the left eyebrow, which later required eight stitches on the outside and two on the inside, was a substantial achievement. But the treatment of the large lump that swelled on the left cheekbone in the third was at least as important. When Buchanan came out for the fifth round it was just about noticeable that he had a slight nick under the lump. The small cut 'wept' gently, relieving the pressure of the swelling and improving the sight of the eye. 'That's lucky,' said someone sitting near me. 'Such a neat little cut. You'd almost think it had been done with a razor blade.' I glanced at him curiously. I knew he had been watching the corner but I had not imagined his eyes were that good.

Making delicate facial repairs in the bedlam of the Garden, where the predictable tension was increased by the ear-splitting competition between a full-scale pipe band and a Panamanian group that featured silver, brass and pulsing drums, was the equivalent of threading needles in an air raid. To do it, Thomas had to be nerveless. Ken Buchanan should not lightly dispense with the services of such a man. Their contract is up for renewal soon, almost certainly before the champion has another match, and there should be no snag big enough to stand in the way of a mutual agreement.

Admittedly, Thomas has weaknesses. 'Those bloody bagpipes drove me crackers,' he said as we ate an Italian meal in the early hours of Tuesday morning. 'You know the Welsh invented the bagpipes and gave them to the Scots and the poor buggers haven't seen the joke yet.' Anyone who says things like that needs to be a good cut-man. He never knows when he will have to work on himself.

Hit by Hard Times

Hugh McIlvanney

While Ken Buchanan bathed his damaged face in the wash-hand basin of a bare dressing-room at Wembley Arena last Tuesday, some among his small, embarrassed audience thought about other nights in other places.

There was one at Madison Square Garden when he, a lightweight, so brilliantly outclassed a welterweight from Canada called Donato Paduano that the lift taking us down to street level afterwards was full of excited comparisons with Sugar Ray Robinson, talk that is the New York boxing crowd's equivalent of canonisation. But that was in 1970, and 1981 has been a very different year for Ken Buchanan. He says it will be his last as a professional fighter, that when he has fulfilled a booking in Lagos, Nigeria, on 19 December, he will retire. His admirers want to believe him, but they do not find it easy. This is a man who quit once before, in the summer of 1975, when he had a record that set him apart from all but a handful of British boxers. He came back four years later in June 1979, on his thirty-fourth birthday, and in the two and a half years since he has scuffled miserably with the remnants of the talent that electrified the Garden. The scuffling reached a nadir at Wembley last week when he came in at short notice to lend a little substance to a promotion that remained so essentially unappealing that, in the old line, most of the audience came disguised as empty seats. He went eight hard rounds with Lance Williams and, although there was a moment early in the fight when he remembered some of the old ways and almost left-hooked Williams out of business, he was legitimately adjudged to have lost narrowly at the end to a man who had barely started primary school when Buchanan began fighting for money.

There was nothing complicated or subtle about the interviews afterwards. We just wanted to know why he was there. 'Money,' he said, as briskly as his battered mouth would allow. The elaboration involved a familiar story of ill-advised investments, a marriage expensively broken, a hotel that could have been a big earner but suffered from haphazard and diffuse supervision. So here he was, taking about £1,600 to impersonate the Ken Buchanan who won the world lightweight championship against Ismael Laguna in San Juan, Puerto Rico, in 1970, and dominated the division for several years afterwards. The quality of his achievement is indicated by the fact that many of his best nights happened thousands of miles from the Edinburgh streets on which he was raised. It was conveyed more succinctly to this reporter in a conversation with Roberto Duran on a day in Las Vegas long before the Panamanian had discredited himself against Sugar Ray Leonard. Duran was reckoned then to be the fiercest man in the game and it was significant that when he was asked to name the opponent who had most impressed him the answer came in an instant growl. 'Buchanan,' he said, with a conviction that was as close as he ever went to saluting an adversary. What Duran had seen at close quarters was something that even good judges were inclined to overlook in the young Buchanan.

Many saw him initially as a richly gifted but rather too Corinthian, stand-up-and-prance-behind-the-jab kind of boxer. What they had to learn about him was that all the fine technique was reinforced by courage and remarkable hardness. He was an out-and-out fighting man.

On Tuesday, Buchanan's body looked much as it did when he warred unsuccessfully with Duran for thirteen rounds, all those years ago. 'He's got a twenty-two-year-old body,' said Paddy Byrne, a warm and inexhaustibly talkative Irishman who works Buchanan's corner, helps to negotiate his purses and spends a lot of time between matches trying to persuade the former champion to be a former fighter. 'At least it looks like a twenty-two-year-old's,' Byrne added, after a pause. 'But the strength isn't there any more. There's nothing to keep young fellas like Williams away. In other days he would have demolished a boy like that. Tonight, Williams kept on coming through Ken's punches.' The effects of that aggression were saddeningly charted on Buchanan's face. Its sharp, rather bony definition has been blurred in the eight engagements since he came back to the ring. The nose has been broadened and on Tuesday his mouth was cruelly bruised and bleeding inside. He has lost four of those eight fights, compared with three losses out of sixty in his real career. His last three outings have been defeats and, although he retains enough of his skill to avoid being dismantled, the punishment has become severe and consistent enough to encourage the Board of Control to make semi-official recommendations about the need to retire soon. The thirty-six-year-old object of their concern says that when he collects his $12,000 for facing Davidson Andeh in Nigeria next month, he will yield to reality and concentrate on acquiring the pub tenancy from which he hopes to make his living in the future.

Watching him duck his aching face into the wash-hand basin on Tuesday, thinking of the practical problems that have accumulated around his life, it was difficult to believe that any sport is as hard as boxing when you're on the way down. The room was full of memories, but they weren't going to pay the man's rent. His father was drifting around, muttering wistfully. Ken had sounded like his previous, rough-edged self only briefly when we first went in, as he bad-mouthed the referee. Even that echo of the better days trailed off, as if he accepted that he is no longer entitled to take decisions against him too seriously.

Soon the present was crowding in on him again. 'I'd better get a move on and catch that sleeper home,' he said. 'Tomorrow is my day for having the children.'

Benny

John Burrowes

The Central Station in Glasgow had never seen anything like it. It was never to know anything like it again. The city had four major stations, Buchanan Street and Queen Street for the north and east; St Enoch and the Central for suburban, steamer links, the Lowlands and England. The Central was the premier station. It was the major link with the outside world. If they came from America, statesmen or sportsmen, actors or aviators, they would come via London and then north to Scotland by the LMS to the Central. Buffalo Bill had got his reception to Glasgow there. So had Tom Mix . . . he even rode his horse Tony right into the Central Hotel. And Harry Lauder, Scotland's first knight of the music hall. And Laurel and Hardy. And countless others. But not all of them together were received as were the occupants of the 2.20 express from Liverpool and Manchester when its big pistons came to a slow clanking halt on Platform Two.

They had been crowding into the station that morning since eleven o'clock singing the same songs they had been singing the night before at the Belle Vue Stadium in Manchester . . . 'Roamin' in the Gloamin', 'Loch Lomond', 'I Belong to Glasgow'. Anything that was Scottish sufficed. For this was a time to be Scottish like it was a time none of them could remember. For one of them had shown the world of what they were made. And they were chanting his name long before he and his party stepped off the train . . . 'Benn . . . neee . . . Benn . . . neee . . . Benn . . . neee . . . Benn . . . neee'. The word had been flashed round the picture screens and announced at the theatres the night before . . . 'Benny Lynch – our Benny – has won the world title.'

Five hundred had travelled south with him to be there on his big night. They had never seen such a crowd of Scottish invaders at an English boxing promotion before. The ringside had all the top celebrities of the day: Jeff Dickson, the famous promoter, Jack 'Kid' Berg, the British lightweight champion, Jimmy Wilde, former world flyweight champion, Jock McAvoy, British middleweight champion, Ted Broadribb, the man they called the 'well-known London sportsman', and Hugh McAlevey, the man they called the 'well-known Irish sportsman'. Further back from the ringside and wearing the big woollen tammy with another one clutched in his hands was Andy Smith, his old friend of the booth days. The spare one was Benny's own, the one he had worn when they had paraded with Len Johnson's troupe at the gaffs. When the pipers marched him into the ring Andy ran up to him; Benny grinned when he recognised him and when he saw the tammy he bowed his head and Andy ceremoniously placed it on him in full view of the huge crowd and the 500 Scots gave Belle Vue a cheer like they had never heard before.

Sammy Wilson fussed over him in the corner, handing him the water bottle he guarded with his life. 'You want to get a boxer nobbled and there's no better way than to "fix" his water,' he would say. He made sure that never happened and even had Tommy McLean, one of their camp, drive a special supply of Gorbals tap water to Manchester in case the local supply affected his charge's stomach. They were taking no chances for this one. Sammy stood before him flapping the towel, more a gesture of support prior to the two fighters being called together. Benny sat in his corner, hands outstretched on the ropes showing no more emotion than he would if it were a fifty-shilling bout at Tommy Watson's.

When referee Moss Deyong called 'seconds out', Sammy Wilson, as he always did, slipped behind Benny, to put his arms round him in order to lift him from the stool at the bell. He had always done this – 'every ounce saved is another punch,' he would say.

Benny didn't need all that much energy this time. Four minutes and forty-two seconds later after he had been on the floor eight times, Jackie Brown, the undisputed flyweight champion of the world for the past three years, had to signal to Mr Deyong that he could continue no longer. The King was Dead. And into the ring stormed the Scots fans to chair their new King, Benny Lynch . . . the first Scot to become a world boxing champion.

'Do you think Brown got a surprise?' asked Benny in the dressing-room after they had cleared it of the first flush of well-wishers and newspapermen.

'Surprise,' replied Sammy. 'Did I no' tell you what happened? Norman Hurst, you know the big-shot sports reporter, well he asked me on the q.t. that time he came up to Glasgow to see you training when I thought you would open up and I told him about halfway through. "You look out for him in the seventh" I says. But I knew he would go right back and tell the Brown camp that. What do they think we are . . . daft bastards?' And the dressing-room filled with laughter at the prospect of Brown copping the onslaught the moment he had advanced on Benny in the very first round.

Benny Beat Them All . . .

All Except John Barleycorn

Frank and James Butler

Some of the most outstanding flyweights who have carried the Union Jack to the highest pinnacle of international pugilism have come out of Scotland. The land of the heather has given us Tancy Lee, Elky Clark, Johnny Hill, Benny Lynch and Jackie Paterson . . . champions all, but the greatest was Lynch. Poor misguided Benny! Invincible against any living flyweight the world could pit against him, yet defenceless against himself . . . himself and John Barleycorn.

If ever a champion committed professional hara-kiri it was the wee Scot who, with the world at his feet, tossed away a golden crown and tumbled off his throne into . . . yes, I'm afraid it is true . . . the gutter. I have seen scores of champions ride the dizzy heights oblivious that they can't abuse nature forever. Eventually the pay-off has struck like a thief at night, and next morning their world has crumbled, leaving them to totter along the already overcrowded cobbles of Dead End Alley.

There have been many tragedies of the ring, but the sudden decline and fall of Lynch surpasses any other boxing drama because the Scot turned his back on fame, fortune, a world crown, good health and self-respect when only twenty-five and at the peak of his career. Today Lynch should be among us . . . a living memorial of the supreme sporting stock produced by Britain. He should be a wealthy and respected citizen. Instead, poor Benny Lynch, once a pocket-Hercules, died in a Glasgow tenement at thirty-three, having lost everything.

I do not wish to dwell too long on the failure and the human weaknesses of the little Scot of whom I was very fond. I would prefer to tell you more about his greatness, his fairness inside the ropes, his ability to box like a wizard and to punch with the power of a featherweight. Above all, it must be remembered this little man who can no longer defend himself against the many charges that have been written against him did little harm to anybody apart from himself. He was his own worst enemy, but I doubt if he had many foes in this world. Had he been born in a different environment, and possessed stronger willpower with which to protect himself from the bad influences of some early acquaintances I might now be writing a different story.

Lynch and Jimmy Wilde were the two best flyweights the world produced. The little Welshman was more amazing because, weighing around 6 stone 10 pounds, he knocked out opponents sometimes nearly two stone heavier. But would he have been able to give away over a stone to the tough Scot with the wicked right-hand punch when both were at their best? This is a question that can never be answered, and a question to which I would not like to have to supply the correct result.

The magnificence of Benny Lynch could only be appreciated when he was fighting for a title. On those occasions he trained religiously, but in some of his non-title bouts he was a shadow of himself for the simple reason that he was often far from fit. Lynch dropped two decisions in overweight matches to Jimmy Warnock, the Belfast southpaw. I don't wish to take any credit from the Irishman who was a grand fighter, but I could not see him beating the Lynch who knocked out Jackie Brown and Peter Kane in title bouts, and who gave as immaculate an exhibition of boxing as has been seen when he outpointed the Filipino. Small Montana, over fifteen rounds at Wembley in the fastest flyweight contest I ever saw.

Those three bouts showed us the Scot at his best. Against Brown at Manchester in 1935, he was a compact destroyer. The Manchester boxer, who had won the world title from the Frenchman, Young Perez, three years earlier, was noted for his speed. For a boxer who moved so quickly, Brown punched exceedingly well. A few months earlier Lynch had held him to a draw in a twelve-round non-title contest, but Brown didn't know what had hit him in the affair at Manchester. The massive-shouldered little Scot released terrible blows and Brown was shattered in two rounds.

His victory over the American champion Small Montana in 1937 satisfied Americans that Lynch was undisputed world champion. The brown-skinned Montana was a smooth boxer. He didn't carry a big punch but had a wonderful defence. The critics were unanimous that to win, the Scot would have to bring over one of his Sunday punches in an early round. Otherwise, they declared, Lynch would never catch up with Montana who would proceed to give him a lesson in speed and science.

So Lynch put on a show of skill that left ringsiders gasping. Every trick Montana revealed was trumped by the Scot. The faster the Filipino set the pace, the more magnificent was Lynch. For fifteen rounds the customers were entertained to one of the most classical and entertaining championship fights it has been my pleasure to watch.

Montana was never disgraced, but Lynch, usually a flat-footed block-buster, this night was the dancing master, the professor of all the arts of self-defence, and at the end, when his right glove was held high in victory, ringsiders stood, clapped and cheered for minutes, carried away like entranced music lovers at a Prom concert.

Nine months later Lynch featured in yet another flyweight epic when he battered Peter Kane, the Golborne blacksmith, to defeat in thirteen rounds at Shawfield Park, Glasgow. This was not a classic like the Montana fistic symphony, but a thrilling and punishing battle showing Lynch again in the role of a terrible ring-slayer. Any Scottish fight fan will tell you this was the greatest flyweight slam in history.

Glasgow certainly was fight-crazy that night. Thousands of men, women and children lined the streets to watch the crowds pass on their way to the football ground. Between 40,000 and 50,000 fans tried to get into Shawfield Park at the same time. There was such congestion outside the main gates that it didn't matter whether or not you had a ticket. You couldn't get inside. Thousands didn't see the fight. On top of this, the heavens opened and it poured all night. But the crowd inside didn't notice the rain as they watched the most destructive pair of flyweights since the days of Jimmy Wilde tear into each other like wildcats. Never have two such punchers of eight stone clashed in the same ring together.

Kane was a raw youngster of nineteen with a terrific punch, but little defence. He had plenty of colour, and danced around the ring at great speed, always moving in on his opponent, staring at him with those large Eddie Cantor-like eyes. Up to now he was undefeated and believed he could lick anything in the world at eight stone.

Lynch, the better boxer and slightly the stronger puncher, was mature and experienced. This was proved in the first seconds. Kane, as usual, came bouncing out of his corner with the enthusiasm of a puppy. Lynch, tucking his chin behind his powerful left shoulder, moved in more cautiously, but as Kane met him, Benny hooked to the body and then struck immediately with a right cross to Peter's chin. Some 33,000 rain-soaked spectators who had managed to squeeze their way into the stadium gasped as the young challenger went into a sitting position. The surprised look on Kane's face told its own story, and so did his action in rising at the count of three. An experienced fighter would have taken another five seconds before going into battle again.

For thirteen rounds, Kane punched away, as game as any fighter who had stepped into any ring, but he revealed after the bout was all over that he didn't remember anything after that first right had smashed against his chin. For a man suffering from a mental blackout, Peter put up a remarkable performance and, although out-generalled, caused some anxious moments for Glasgow fight fans and for the men in Lynch's corner.

Even in the second round he let go a number of hammer-like right-handers on the Scot's chin, and although Lynch wasn't in danger of being knocked out, he was shaken. Kane kept on moving in round after round fighting instinctively, trying to smack down the calculating slayer facing him. All the time, Lynch remained cool. The difference between the two men was that, whereas the Golborne battler's punches were often wild, Benny seldom wasted a blow.

By the twelfth round the patient Lynch could see Kane was just about all-in and so the Scot rushed from his corner and battered the blacksmith against the ropes, so that Peter was reeling drunkenly although still refusing to go down, but the human body cannot always hold up a game heart for ever, and a left hook dropped Peter for three. He rose and chased after Lynch still by instinct as blood poured from cut lips and nose. The bell saved him . . . for one more round at least.

The thirteenth was to be the end. Kane waded – or rather staggered – towards the champion. Lynch steadied himself before releasing a left hook which dropped the Lancashire boy in a heap. He was up at seven, but incapable of defending himself, and so the Scot took careful aim, and a smashing cross to the chin sent Peter crashing to remain lying across the bottom strand of the ropes, out to the world. A grand little battler had been annihilated by a superb champion.

Lynch was never the same fighter again. He was drinking heavily, and didn't seem to care that he was the most outstanding flyweight in the world. Five months later he boxed Kane in a non-title fight, and Peter shared the decision.

I travelled to Glasgow to see him defend his title against the American champion Jackie Jurich of California. Benny hadn't trained. There was a gasp at the weigh-in when it was announced he was $6^{1/2}$ pounds overweight. Poker-faced Lynch showed no emotion, although he knew he had lost his world crown on the scales.

The fight went on at catch-weights, and Lynch, in spite of his lack of condition, chopped down Jurich in twelve rounds. In another three months Benny had deteriorated still more and lost to Kayo Morgan over twelve rounds at Glasgow.

One more month saw him reach the depths in his last fight – the tragic affair against Aurel Toma, a fair bantamweight from Romania, who would have been easy prey for the Lynch who had knocked out Kane only twelve months earlier.

This was the most tragic fight I ever watched. Benny had gone completely round the bend of the road. He was bloated and far from fit and what is more he had been drinking. I called to see him in his dressing-room before the fight. He had lost every bit of self-respect as a fighter.

As a contest it turned out to be a farce . . . or rather a tragedy. Benny stumbled round the ring incapable of throwing a serious punch, and an open target for the little Romanian who, as a fighter, was not fit to wipe the boxing boots of the Lynch we had known some six months earlier.

Efforts were made to save Benny from himself, but he was beyond rescue. He never looked forward again. All that remained was a wonderful past, a shameful present, and no future. He died still a young man in Glasgow in 1946.

(from *The Fight Game*)

ROUND 5

The Man they Couldn't Gag

Controversy is nothing new in the world of professional boxing. Dubious decisions abound throughout the history of the game, and many a heartfelt cry of 'Fix' has ricochetted round the cavernous reaches of smoke-filled fight arenas. Even today, in the full glare of television lights, some decisions are, to say the least, open to debate.

One man gave very short shrift indeed to such doubtful shenanigans. In a brilliant journalistic career spanning more than forty years, the British sportswriter Peter Wilson called the shots exactly as he saw them, without fear or favour. Though he wrote knowledgeably on many sporting events, it was in his big-fight reports that he really excelled. A familiar sight at ringside, greeting friends while simultaneously pounding out his dispatches, he epitomised the old-fashioned school of journalism and truly earned the epithet of 'The Man they Couldn't Gag'. Here are just two examples of his punchy and appealing style.

I'll Swear on Oath that Joe Louis Was Licked

Peter Wilson

Have you ever attended an execution and seen the condemned man turn round and shoot the firing squad? Have you ever gone to a bullfight and seen the bull tantalise the matador and make him look like a dumb beast? Have you ever seen Joe Louis made to look like a novice, made to fight fifteen full rounds and then have to stand in the ring and take the worst punishment he's ever received – the booing of close on 20,000 of his fans? Well, I saw the last of these sensations at Madison Square Garden when Jersey Joe Walcott – who was a 9-to-1 underdog in betting before his world heavyweight tilt at Louis – twice floored the champion, closed his left eye, made his nose leak and dribble blood for the last quarter of an hour, and finally won the decision according to everyone's opinion except that of two judges. In my opinion, this was the greatest robbery since Colonel Blood stole the Crown Jewels. Referee Ruby Goldstein, former near-champion fighter, gave seven rounds to Walcott, six to Louis, and two even. Judge Frank Forbes gave Walcott six rounds, Louis eight, and one even. The other judge, Marty Monro, gave nine rounds to Louis and six to Walcott. All I can conscientiously say is that I hope I never come up in front of a judge named Monro if those are the sort of verdicts he gives. I'd reckon to get a life sentence from him. Louis thus retained his title on the majority vote of officials – in New York State a referee and two judges each have a vote.

As to the fight itself, it wasn't a fight, it was a sensation even before it started. First there was the parade of champions. Arturo Godoy who, apart from our own Tommy Farr, was the only other man ever to have gone fifteen rounds with Louis. Joe Baksi, looking as though he weighs about 18 stone now. Gus Lesnevich, world light heavyweight champion, likely to be voted fighter of the year here. Olle Tandberg, the Swede, who beat Baksi and who may fight Lesnevich here soon. Ike Williams, world lightweight champion, who ruined our Ronnie James. Then all the lights went out and a girl's voice singing America's national anthem, 'The Star-Spangled Banner'. Then the bell, clanging and compelling, and Walcott alone in the loneliest place in the world with the greatest man-killer for twenty years.

Would he freeze as so many of Louis's opponents have done? Would he hell! Louis stalked him. Shades lighter in colour than nearly-thirty-four-year-old Walcott, over a stone heavier, and very conscious of being the champion, Louis padded round the ring trying to skewer Walcott on the end of his long left and open him up for the meat-axe right. Halfway through the round it looked as though it was all over. Louis landed a right-hand shot to the chin. Walcott's mouth flew open. He jerked backwards like a marionette on a string. Walcott fought back, and you can spell 'fought' as g-u-t-s. He swung a right and hooked a left – and Louis was down. He got up at two, throwing right hands crazily, but Walcott caught him again, this time with a right to the chin, and Louis was reeling on the ropes. Then the round was over and we remembered to start breathing again. The second round was even more decisively Walcott's.

People had been betting on how many rounds it would go. They stopped betting now. Everyone was with the challenger, the old guy with six kids, who had been on the dole not so long ago, who had been cheated and twisted and chiselled, and who had only got his chance when he should have been way past his best and who, by heaven, had told me that he wasn't going to be frightened of Louis or anyone else, and who, by the almighty gods of sport, was putting up the greatest surprise of our sporting generation. Now it's the fourth round, Louis is puzzled, indecisive, amateurish. Walcott is cheeky, impertinent with him – but never careless. Louis is out of distance with pawing left leads, which are like a blind man feeling his way round an unfamiliar room. Then smash, Walcott lands a terrific right-hander flush to the champion's beefy jowl. Louis is down. In the first round the fans had said he was off balance. You couldn't say that this time. Louis took a count of seven, and he was glad of every second. But still he fought like a champion. He was always going forward except when he was going down.

Round after round reeled off. Walcott bemused the champion. He would face him, then break stance, do a sort of jig, bob and weave or just walk away from him. Sure, he was on the defensive, but every time you could hear Louis's brain grinding out the message, 'This guy's a soft touch. I'll just wade in an' mash him up,' Walcott would unleash one of his numbing rights. By the end of the eighth Louis looked an old man. His features, which appear almost Mongolian when he's in action, were puffy and red-raw in patches. Sweat was pouring off him as though his body were a sponge being squeezed dry. His left eye had had shutters put on it. Louis was always full of menace, but each time he got set to do a blasting job Walcott would go into his jiggling, jerking walk and leave the champion flatfooted. In Louis's corner they were jabbering frantically. But the champ was old, old, old. I'll never forget the last minute of the ninth round. Louis got his shifty tantalising opponent just where he wanted him. Walcott was on the ropes. There was no way out. He had to fight or finish – flat on his back looking up through the knockout mist at Louis's gigantic thighs. That's the traditional way for Big Joe's opponents to end. But Walcott fought back. Fifteen stone one pound, Louis used all $16^{1/2}$ pounds extra weight advantage to bore Walcott back into the ropes. For sixty seconds Louis gave everything he had. And Walcott gave it right back. Big Bronze walked back to his corner stiff-legged. I think he knew that he hadn't got it any more. A lighter, older man had taken the best he could give – punches with which he had halted the last five world heavyweight champions – and was still coming back for more give and take. There were other highlights. In the eleventh, when Louis landed his hardest blow, a right with 'poison' stencilled all over the glove, Walcott came back with overhand rights to even the round. The unlucky thirteenth came and went with Walcott down for the only time in the fight – but from a slip and proving it was such by bouncing up and shaking Big Joe with a left hook. Then the fourteenth and just for a few seconds it looked as though Louis would still win in the traditional way, for he had Walcott weaving and tottering under his attack. Fifteenth round and Louis had only three minutes to keep his all-time great record untarnished. He tried to do it – and oh, how he tried. Walcott ran unashamedly. Only fools and gamblers could blame him. He must have felt that he had the fight won on points. He must have remembered how Billy Conn blew away his chance of winning sport's richest prize by trying to slug it out. The final bell –

and the last sensation. Louis stepped through the ropes as though to leave before the decision was announced. His handlers grabbed him and muttered madly in his ear. I really think Louis thought he had lost, or maybe he just did not know what was going on. I'll swear on oath he was licked by the cagey, shifty, game guy they call Jersey Joe Walcott.

The Weary Champion

Peter Wilson

The man who had been middleweight champion of the world for less than two hours just managed to open his eyes and whisper: 'I'm tired, oh, I'm so tired.' He was wearing the sort of woollen pyjamas they put on you when you are in hospital recovering from a major operation. His thin brown right hand was folded across his breast – a broken tool of his trade.

Sugar Ray Robinson, who had achieved the incomparable by winning the world's 11 stone 6 pounds title for the fifth time, back in his hotel bedroom was a weary, ageing Negro. After nearly eighteen years of ring warfare, comprising 150 professional fights, he had just beaten Carmen Basilio over fifteen rounds in front of a crowd of 17,976 people who paid roughly £125,700 to see him do the job.

And now the sepia-stained architect of victory could only whisper: 'Mr Wilson, I don't know whether I shall ever fight again. I'm so tired. So tired. I shan't make up my mind about anything for days . . . maybe a week or more.' Only once did his voice reach anywhere near a normal pitch. That was when he talked of the referee's decision – for in Chicago, as in most other parts of the States, there is a referee and two judges to give the decision. And referee Frank Sikora had voted for Basilio, being overruled by judges Spike McAdams and John Bray. Sikora's score card made Basilio the winner by sixty-nine points to sixty-six. Both McAdams and Bray gave it to Robinson seventy-two to sixty-four. Scoring in the British fashion, I made Robinson the winner by 74 1/4 to 72 3/4. If you translate that into the Chicago markings it would be seventy-two to sixty-six. On rounds I had Robinson ahead by eight to three and four even.

Robinson's exit from the ring was no conqueror's progress. He had to be supported between two of his handlers, his chin sagging on his breast, his legs hosepiping under him, his toes scuffing the long corridor to the dressing-room – I nearly wrote 'the casualty station'. For an hour no one was allowed to see him except his family and his doctor. Basilio was in no better plight. With tears streaming from his one good eye he had to be guided to his place of haven. He was a blinking, winking gnome, a half-blinded Samson.

And that was the turning-point of the whole battle – when Basilio became a one-eyed fighter. In the fourth there was a graze by his left eye. By the sixth it was completely blotted out. From that moment I felt that though the years might conquer Robinson, Basilio surely would not. But before that – almost before the fight had drawn breath – naked hate had been unleashed in the lonely ring, shimmering under the glare of thirty-six sizzling arc lamps. Scarcely had referee Sikora given his final instructions demanding no kidney or rabbit punches, before the two men were locked in a vicious clinch. They were chopping away at the back of each other's necks as though their gloves were guillotine blades, banging away at the kidneys, spraying punches far below the mythical belt. When the bell sounded for the end of the round they fought more furiously than ever, smashing at each other before being separated. The smaller, lighter, shorter-reaching Basilio was forcing the fight. But from the moment Robinson had a specific weakness at which to aim – the damaged left eye – his superior boxing and target punching added confidence to his skill. It became a fight between a shambling crab and a flashing swordfish. Because of the blindfold of taut-drawn skin over it, Basilio had to stand four square to his man. It meant that he presented a larger target and also lost leverage for his most effective punches – his left hooks. At the end of the ninth I made them dead-level on points – three rounds to Basilio, three to Robinson, three even. The tenth was thunder, Robinson pecked with his flicking left until you expected to see Basilio's eye staring through the back of his head.

It was a great round, and it was Robinson's – and perhaps that clinched the fight for him. So it went on. Blind Basilio – weary Robinson. The left jab pea-shootered into the plodding gnome's face. Inside, Robinson unabashedly held while Basilio corseted him with a flaming red rim round the ribs. But how well he had paced his fight. Although I thought in the twelfth he might collapse as he did in the heat against Joey Maxim, he had the vital sprint for the tape left in him. He won the thirteenth. He won the fourteenth. And in the fifteenth he put it beyond all doubt. A terrific right dazed Basilio, and he was booed for butting.

He continued to flail away inside, but now his left eye – the one from which he had scar tissue removed some four months ago – had turned into a river of blood having finally split after being bunged up for over half an hour. Robinson threw right hands as though he never wanted to see his fist again. Basilio was in bad, bad trouble on the ropes at the final bell. But Robinson was holding on to them, pinioning the little man between the black brackets of his arms and refusing to be torn off the strands, try though the referee might. Thus the end. And what now? A rubber match in New York in June? Basilio wants it. He believes he would have won had it not been for the injury to his eye. But Robinson is the key character. I believe that he would now like to retire – for the second time – as champion. His share of the total profits accruing from the gate-money to radio and the film of the fight should be in the region of £80,000. So he should be able to afford the luxury of a ringside seat instead of a stool within the ropes.

But he talked vaguely of coming to England, perhaps to renew his rivalry with Randolph Turpin. He has been promised forty-two-and-a-half per cent of all the take from a third battle with Basilio. When the weariness leaves his limbs and his essential egotism returns, will he be able to relinquish that glittering bauble, the world title – and the hundreds and thousands that go with it? To read Robinson's mind is as impossible as to out-think him in the ring. Only time and Sugar Ray Robinson can tell.

ROUND 6
The Harder they Fall

It is a story as old as boxing itself. The poor kid from the sticks who made his way to the big city, and fought his way up to the championship of the world. A fascinating story. A novel, perhaps? Or a film script? No. In this case, it really happened that way.

His name is Beau Jack, and once he was the lightweight champion. He started out as a shoeshine boy, made the big time, and when the career was over, the money gone, he found himself back where he'd started. On his knees, shining other men's shoes. Beau Jack, who had it all and lost it all. The big money, the beautiful women, the fancy cars, and all the other trappings that are the rightful provenance of the champion of the world. Beau Jack, who could fill the Garden as no other, before or since; who still can cherish the mementoes of his past glories, and talk of friends in high places. Beau Jack, who despite the travails of a long and eventful life, can still say with simple sincerity: 'Boxing is a fine sport.'

In the piece which follows, Gary Smith meets the legend. It is a marvellous story, wonderfully told. But, more than that, it is a moving testament to the invincible qualities of the human spirit.

Still Fighting Old Wars

Gary Smith

They told me he had guts as nobody since has had guts. They said you had to fight him or jump out of the ring or curl up in a ball and get killed. They told me that the bell would ring and he would be throwing punches as soon as he stepped out of his corner, before he even got near the centre of the ring. They said they saw him break his knee, crumple, stagger up on to his other leg and hop after his opponent, wincing horribly, still throwing punches.

They told me it was wartime then, and the only light during Friday-night air-raid blackouts in New York was the orange glow from the vacuum-tube radios that people huddled around, listening to his fights. They said he sold out Madison Square Garden more times than any man in history – attracted the largest live boxing gate ever, $35 million, and ended up without a penny, on his knees, shining men's shoes. They told me these things in a way that made me think he was dead. People like that don't ever seem to be alive.

One day not long ago, I walked up a stairway into the Fifth Street Gym in Miami Beach. Four decades of fighters had spilled their body fluids there. It was hot and close in the room, and you could smell every drop of those juices. In the ring, something strange was happening. Three large men were taking turns beating up a fourth.

'Throw punches! Throw punches! You don't throw punches, you gonna get hit! Throw punches! Oh My God, have mercy, throw punches! Next! Your turn! Throw punches! Stop huggin' that man like he's your wife, goddam! Throw the left hook! Now! Oh, maaaaaan. Oh My God! Throw punches! Get out! Next! *Throw punches!*' The words poured from a small, coffee-coloured man standing on the apron of the ring.

The victim's arms sagged from exhaustion, uncovering his head. His jaw fell slack from the blows. 'Get out!' the coffee-coloured man shouted again. 'Next!' The aggressor turned away, and one of the other two fighters, refreshed, stepped in and continued the beating.

'If you can't stand this, you're nothin'!' the small man roared at the helpless one. 'You gotta get in shape if you wanna fight. Throw punches! Teach him a lesson! Throw it–throw it–throw it! Get out of that cover-up! Goddawg, throw punches! *Throw punches!*'

I licked the dry roof of my mouth. 'What the hell is . . . ?'

A bystander pointed to the boxer getting beaten on. 'He's training for a fight this weekend in Vegas,' he said.

'*This* weekend?'

The man nodded towards the small blinking man on the apron, whose lips were drawn back to show his toothless gums, whose wrist veins bulged as thick and as taut as the ropes he was clutching. 'And that,' he said, as if it explained everything, 'is Mr Beau Jack.'

So he wasn't dead. He was managing the Fifth Street Gym. My eyes left the men in the ring and fixed on him. He had wide, flaring Indian cheekbones, eyes wrapped in hoods of thick scar tissue and magnified by soda-pop-bottle lenses, sitting crooked on his flattened nose. His head and shoulders bobbed with the action; now and then he threw two short, vicious uppercuts at the air, grunting with them: 'Ah . . . ah!' The bell rang. Beau Jack screamed at the fighters to continue: he was working inside his own space and time.

I heard the helpless one get clubbed again, turned and saw him stumble against one of the other fighters who awaited his turn. And then I remembered: hadn't they told me Beau Jack got his start fighting in battle royals – an old tradition in which a group of five to ten teenage blacks, for the amusement of southern gentlemen, were blindfolded and sent into a ring en masse for a free-for-all. I had read an account of one in Ralph Ellison's *The Invisible Man*:

> . . . now I felt a sudden fit of blind terror. I was unused to darkness. It was as though I had suddenly found myself in a dark room filled with poisonous cottonmouths. I could hear the bleary voices yelling insistently for the battle royal to begin . . .
>
> I wanted to see, to see more desperately than ever before. But the blindfold was tight as a thick skin-puckering scab and when I raised my gloved hands to push the layers of white aside a voice yelled, 'Oh, no you don't, black bastard! Leave that alone!'

. . . And I heard the bell clang and the sound of feet scuffling forward. A glove smacked against my head. I pivoted, striking out stiffly as someone went past, and felt the jar ripple along the length of my arm to my shoulder. Then it seemed as though all nine of the boys had turned upon me at once. Blows pounded me from all sides while I struck out as best I could. So many blows landed upon me that I wondered if I were not the only blindfolded fighter in the ring . . .

Blindfolded, I could no longer control my motions. I had no dignity. I stumbled about like a baby or a drunken man . . . A glove connected with my head, filling my mouth with warm blood. It was everywhere. I could not tell if the moisture I felt upon my body was sweat or blood. A blow landed hard against the nape of my neck. I felt myself going over, my head hitting the floor. Streaks of blue light filled the black world behind the blindfold. I lay prone, pretending that I was knocked out, but felt myself seized by hands and yanked to my feet. 'Get going, black boy! Mix it up!'. . . Pushed this way and that by the legs milling around me, I finally pulled erect and discovered that I could see the black, sweat-washed forms weaving in the smoky-blue atmosphere like drunken dancers weaving to the rapid drum-like thuds of blows . . .

In one corner I glimpsed a boy violently punching the air and heard him scream in pain as he smashed his hand against a ring post. For a second I saw him bent over holding his hand, then going down as a blow caught his unprotected head . . . The smoke was agonising and there were no rounds, no bells at three-minute intervals to relieve our exhaustion. The room spun round me, a swirl of lights, smoke, sweating bodies surrounded by tense white faces. I bled from both nose and mouth, the blood spattering upon my chest.

The men kept yelling, 'Slug him, black boy! Knock his guts out!'

I watched Beau Jack climb down from the ring apron and move in a half-trot across the floor, shoulders swaying with his rolling gait, right leg dipping to accommodate old pain. I approached him. 'You fought in battle royals, didn't you?' I asked.

'Yes, sir,' he said, eyeing me.

'How did it feel?'

'They should still have them,' he said. 'They'd be a lot of fun for people who ain't seen them. But they can't. Guys ain't tough enough any more.'

'I'd like to write a story about you,' I said.

'All right, sir,' he said quietly. A maroon cap hid most of his balding head with its white stubble of hair, and a T-shirt with the words 'FORWARD MOTION' covered his still-muscular chest. 'They think they can tire me out,' he said, as if he had been one of the men in the ring. 'They can't. I can outlast them all. They try to kill me, and I be relaxin'. I know how to breathe and how to throw punches. You're not in condition, you're gonna get your brains scattered to the wrong part of your head. Can't never quit in a ring. All that crap about defence – take it and put it up your butt. *Conditioning.*' He threw a combination at a heavy bag and walked over to two women lying on tables, doing leg lifts. 'Everybody gets sick when they first come here,' he warned one. 'It'll go away. Tomorrow I'm gonna murder you.'

His tone turned gentle now, as if he were an old man telling his assembled grandchildren a story before bed. I moved closer to hear. 'You know, if you didn't get your ticket before Friday when I fought,' he said, 'forget about it. They was none left. I had 2,000 ladies came to see me. They'd yell, "Uh-oh, here comes that tiger again." And anyplace I go now I hear people say these same words: "We been watchin' and we been lookin', tryin' to find another Beau Jack, but we ain't never seen another one. How did you keep throwing punches from one end of the bell to the other, Beau Jack?"

'Well, you have to love people to do that. They kept screamin' "Beau Jack, Beau Jack"' – his fists began to punch the air – 'so I loved 'em and had to fight harder and harder and harder. Didn't want no people talkin' about me like I was a dog. I had to do good for my guests. I love every human being God put on this earth. We're here for one reason – to attract each other. I fought that way, for love.'

Pools of dusk had begun to form in the corners of the gym; in ones and twos the boxers towelled their sweat, called goodbye to Beau Jack and departed. 'That bone tried to jump up and get away, but I chased it down and caught it, and I ain't even got no teeth, that's how good that chicken was you cooked for me,' he said to one of the two women he was conditioning. 'You comin' back to work out tomorrow, aren't you?'

When she was gone, I asked if I could accompany him home. I wanted to meet his wife and the fifteen children that people said he had fathered. 'No need for that,' he said. 'We disbanded. Sometimes it's best to just disband yourself.'

'Who do you live with?'

'Nobody. Myself.'

'Where?'

'One-room place, few blocks from here. Don't need nothin' else.'

I asked what he did alone at night.

'I play blackjack against a dead man's hand,' he said. 'When I win, I put the cards on my side. He wins, I put 'em on his side. Funny, ninety-nine times out of a hundred, the dead man wins.'

Carefully he reached under a desk in his shabby corner cubicle, pulled out his boxing plaques and awards, and tucked them into a black bag. He placed it on his shoulder, locked up the gym and headed home. A block away, he paused. At the night air, he threw a pair of punches.

Most of the newspaper stories about Beau Jack were yellowed and smelt like your grandfather's attic. Gingerly I held them under a light, to learn how a life starts that ends this way.

He was born in 1921 on a Georgia farm where the roosters scratched at dust and the breeze banged the doors. His mother and father gave up trying to love when he was trying to crawl, so his grandma, Evie Mixom, raised him. She called him Beau Jack instead of Sidney Walker, and did there have to be a reason? Evie told people that Beau would be a fighter or a preacher. She knew what most smart folks didn't, that furthest opposites were the closest kind of kin.

By the time he was eight, Beau would awake at five each morning so he could walk the three and a half miles to Augusta and be the first at Ninth and Broad, the best shoeshine corner spot because the cotton farmers entered the city there. The money he earned made him a target, and one day he came home in tears. Five boys had threatened him into surrendering the three dollars he had earned, he sobbed to his grandmother. Evie took off all his clothes and beat him. 'You better fight till the blood runs out your shoes,' she said. 'No

Walker is supposed to be runnin' nowhere.' She also told him she preferred that he be a preacher. A week later a gang demanded a tip he had earned. Beau attacked the leader, smashed his head against the concrete and kept the coin.

Not long after that came the battle royals. The winner got to keep all the coins that the amused southern gentlemen tossed into the ring. Invariably Beau Jack, the littlest one in there, would win, and the gentlemen cheered.

Once, one man got so excited watching Beau Jack punch, he handed him a hundred-dollar bill. Anything a kid like Beau Jack got in life beyond the necessities made him vulnerable; another boy skulked up and snatched the bill away. Beau Jack spun and knocked him out, too.

Funny thing about fighting blind. Made a guy feel scared, but took a weight off him, too. If a guy couldn't see what he did, there weren't any complications. A guy couldn't see, how could any of the responsibility be his?

One day, Beau Jack's grandma called him to her, told him to be a good boy and go fetch her a bowl of soup. When he came back, she was dead.

By fifteen, he was married and making his own children: he loved the feel of their little arms around his neck. He had a job shining shoes at Augusta National, the golf club where the Masters is played, and there he made the sportsmen stand and holler each time they staged a battle royal. A group of them, including the famous golfer who started the club, Bobby Jones, pitched in fifty dollars each to send Beau Jack north and start his boxing career.

For the first few years, he fought in a converted gasoline storage tank in Holyoke, Mass. 'People called it boxing. I called it fighting,' he told a reporter. 'He had no pity,' said a sparring partner. 'A jungle cat,' a writer called him. 'A bum . . . not nothing . . . never will be nothing,' his trainer, Sid Bell, kept sneering at him. 'Your best ain't good enough. Rip their mouths out.' Twelve straight uppercuts, left hook, right cross, bolo punch, *uppercutuppercutuppercut* . . . A man who never stopped attacking was never vulnerable. A man who never stopped attacking was blind.

It was wartime, and the men who stayed home needed to see some violence. Soon Private Beau Jack was fighting main events at Madison

Square Garden, and the house was SRO with love. He beat Henry Armstrong in front of 19,986. Twice he was lightweight champion of the world. In 1944, to see him fight Bob Montgomery, people had to buy US war bonds. The gate was $35,864,900. Each fighter was paid one dollar. In 1944 Beau Jack sold out the Garden three times in a single month.

Now he was sixty-six. He passed his nights in the tiny efficiency, his days a few blocks away in the dying gym. I headed there the next day, noticing all the tattoos on the transients in his neighbourhood, all the missed belt-loops of old people who had no one to let them know.

Near the doorway of the gym, a drifter stood. He had the sunken cheeks and dazed eyes of a man nudged awake all night by a cop's shoe. The building housing the gym seemed deserted at this early hour, a good place to sleep. The drifter wandered inside and curled up at the foot of the stairway. I stepped over him and headed up the steps.

'Youuuuuuu! *Get out of my building!*' The scream pierced the stairwell. I looked up and saw Beau Jack, legs spread and braced, fists taut, eyes burning. He pounded down the steps and stood above the drifter.

Groggily the man rose. Now you could see and smell all of his loneliness. It drove Beau Jack berserk.

'Get the f– *out of my building! Get your ass out of my building before I put you through the wall!*'

'I'm a man,' said the drifter, 'just like you. Don't talk to me like a dog.'

'You ain't no man! *Prove it, prove it, prove it!*' Beau Jack ripped off his glasses, raised his fists, thrust out his jaw. His chest grew large and small, large and small, like a bellows. '*This don't belong to you! It belongs to me! I'll put you through the wall!*'

The drifter's eyes focused. He looked at Beau Jack and saw what it meant to him. He shook his head and walked away.

I accept fate. I began as a shoeshine boy and I'm resigned to end as one. All the good things that happened to me in between have been a blessing. Lovingly he swept the gym after evicting the drifter, while I sat to the side of the ring reading photocopies of the old newspaper stories. This last comment, he made to a writer in 1980.

Every now and then after he had retired in 1955, reporters came upon Beau Jack bent over a man's shoes in a Miami Beach hotel –

sometimes at the Fontainebleau, other times at the Doral – and wrote stories steeped in pathos about the sorry fate of the former champion. Cameramen and documentary-makers came too. Beau Jack became the stereotype of the penniless ex-fighter, exploited by his managers.

I waited for Beau Jack and asked him how he felt about being robbed so cruelly. He paused, grinned and said, 'Mistah, sah, ain't no use bothering about what they done with that money. I don't grieve no more. That being world champion was worth all I done and all they done to me. Mistah, sah that was just the greatest.'

That's what one man wrote. And another: *Business is slow, but Beau Jack the Boxing Champion still has to eat, and that means he must wait in a hard-backed chair and pray for a chance to drop to his knees and scrape out his living . . . This is where Beau Jack works fourteen hours a day, sometimes more, where he barely makes enough money to catch the 1 a.m. bus back downtown to his little house on the mean streets . . .*

He laid aside the broom and took a few punches at a heavy bag, watching it sway from the corner of his eye as he bounced away. 'Sometimes,' a man there told me, 'he punches himself in the guts, to see if he can take it.' Beau Jack passed me, gave my knee an affectionate squeeze and smiled.

With his gums Beau gnawed at something chunky from a take-out bowl of oxtail soup. He had tried false teeth once and didn't like them, so he had gnawed and winced until he had turned his own softness hard.

'You know, sir,' he said, pulling out a Bible and a pamphlet about Jesus, 'I don't have no control of me. God have all of it. If there ain't no God, what about the night, the cool, the hot? How they be, sir? If I go, I don't need anything else in life but what I got now. I got friends I don't even know about. Rocky Marciano would never come this way without saying hello to me. Frank Sinatra, he still hugs me every time he sees me and says, "This is my Beau Jack." He was there that night I broke my knee. You see, I'd broken it three months before that night, during training. My trainer didn't want me to fight so soon, sir, but I sure wanted to.

'Fourth round, I threw a left hook at Tony Janiro. My foot got caught on something loose in the canvas. My body went with the punch but my leg didn't move. My knee made a terrible pop, split like it was sawed in half. Busted in five places, doctor told me. I could put my fist in the hole in my knee. I said, "I'm all right." I tried to push it back together. I got up and kept hoppin' on one knee, throwin' punches. But the referee, he made me stop. I tried to push him out of the way. I felt ashamed to lose that way. They took me off in a stretcher.'

His career essentially ended that night; he fought on but could no longer be the blind attacking dervish who had filled the Garden with violence and love. 'Frank Sinatra walked into the dressing-room, looked at me and started cryin',' he continued. 'If that man needed me any hour, any day, I'd go to him. Not walkin'. Runnin'. After I'm gone, I'm gonna remember him. When he came to Miami he would try to give me his shoes when I shined 'em, but they was so small I couldn't get two toes in. He was always worried that I didn't have money.'

'How do you get by, Beau? You don't make much here, do you?'

'I get by.'

'How?'

'Don't you worry. There's a famous man sends me a cheque every month, enough to live on.'

'Who? How much?'

He looked down and fidgeted with something inside a desk drawer. 'I promised I'd never tell that. Shouldn't even told you what I did.'

I asked him for the names of his friends. 'Frank Sinatra, Dean Martin. Jackie Gleason was a friend,' he said. 'Rocky Marciano was a friend.'

'I mean, ones you see more often.'

Abruptly, as if he'd just remembered something, he headed towards the cubicle door.

'Who . . . ?'

He stopped. 'If you see me, I'll be by myself. I travel alone. If I'm with someone, I'm responsible for someone. If I'm alone, I'm only responsible for myself.'

I asked about the two women he had married. 'You can't out-argue no lady,' he said. 'They can blast their mouths off ninety-nine billion times, all day, all night, same voice, same words, and you get tired. I just walked out. Don't like the way the pot's boilin', turn the fire out.'

I asked him for the names of his fifteen children. 'Georgianna . . .

Shanita . . . Michael . . . Jonathan.' He peered out the door, towards the ring.

'And the others?'

'That's enough.' He walked out and turned back. 'No need for you to come home with me after work tonight,' he said.

Someone who slept next to a man like that, I thought – they could tell you things. The next afternoon his daughter came up the steps to pass him a message from her mother. 'Where is she?' I asked. 'In the car outside,' the daughter said. I ran down and asked if I could come talk to her one afternoon.

Back in my hotel I started calling people who knew Beau Jack. Maybe they could help me understand him.

'His manager,' one man said, 'I heard he'd dump a big bag of one-dollar bills on Beau's bed after a fight – five thousand of them! – and Beau would get so excited he wouldn't realise he was supposed to get $10,000. I hear sometimes they'd have him practise writing his name on blank cheques. Robbed the poor guy blind.'

'Gave half the money away,' claimed another man. ' "Hey, Mr Beau Jack, I'm hungry, I need a drink," people would say to him, and he'd give them hundreds and fifties and tens. Awful lot of people crossed that man.'

Kept pictures of fat ladies on his walls, claimed one man.

Always talking about Jesus Christ, said another.

Never much for nightclubbing, an old sparring partner said. Didn't drink. Stayed to himself.

The homeless boy who was so used to poverty discovered the fun of buying fancy clothes, nightclubs and entertaining a gang of friends . . . Beau Jack's chief interest in life out of boxing . . . became the sleek beauties of Harlem who were only too pleased to entertain the champion. So said a 1955 story in *Ring Digest*.

'Carries his plaques back and forth from his apartment to the gym every day,' said Roosevelt Ivory, the man who hired Beau Jack a year ago to run the gym. 'Lot of times I try to give him his pay cheque and he says to give it to the fighters, he doesn't need it.'

'Ain't worth a quarter!' *Punch.* 'Ain't worth a dime!' *Punch.* 'Goddammit, look at you!' *Punch.* 'My grandfather got more.' *Punch.* 'I know what you done with it.' *Punch.* 'You're hidin' it out on the river!' *Punch.* 'You've given it to the girls!' *Punch.* Beau Jack was wearing flat, padded mitts when I got to the Fifth Street Gym the next day, catching the punches of a young man who was reeling from exhaustion.

'What's wrong with you?' he screamed at the boxer.

'Too hot.'

'I'd burn up in the fields, 184 degrees, it didn't stop me! Lord have mercy! The old man's got you!'

The young man bent in half with his gloves on his knees, panting, crimson. Beau Jack staggered around him like a drunk man, cackling, triumphant.

I stared and shook my head. How could someone so vulnerable cackle? How does a man who fought so frantically to fill the Garden with love, who surrounded himself with fifteen children, end up without . . .

The phone rang in his cubicle and Beau Jack bounced away. I waited a little while, then went in to find out. I stopped short. Beau Jack turned his eyes towards the window behind his desk. I came a step closer. He corkscrewed in his chair, legs still pointing forward but his torso and head twisted backwards. What's out that window? I wondered, moving next to him. And then I could see. He was trying not to cry.

'Something wrong with your dad?'

'No, not that I know of.'

'Nothing wrong in the family?'

'No, everything's fine. Why?'

'He seemed upset yesterday.'

Beau's son Jonathan is twenty-four and lives in Miami. He shrugged. 'He gets in moods.'

'Tell me,' I said. 'Did you ever see your father fight?'

'On tape. I thought he was crazy when I saw it. But I have seen him train guys. Ninety-eight per cent of them are gone after a few months. I've seen him swing a stick under their legs, making them jump, and when they can't pick up their legs any more, he's hitting their legs with the stick. They'll say, "You're stupid, you're trying to hurt me." He says, "That's right. They're gonna try to kill you in the ring." Funny thing, my dad never even spanked us.'

'Must have been pretty rough growing up,' I said. 'Moneywise, I mean.'

'Not really. My dad didn't need to shine shoes. He just went back to what he knew before boxing. Five of us were in private school while he was shining shoes. He must have a hundred suits in his closet at my mother's house. Never wears them, but he's got them. We could get anything from my dad – all we had to do was ask. I tested him once. I asked him to buy me a DeLorean. He looked at me for two minutes. "Are you a good son?" he asked. I said, "I guess so." He said, "Listen to your mom, and I'll get it for you." I started feeling guilty. I said, "No, that's okay, Dad." So he bought me a Mustang instead.

'His manager ripped him off, but not *everything*. He's got land in Georgia, some investments. And he doesn't spend money, lives real simple. I've begged him to move out of that place where he lives; that's not a good area. But he told me, "Son, always play broke. Don't let people know you have a cent."'

I lingered near his door again, looking into his cubicle. In the day that had passed, it seemed he hadn't stirred. His body was still contorted in the chair, twisted back so he could stare out the window and not show his face. 'Beau,' I called. He didn't move or reply. I left, bewildered.

I waited another day, then returned the next morning. He was staring out a window near the ring. Then he noticed me. He sprang from his seat, gesturing wildly to the few other people in the gym. 'Don't talk to him!' he screamed.

I looked around. Me. He was screaming about *me*.

'I'm finished with you! No more! I gave you everything you need to know!'

He waved me inside his cubicle and turned on me. 'My wife called the other day – told me you'd talked to her!'

'I haven't talked to her yet. I only arranged to meet her.'

'Makes no difference. I told you everything; you got no reason to talk to her. I got nothing more to say to you.'

'Beau . . .'

'No!'

His body was braced. His chest grew large and small, large and small, like a bellows. I looked at him and saw what it meant to him and walked away. Perhaps he was right. Now that he was used to fighting with a blindfold, what right had I to tug it off?

I walked the streets full of tattoos and missed belt-loops, and wondered how a judge would score Beau Jack's life. At the beginning of the fight they didn't let him see, then took advantage of his money and his feelings. But he fooled them all. Now, near the end, he had his dignity, more money than people realised and was free from people who might hurt him. I guess that meant he had won.

❝I work here at the Fontainebleau Hotel now and I enjoy my work that I do. This is where I make my living for my family, and that's where I'll be. I could be in New York, Chicago, I have a lot of friends all over the world that I could get a job anyplace I go, but I like it there. People from all over the world, everybody come in, they come by and say hello. That means a lot to you. That's worth more to me than money. I wish you'd tell all my friends in New York and all over America, I say God bless all of you. I loved boxing better than anything that I know but my family. Boxing is a good sport.❞

Beau Jack (from *In this Corner* by Peter Heller)

ROUND 7
Requiem for a Heavyweight

They called it 'The War at the Shore'. For big Gerry Cooney it was to be his swansong, the last hurrah of yet another White Hope.

Great White Hope. The phrase is an anachronistic one yet still potent enough, at least in America, to draw a crowd. In a heavyweight division still dominated, for the most part, by black boxers, the dream still persists that somewhere, someday there will be another Dempsey, another Marciano.

As fixations go, it has a long history, dating back as it does to the Jack Johnson era. But history moves on and such considerations, one might think, are no longer valid in the 1990s. But old prejudices die hard, and Gerry Cooney would do his utmost to thwart the ring ambitions of Michael Spinks. Not that Cooney was in any way racially motivated. Not even his worst enemies could justly accuse him of that. Rather he was lured back by outside pressures and the undoubted glitter of a multi-million-dollar pay day, and the doubtful honour of being eventually served up to the tender mercies of one Mike Tyson. In the event, that 'honour' went to Spinks, all ninety-one seconds of it! But that's another story.

Looking at all of this in a dispassionate manner, and from the point of view purely of boxing, the question is surely this: a great champion is still a great champion, is he not, be he black, white, yellow or polka-dot?

The marvellous Budd Shulberg here recounts the story of that final bell that tolled the death knell on a once-promising heavyweight career.

Gerry Cooney. He Coulda Been More than a Contendah

Budd Schulberg

When I first met Gerry Cooney, he was a kid, an overgrown twenty-four-year-old who had won his battle with adolescent acne and knock-kneed awkwardness. He was an odd mix of shyness and teenage prankishness, with a dark Irish ambivalence towards the public recognition thrust upon him after he cast a white shadow on the black world of heavyweight champions.

Since the Joe Louis–Ezzard Charles–Joe Walcott days, there has been only one Caucasian interruption to the steady march of Afro-American heavies. That was the indestructible Rocky Marciano. But then came Patterson, Liston, Ali, Foreman, Frazier, Norton, Holmes, Weaver, Spinks and Tyson. Even the contenders, the overweights, the momentary champions, were black – Page and Thomas, Witherspoon and Tubbs, Berbick, Tucker and Dokes.

For a generation, honkies have been relegated to trial horses and rugged losers like Jerry Quarry and George Chuvalo. White Hopers barely had time to learn his name before Duane Bobick was exposed in less than a round by Ken Norton.

So in a sport/business that has never outgrown its traditional ethnic rivalries, there is still an appeal to primitive emotions most fans have overcome in baseball and football. Cooney, in the early 1980s, was a very hot ticket. On the eve of the Norton fight in the Garden, sensing the left hook would do to this ageing Kenny what it had already accomplished with two other prestigious senior citizens – Jimmy Young and Ron Lyle – we talked about the fame and fortune that was about to descend on him like a flash storm.

One day, he's just a big kid commuting from what was then blue-collar Huntington to the traditional grime of Gleason's Gym in downtown Manhattan. But before his fast-talking manager could say 'God Bless America', Gerry is training in posh Palm Springs, with movie stars taking the place of the beery aficionados who had seen the good ones come and go at the old gym that stank so sweetly of blood and sweat and dead cigars.

Almost before he knew what hit him – because he hadn't been hit that hard or that often in an upwardly mobile career that had never taken him beyond round eight, with nineteen of his twenty-five fights not even going four – the 6 foot 7 inches boy-next-door was in there for a mere nine million bucks with Larry Holmes, a true heavyweight champion. Holmes had gone fifteen with a vintage Norton, a punishing twenty-three in two bouts with Shavers, had been left for dead by both Weaver and Snipes, and had proved himself a fistic Lazarus who could not only rise from the dead but bury them in his place.

Having paid his dues, Holmes broke out in verbal hives at the sight of the young, white Gerry-come-lately upstaging him on the cover of national magazines and getting parity on the pay night despite the fact that this Long Island honker had been an awkward kid in the Golden Gloves when Larry was punching and getting punched for a living from San Juan to Manila.

Holmes got even in that pivotal fight with Cooney five years ago, jabbing him mercilessly (though whoever heard of a merciful jab?) and setting him up for the straight right hand until after a while Gerry's face became a sickeningly easy target for the champion's right-hand rifle shots.

Anyone who questioned Cooney's readiness to climb through the ropes against Holmes was on solid ground. Less solid were those who questioned Cooney's heart. Heart, or courage, or bottom as it used to be known in the bare-knuckle days, is a necessary ingredient of every sport. As they sang in *Damn Yankees*, 'You gotta have heart . . . miles 'n' miles 'n' miles 'n' miles of heart . . .' But since boxing is the most personal, naked, one-on-one sport ('a chess game with blood', we once described it), heart, grace-under-pressure, true grit are not only exposed but revealed on a giant magnifying glass under blinding lights. And so in this intensely personalised sports/combat, the contestants are more inclined to hypersensitivity than most athletes in other fields.

In a lifetime of watching and knowing professional fighters, I've been struck by their kinship with poets rather than tobacco-chewing outfielders from Georgia, or teenage wonders at Wimbledon. 'I'm not hurt, just embarrassed,' a friend of mine told me after the referee stepped in to save him from further punishment. In the dressing-room at the Garden, Archie McBride, a heavyweight I co-managed, stared at the floor after being stopped by Floyd Patterson in seven and mumbled 'I'm okay. I'm okay. I just feel bad you and all your friends had to see me like that.'

When Floyd Patterson lost his title in the most humiliating way a champion can, KO'ed in one, he donned a disguise complete with false beard and sneaked out of Chicago like a serious bank thief on the lam. Losing fighters have been known to go out and get drunk, or in these days snort a line, or hole up in a brothel or a monastery.

So what Gerry Cooney did after the Holmes fight, after his corner decided to abort Larry's moving in for the *coup de grâce* in the thirteenth, wasn't a total break with boxing tradition. Gerry went off and hid. After the Holmes fight Cooney wanted to be alone or with his in-group high school buddies. He felt he had let the 'Cooney Country' people down. He brooded, he drifted, a fistic Hamlet asking himself into the night, 'To fight or not to fight?' And getting no answers. He was famous, even in defeat, and an overnight millionaire, but – son of tough Tony Cooney, who had trained him and his older brother, Tommy, to be fighters before their teens – he didn't know where he was going, or who he was.

His sabbatical from boxing went on for months, and months that grew into years. His diehard fans began to wonder: Was Gerry Cooney hanging them up at age twenty-eight? Was the last White Hope (although that peg truly revolted him) packing it in because he had enough bread and couldn't get his head together after losing to Holmes? Some boxing-writers were on his back, and some of the Cooney-lovers were losing patience, too. He could have challenged Mike Weaver for the WBA title, or Dokes, when 'Dynamite' or 'Cokeamite', took Weaver by a suspicious one-round KO and then 'successfully' defended that title via a highly questionable draw. Into such bathos had the once vaunted heavyweight crown descended. Gerry would have been a lively candidate to pick up the pieces. But it seemed as if the heart that had carried him through thirteen bruising rounds against the crafty and vengeful Holmes was no longer where his hard-minded father had wanted it to be – in the prize ring.

And when, after twenty-seven months, he finally decided to put on the gloves for real, it was only half for real. It wasn't against Snipes or Berbick or even a Quick Tillis. No, for this auspicious comeback, his cautious manager Dennis Rappaport and his surrogate father, trainer Victor Valle, chose a former sparring partner, Phil Brown, whose main interest in the fight seemed to be what corner of the ring would be most comfortable for a declining figure. And when even that 'fight' was postponed again and again, due to well publicised and chronic injuries to knuckle, shoulder and eye, the Anti-Cooney Club grew rapidly. Nor did things improve when Cooney made short work of another journeyman, George Chaplin.

When Gerry followed up that stirring victory not with a challenge of a top-rated contender but with yet another retirement, even the most loyal Huntingtonian was taking down the green flag and hoisting the white. 'Forget Cooney, he's got his millions, he's in the disco, he's a joke,' a bar-tending ex-boxer exploded at the mention of his name.

A few weeks before his comeback fight against recently-defrocked IBF heavyweight champion, Michael Spinks, at a spacious but Cooney-cluttered condo at the brand new super-yuppie spa at Great Gorge in upper New Jersey, Gerry nodded philosophically at the criticism that's shadowed his curious career since the Holmes fight, just three bouts (lasting less than seven rounds) in five years. In that same period Spinks had fought fifty-three rounds, including two fifteen-round razor-thin wins over an ageing Holmes, eight with the hard-hitting Jim MacDonald and, three years ago, a bristling twelve for the light heavyweight title with ringwise Long Islander Eddie Davis.

'Did you see what one of the columnists wrote about me the other day?' Gerry said softly. 'That "if I were George Washington we'd still be part of the British Empire because I'd have said it's too cold to fight in winter"? That hurt. And I said something to the writer I shouldn't have said. I guess I shouldn't let it get under my skin. But in a lot of ways, while it may have looked as if I just took the money and ran, these have been tough years for me. They can laugh at the injuries and the postponements, but the knuckle problems and the shoulder weren't excuses. They were frustrating and they took time. Training, and then having to stop and heal and then start again, and stop again – it can drive you crazy. I'll admit I had moments when I started asking myself, "Maybe I wasn't meant to be a fighter."

'And there were so many other distractions. I honestly think if I had won the Holmes fight I wasn't ready for it. I was still a kid – it's taken me these years of frustration and trouble to grow up and feel like a man. The writers, they have a right to write whatever they please, but sometimes they just ask the obvious questions they already know the answers to, and don't take the time or the trouble to go deeper.'

Gerry didn't hide from a hard question about his brother.

'Okay, my brother. It's easy to write a line about having family problems. That goes in one ear and out the other. But I wonder how well the writers would be doing their job if their brother was on hard drugs – if it was driving their family crazy – if they opened a restaurant-bar where the brother would go to the cash register to put in his arm. When you're in training for a fight that's all you should think about. But even getting ready for the Holmes fight – the night my father would've dreamed about – that's when my brother Tommy got into the heavy stuff.

'I know they keep saying, "Excuses, excuses", but how can you keep your mind on fighting when your brother comes into the house we grew up in, wants money again, and in front of our own mother, goes in the kitchen, gets a knife and slashes his wrists!' Gerry puts his head down and relives it. 'It was a nightmare. I had to call the police. He's in a rehab now and doing okay. But it's tough, it's tough, I hope he'll be okay. But those things take energy, the energy you need to be a fighter.

'Another thing. Fighters who get into big money aren't prepared. So many things come at them. So many distractions. I think there should be some kind of education for fighters, so they know what to do with the rest of their lives.

'And there's so much BS in the fight game. Like King trying to corner the market on the heavyweights. Witherspoon fights Smith and Carl King manages one of them and co-manages the other. But King doesn't control Spinks, Butch Lewis does, and Dennis (The Menace) Rappaport kept me independent. Believe me, I like boxing. I love to fight. I really wanted Holmes again – I learned a lot in that fight, what not to do, and press him more when I had him hurt, like in the tenth, and how to move away from the right hand.

'They say all things come to those who wait. I was overconfident for Holmes. Now I'm confident in a more mature way. I've got to win this fight. Winning now means more to me than it did then. So it isn't Holmes, but it's Spinks who beat Holmes. And if Holmes was the champion, no matter what all those commissions say, then it's not just hype to consider this a fight for the heavyweight championship. I've got to win this fight.'

The title of the fight – since fightbiz and showbiz are more and more interchangeable – was 'The War at the Shore'. Only, just short of five rounds of non-stop, non-clinch, take-no-prisoner intensity, a new title popped up on our screen for Michael Spinks's dramatic victory over the greatest heavyweight to fight out of Long Island since John Morrisey tried it in the nineteenth century.

So credit the winner-and-still champion Spinks the Jinx with writing a new title to the unexpected five-round war: *Requiem for a Heavyweight*. And, putting vanity aside in this moment of emotion, after watching the brains and heart of a true fighter overcome the size and starboard power of an almost, a Could-Have-Been, and now a Never-Will-Be, The War at the Shore wound up with Cooney at the Shore retitled, 'The Harder they Fall'.

Boxing may be the most misunderstood of all sporting events. It would seem, unlike baseball or basketball or even water polo, that it is a confrontation of brawn, physical brutality, matter over mind. Wrong. Victory is not to the strongest or to the fleetest, it is to the man who has the unique gift of matching brain to body and hand movement, who is able to think two or three moves beyond his hurt. That ability separates the men from the boys, and in the climatic meeting between the ongoing Spinks and the no-going Cooney, it was the 200-pound Spinks, the punching man's thinker and finally the thinking man's puncher, who proved himself the man, and Cooney, who should have destroyed him in four, finding himself out-fought, out-manned, alas no longer a contender but a 6-to-7 boy suddenly over his head at the shore.

Now, with philosophy behind us, and the technique of a very interesting contest ahead, let's, in the style of that extravagantly paid sports commentator, 'go to the videotape'. The picture we see shows a scowling and very serious Gerry Cooney going forward and pressing, jabbing, but (in the notes of this ringside table) 'not too effectively'. He's throwing lefts, but Spinks is moving smartly away from them, and then deciding he has to do something, moves in and smacks Cooney's still-inviting jaw (the same one that appealed to Larry Holmes five years ago). Round one to Huntington, but this is no Ken Norton, no standing target like Eddie Gregg. Ringside reporters turned to each other in agreement: 'This is a fight.'

It's still a fight in the second round with Cooney so-so jabbing and scoring with lefts softened by Spinks's knowing movements away from Cooney's predictable one-at-a-time left-hand shots. The fighter-thinker Spinks (you feel-see-think-see this with him at ringside) tells him to send Cooney a message: you think you're winning this fight, you think you're bigger and stronger, so wham! – my notes read: 'three-punch combo – one, two – flush – Gerry's nose, Gerry's jaw'. The round goes to the slower, shorter, lighter, smarter Spinks who says, 'I'm here! I'm here!,' even as blood begins to trickle from a torn right eyebrow. Pierce Egan, who might have been doing this piece if it had been around in the late eighteenth century or early nineteenth century, would have said for round three, 'Spinks comes out gaily.' A worried and slightly confident Cooney catches him with glancing left hooks but the fighting mind of Michael brings him in and out. Cooney fights back awkwardly, ineptly, bravely, but once again the writers turn to each other because they are concerned with the entertainment value of a close fight and not with the futures of the contestants after this match, or maybe that the careers of one or the other is over: 'This is a fight!'

The fourth round is the key, and it looks as if the key is in Cooney's hand, and he's ready to open all the doors in Trump's Plaza Hotel, Casino and Roman Coliseum.

Spinks is retreating, Cooney is coming forward, Cooney is winning, and he's not fighting an all-out knockabout as he did against the Nortons and Ron Lyles and Jimmy Youngs. He seems to know what he's doing. Spinks goes back to his corner on what appear to be weakening legs. One more round . . . the bigger, stronger banger is ready to take him out in five.

Only, wait! Round five tells us what boxing-fighting-mental-physical-heavyweight fighting is all about. Just when you think Cooney is coming on, Spinks and his ringwise corner know what Michael has to do to save and win this fight. We were close but not close enough to hear what Eddie Futch was telling Spinks, but it must have been, 'Look, Michael, you know he's wide open for right hands, you know you can catch him with combinations that will confuse and bemuse and abuse him. Forget legs, forget tired, get off first and take him out. He discourages. He's brave, he takes a punch, a fair punch, but give him a bunch of punches and . . .'

And round five is two minutes in and Big Gerry Cooney is in very big trouble. He's forgotten everything he's learned in all those months from Victor Valle, or maybe he's remembered what he's dis-remembered what Victor Valle forgot to tell him.

Anyway, with fistic fate thumbing its nose at all the experts – those who had Cooney winning early or Spinks winning by decision late – with two handfuls of seconds left in round five, Spinks is beating the deleted out of Cooney, hitting him with so many punches only a computer can count them. And Cooney is down. And down again. And a very nice boy/man or man/boy from Long Island is not only down, but out of the fight game and into the rest of his life.

ROUND 8
The Foreman Meets the Boss

After many long years in the wilderness, Muhammad Ali was on the comeback trail. Here and now, in far-flung Zaïre, of all places, about as far as one could reasonably imagine from Louisville, Kentucky, the usurped king would stake his claim to his rightful crown. Standing full square in his path was the formidable and, some said, insurmountable obstacle of George Foreman; a dark nemesis of such fearsome reputation that many felt he would destroy Ali or, at the very least, send him to the nearest hospital.

For how could the former champion, at thirty-two, no longer the dancing master of old, no longer using the left, seriously hope to defeat the man who had virtually dismantled Joe Frazier to win the title? Seasoned ring commentators, who should have known better, echoed the doubts, as Ali went into his 'rope a dope' tactics. 'This is crazy,' they told their listeners, 'you can't take these kind of chances with a man like Foreman!'

But, came the momentous eighth round and that tremendous Ali right, accurate and deadly as a heat-seeking missile, and the cry went up from those same quarters: 'My God, I don't believe it! Ali's got him! This man is amazing!' Amazing indeed. But to those who had kept the faith it was only as it should be. Fitting, proper, and preordained. Here, under a lowering African sky, the prodigal son had returned to claim his birthright, and to proclaim to the world that that which had seemed a dethronement was, after all, merely an interregnum. The King was Dead. Long live the King!

The story of that historic night is here recalled in the sinewy prose of Norman Mailer, one of America's greatest men of letters, Pulitzer Prize winner, novelist, sometime film director, and inveterate fight fan.

An Appreciation of Cassius Clay

Norman Mailer

I'm working on something else now, so don't want to get started writing about Muhammad Ali, because I could go on for a book. Suffice it that the most interesting original talented and artistic prizefighter to come along in at least a decade has been cut off by the bully-boy mentality of the American sporting world. A great athlete is almost always an extraordinary man, but a mediocre athlete has a character which is usually no prettier than the lifestyle of a mediocre writer. The sort of mugs and moguls who run our amateur and professional sports and write about them are invariably mediocrities, second-rate athletes, rich boys – they gravitate to running sports and writing up the canons of sports, and they ran Muhammad Ali right out of boxing. Their basic reflex is, after all, to kiss ass (it is their connection to the primitive) and patriotism is thus their head-on sublimation for such kissing. Therefore we are all deprived of an intimate spectacle which was taking place in public – the forging of a professional artist of extraordinary dimensions. Yes, I could write a book about Cassius: he was bringing a revolution to the theory of boxing, and bringing it into the monarchical spook-ridden class where every theory runs into a bomb – the heavyweights. Those who don't know boxing don't know the frustration one feels that he couldn't have the run of his own true career, for the knowledge he offered was mint.

(from *Partisan Review*)

The Fight

Norman Mailer

'Five minutes,' somebody yelled out, and Youngblood handed the fighter a bottle of orange juice. Ali took a swig of it, half a glass worth, and stared with amusement at Broadus. 'Tell him to hit me in the belly,' he said.

George would. George was certainly going to hit him in the belly. What a battle was to follow. If the five-minute warning had just been given, it passed in a rush. There was a bathroom off the dressing-room and to it Ali retired with his manager, the son of Elijah Muhammad, Herbert Muhammad, a round-faced benign-looking man whose features offered a complete lack of purchase – Herbert Muhammad gave the impression nobody would know how to take advantage of him too quickly. He was now dressed in a priestly white robe which ran from his shoulders to his feet, a costume appropriate to his function as a Moslem minister, for they had gone into the next room to pray and their voices could be heard reciting verses of the Koran – doubtless such Arabic was from the Koran. In the big room, now empty of Ali, everybody looked at everyone and there was nothing to say.

Ferdie Pacheco returned from Foreman's dressing-room. 'Everything's okay,' he stated. 'Let's roll.' In a minute Ali came out of the bathroom with the son of Elijah Muhammad. While he shadow-boxed, his manager continued to pray.

'How are things with Foreman?' someone asked Pacheco, and he shrugged. 'Foreman's not talking,' he said. 'They got him covered with towels.'

Now the word came down the line from the stadium outside. 'Ali in the ring, Ali in the ring.'

Solemnly, Bundini handed Ali the white African robe which the fighter had selected. Then everybody in the dressing-room was on their way, a long file of twenty men who pushed and were hustled through a platoon of soldiers standing outside the door and then in a

gang's rush in a full company of other soldiers were racing through the
grey cement-brick corridors with their long-gone echoes of rifle shots
and death. They emerged into open air, into the surrealistic bliss and
green air of stadium grass under electric lights, and a cheer of no vast
volume went up at the sight of Ali, but then the crowd had been
waiting through an empty hour with no semi-final to watch, just an
empty ring, and hours gone by before that with dancers to watch,
more dancers, then more tribal dancers, a long count of the minutes
from midnight to four. The nation of Zaïre had been awaiting this
event for three months, now they were here, some 60,000, in a great
oval of seats far from that ring in the centre of the soccer field. They
must be disappointed. Watching the fighters would prove kin to
sitting in a room in a housing project studying people through a
window in another housing project on the other side of a twelve-lane
freeway. The fighters would work under a big corrugated tin shed roof
with girders to protect the ring and the 2,500 ringside seats from
tropical downpour, which might come at any minute on this night so
advanced already into the rainy season. Heavy rains were overdue by
two weeks and more. Light rain had come almost every afternoon and
dark portentous skies hung overhead. In America that would speak of
quick summer storms, but the clouds in Africa were patient as the
people and a black whirling smoky sky could shift overhead for days
before more than a drop would fall.

Something of the weight of this on-coming rain was in the air. The
early night had been full of oppression, and it was hot for so early in
the morning, eighty degrees and a little more. Thoughts, however, of
the oncoming fight left Norman closer to feeling chill. He was sitting
next to Plimpton in the second row from the ring, a seat worth
travelling thousands of miles to obtain (although counting two round
trips, the figure might yet be 25,000 miles – a barrel of jet lag for the
soul). In front of them was a row of wire-service reporters and
photographers leaning on the apron of the ring; inside the ropes was
Ali checking the resin against his shoes, and offering flashes of his
shuffle to the study of the crowd, whirling away once in a while to
throw a kaleidoscope-dozen of punches at the air in two seconds no
more – one-Mississippi, two-Mississippi – twelve punches had gone
by. Screams from the crowd at the blur of the gloves. He was all alone
in the ring, the challenger on call for the champion, the prince

waiting for the pretender, and unlike other fighters who wilt in the long minutes before the title-holder will appear, Ali seemed to be taking royal pleasure in his undisputed possession of the space. He looked unafraid and almost on the edge of happiness, as if the discipline of having carried himself through the two thousand nights of sleeping without his title after it had been taken from him without ever losing a contest – a frustration for a fighter doubtless equal in impact to writing *A Farewell to Arms* and then not being able to publish it – must have been a biblical seven years of trial through which he had come with the crucial part of his honour, his talent, and his desire for greatness still intact, and light came off him at this instant. His body had a shine like the flanks of a thoroughbred. He looked fully ready to fight the strongest meanest man to come along in heavyweight circles in many years, maybe the worst big man of all, and while the prince stood alone in his ring, and waited out the minutes for the champion to arrive and had his thoughts, whatever they were, and his private communion with Allah, however that might feel, while he stood and while he shuffled and while he shadow-boxed the air, the Lord Privy Seal, Angelo Dundee from Miami, went methodically from ring post to ring post and there in full view of ringside and the stadium just as methodically loosened each of the four turnbuckles on each post which held the tension of each of the four ropes, and did it with a spoke and a wrench he must have put in his little carrying bag back at Nsele and transported on the bus and carried from the dressing-room to this ring. And when the ropes were slack to his taste, loose enough for his fighter to lean way back, he left the ring and returned to the corner. Nobody had paid any particular attention to him.

Foreman was still in his dressing-room. Later Plimpton learned a detail from his old friend Archie Moore. 'Just before going out to the ring, Foreman joined hands with his boxing trust – Dick Sadler, Sandy Saddler, and Archie – in a sort of prayer ritual they had practised (for every fight) since Foreman became champion in Jamaica,' Plimpton wrote. 'Now they were holding hands again in Zaïre, and Archie Moore, who had his head bowed, found himself thinking that he should pray for Muhammad Ali's safety. Here's what he said: "I was praying, and in great sincerity, that George wouldn't kill Ali. I really felt that was a possibility."' So did others.

Foreman arrived in the ring. He was wearing red velvet trunks with a white stripe and a blue waistband. The colours of the American flag girded his middle and his shoes were white. He looked solemn, even sheepish, like a big boy who as Archie said 'truly doesn't know his own strength'. The letters GF stood out in embossed white cloth from the red velvet of his trunks. GF – Great Fighter.

The referee, Zack Clayton, Black and much respected in his profession, had been waiting. George had time to reach his corner, shuffle his feet, huddle with the trust, get the soles of his shoes in resin, and the fighters were meeting in the centre of the ring to get instructions. It was the time for each man to extort a measure of fear from the other. Liston had done it to all his opponents until he met Ali who, then Cassius Clay at the age of twenty-two, glared back at him with all the imperative of his high-destiny guts. Foreman, in turn, had done it to Frazier and then to Norton. A big look, heavy as death, oppressive as the closing of the door of one's tomb.

To Foreman, Ali now said (as everybody was later informed), 'You have heard of me since you were young. You've been following me since you were a little boy. Now, you must meet me, your master!' – words the press could not hear at the time, but Ali's mouth was moving, his head was twelve inches from Foreman's, his eyes were on the other. Foreman blinked, Foreman looked surprised as if he had been impressed just a little more than he expected. He tapped Ali's glove in a move equal to saying, 'That's your round. Now *we* start.'

The fighters went back to their corners. Ali pressed his elbows to his side, closed his eyes and offered a prayer. Foreman turned his back. In the thirty seconds before the fight began, he grasped the ropes in his corner and bent over from the waist so that his big and powerful buttocks were presented to Ali. He flexed in this position so long it took on a kind of derision as though to declare: 'My farts to you.' He was still in such a pose when the bell rang.

The bell! Through a long unheard sigh of collective release, Ali charged across the ring. He looked as big and determined as Foreman, so he held himself, as if *he* possessed the true threat. They collided without meeting, their bodies still five feet apart. Each veered backward like similar magnetic poles repelling one another forcibly. Then Ali came forward again, Foreman came forward, they circled, they feinted, they moved in an electric ring, and Ali threw the first punch, a tentative left. It came up short. Then he drove a lightning-strong right straight as a pole into the stunned centre of Foreman's head, the unmistakable thwomp of a high-powered punch. A cry went up. Whatever else happened, Foreman had been hit. No opponent had cracked George this hard in years and no sparring partner had dared to.

Foreman charged in rage. Ali compounded the insult. He grabbed the champion around the neck and pushed his head down, wrestled it down crudely and decisively to show Foreman he was considerably rougher than anybody warned, and relations had commenced. They circled again. They feinted. They started in on one another and drew back. It was as if each held a gun. If one fired and missed, the other was certain to hit. If you threw a punch, and your opponent was ready, your own head would take his punch. What a shock. It is like seizing a high-voltage line. Suddenly you are on the floor.

Ali was not dancing. Rather he was bouncing from side to side looking for an opportunity to attack. So was Foreman. Maybe fifteen seconds went by. Suddenly Ali hit him again. It was again a right hand. Again it was hard. The sound of a bat thunking into a watermelon was heard around the ring. Once more Foreman charged after the blow, and once more Ali took him around the neck with his right arm, then stuck his left glove in Foreman's right armpit. Foreman could not start to swing. It was a nimble part of the advanced course for tying up a fighter. The referee broke the clinch. Again they moved through invisible reaches of attraction and repulsion, darting forward, sliding to the side, cocking their heads, each trying to strike an itch to panic in the other, two big men fast as pumas, charged as tigers – unseen sparks came off their moves. Ali hit him again, straight left, then a straight right. Foreman responded like a bull. He roared forward. A dangerous bull. His gloves were out like horns. No room for Ali to dance to the side, stick him and move, hit him and move. Ali went back, feinted, went back again, was on the ropes. Foreman had cut him off. The fight was thirty seconds old, and Foreman had driven him to the ropes. Ali had not even tried to get around those outstretched gloves so ready to cuff him, rough him, break his grace, no, retreating, Ali collected his toll. He hit Foreman with another left and another right.

Still a wail went up from the crowd. They saw Ali on the ropes. Who had talked of anything but how long Ali could keep away? Now he was trapped, so soon. Yet Foreman was off his aim. Ali's last left and right had checked him. Foreman's punches were not ready and Ali parried, Ali blocked. They clinched. The referee broke it. Ali was off the ropes with ease.

To celebrate, he hit Foreman another straight right. Up and down the press rows, one exclamation was leaping, 'He's hitting him with rights.' Ali had not punched with such authority in seven years. Champions do not hit other champions with right-hand leads. Not in the first round. It is the most difficult and dangerous punch. Difficult to deliver and dangerous to oneself. In nearly all positions, the right hand has longer to travel, a foot more at least than the left. Boxers deal with inches and half-inches. In the time it takes a right hand to travel that extra space, alarms are ringing in the opponent, counter-attacks are beginning. He will duck under the right and take off your head with a left. So good fighters do not often lead with their right against another good fighter. Not in the first round. They wait. They keep the right hand. It is one's authority, and ready to punish a left which comes too slowly. One throws one's right over a jab; one can block the left hook with a right forearm and chop back a right in return. Classic maxims of boxing. All fight-writers know them. Off these principles they take their interpretation. They are good engineers at Indianapolis but Ali is on his way to the moon. Right-hand leads! My God!

In the next minute, Ali proceeded to hit Foreman with a combination rare as plutonium: a straight right hand followed by a long left hook. Spring-zing! went those punches, bolt to the head, bolt to the head; each time Foreman would rush forward in murderous rage and be caught by the neck and turned. His menace became more impressive each time he was struck. If the punches maddened him, they did not weaken him. Another fighter would be staggering by now. Foreman merely looked more destructive. His hands lost no speed, his hands looked as fast as Ali's (except when he got hit) and his face was developing a murderous appetite. He had not been treated so disrespectfully in years. Lost was genial George of the press conferences. His life was clear. He was going to dismember Ali. As he kept getting hit and grabbed, hit and grabbed, a new fear came over

the rows at ringside. Foreman was awesome. Ali had now hi
about fifteen good punches to the head and not been caught or
return. What would happen when Foreman finally hit Ali? No
heavyweight could keep up the speed of these moves, not for
fourteen more rounds.

But then the first was not even over. In the last minute, Foreman
forced Ali to the ropes, was in on him, broke loose, and smashed a
right uppercut through Ali's gloves, then another. The second went
like a spear through the top of Ali's skull. His eyes flew up in
consternation, and he grabbed Foreman's right arm with his left,
squeezed it, clung to it. Foreman, his arm being held, was still in a
mood to throw the good right again, and did. Four heavy half-
smothered rights, concussive as blows to the heavy bag, went up to
the head, then two down to the body, whaling on Ali even as he was
held, and it was apparent these punches hurt. Ali came off the ropes
in the most determined embrace of his life, both gloves locked
around the back of Foreman's neck. The whites of Ali's eyes showed
the glaze of a combat soldier who has just seen a dismembered arm
go flying across the sky after an explosion. What kind of monster was
he encountering?

Foreman threw a wild left. Then a left, a right, a left, a left and a
right. Some to the head, some to the body, some got blocked, some
missed, one collided with Ali's floating ribs, brutal punches, jarring
and imprecise as a collision at slow speed in a truck.

With everybody screaming, Ali now hit Foreman with a right.
Foreman hit him back with a left and a right. Now they each landed
blows. Everybody was shaking their head at the bell. What a round!

Now the press rows began to ring with comment on those right-
hand leads. How does Ali dare? A magnificent round. Norman has
few vanities left, but thinks he knows something about boxing. He is
ready to serve as engineer on Ali's trip to the moon. For Ali is one
artist who does not box by right counter to left hook. He fights the
entirety of the other person. He lives in fields of concentration where
he can detect the smallest flicker of lack of concentration. Foreman
has shown himself a lack of quiver flat to the possibility of a right.
Who before this had dared after all to hit Foreman with a right? Of
late his opponents were afraid to flick him with a jab. Fast were
Foreman's hands, but held a flat spot of complacency before the

right. He was not ready for a man to come into the ring unafraid of him. That offered its beauty. But frightening. Ali cannot fight every round like this. Such a pace will kill him in five. Indeed he could be worried as he sits in the corner. It has been his round, but what a force to Foreman's punches. It is true. Foreman hits harder than other fighters. And takes a very good punch. Ali looks thoughtful.

There is a sound box in the vicinity, some small loudspeaker hooked into the closed circuit, and on it Norman can hear David Frost, Jim Brown, and Joe Frazier talking between rounds, an agreeable sense of detachment thereby offered for they are on the other side of the press rows. Listening to them offers the comfort of a man watching a snowstorm from his fireplace. Jim Brown may have said last night that Ali had no chance, but Brown is one athlete who will report what he sees. 'Great round for Muhammad Ali,' he comments. 'He did a fantastic job, although I don't think he can keep up this pace.'

Sullenly, Joe Frazier disagrees. 'Round was even . . . very close.'

David Frost: 'You wouldn't call that round for Ali?'

Joe is not there to root Ali home, not after Ali called him ignorant. 'It was very close. Ali had two or three good shots to the face while George been landing body shots.'

Foreman sits on his stool listening to Sadler. His face is bemused as if he has learned more than he is accustomed to in the last few minutes and the sensation is half agreeable. He has certainly learned that Ali can hit. Already his face shows lumps and welts. Ali is also a better wrestler than any fighter he has faced. Better able to agitate him. He sits back to rest the sore heat of his lungs after the boil of his fury in the last round. He brings himself to smile at someone at ringside. The smile is forced. Across the ring, Ali spits into the bowl held out for him and looks wide awake. His eyes are as alive as a ghetto adolescent walking down a strange turf. Just before the bell, he stands up in his corner and leads a cheer. Ali's arm pumps the air to inspire the crowd, and he makes a point of glowering at Foreman. Abruptly, right after the bell, his mood takes a change.

As Foreman comes out Ali goes back to the ropes, no, lets himself be driven to the corner, the worst place a fighter can be, worst place by all established comprehension of boxing. In the corner you cannot slip to the side, cannot go backward. You must fight your way out. With the screech that comes up from a crowd when one car tries to pass another in a race, Foreman was in to move on Ali, and Ali fought the good rat fight of the corner, his gloves thrown with frantic speed at Foreman's gloves. It became something like a slapping contest – of the variety two tall kids might show when trying to hit the other in the face. It is far from orthodox practice, where you dart out of a corner, duck out of a corner, or blast out. Since Ali kept landing, however, and Foreman did not, George retreated in confusion as if reverting to memories of fights when he was ten years old and scared – yes, Ali must have made some psychological choice and it was well chosen. He got out of the corner and held Foreman once again by the head in a grip so well applied that Foreman had the pensive expression of a steer being dogged to the ground by a cowboy.

Once the referee separated them, Ali began to back up across the ring. Foreman was after him throwing fast punches. 'Show him,' George's corner must have instructed, 'that your gloves are as fast as his.' Suddenly Foreman hit Ali with a straight hard right. Ali held on to Foreman to travel through the shock. After the fight he would say that some of Foreman's punches went right down to his toes, and this must have been one of them. When the fighters were separated, Foreman chased Ali to the ropes, and Ali pulled out a new trick, his full inch and a half of reach. He held his arms in Foreman's face to keep him off. The round was almost a minute gone before Ali got in his first good punch, another right. But Foreman charged him and pushed him, driving down on Ali's gloves with his own gloves, stalking him back and back again, knocking Ali's gloves away when he didn't like the character of their moves. Foreman was beginning to dictate how the fight should be. If a bully, he was a master bully. He did not react to the dictation of others, liked his own dictation. The force he sought in serenity had locked him on a unilinear road; it was working now. Ali kept retreating and Foreman caught him again. Hard! Once more, Ali was holding on with both hands, back of the neck, back of the bicep, half writhing and half riding with the somewhat stifled punches Foreman kept throwing. Foreman had begun to dominate the action to the point where Ali's best course seemed to be obliged to take what was left of each punch after the attempt to smother it. He kept trying to wrestle Foreman to a stop.

But then Ali must have come to a first assessment of assets and weaknesses, for he made – somewhere in the unremarked middle of the round – he must have made a decision on how to shape the rest of the fight. He did not seem able to hurt Foreman critically with those right-hand leads. Nor was he stronger than Foreman except when wrestling on his neck, and certainly he could not afford any more of those episodes where he held on to Foreman even as George was hitting him. It was costly in points, painful, and won nothing. On the other hand, it was too soon to dance. Too rapid would be the drain on his stamina. So the time had come to see if he could outbox Foreman while lying on the ropes. It had been his option from the beginning and it was the most dangerous option he had. For so long as Foreman had strength, the ropes would prove about as safe as riding a unicycle on a parapet. Still, what is genius but balance on the edge of the impossible? Ali introduced his grand theme. He lay back on the ropes in the middle of the second round, and from that position he would work for the rest of the fight, reclining at an angle of ten and twenty degrees from the vertical and sometimes even further, a cramped near-tortured angle from which to box.

Of course Ali had been preparing for just this hour over the last ten years. For ten years he had been practising to fight powerful sluggers who beat on your belly while you lay on the ropes. So he took up his station with confidence, shoulders parallel to the edge of the ring. In this posture his right would have no more impact than a straight left but he could find himself in position to cover his head with both gloves, and his belly with his elbows, he could rock and sway, lean so far back Foreman must fall on him. Should Foreman pause from the fatigue of throwing punches, Ali could bounce off the ropes and sting him, jolt him, make him look clumsy, mock him, rouse his anger, which might yet wear Foreman out more than anything else. In this position, Ali could even hurt him. A jab hurts if you run into it, and Foreman is always coming in. Still, Ali is in the position of a man bowing and ducking in a doorway while another man comes at him with two clubs. Foreman comes on with his two clubs. In the first exchange he hits Ali about six times while Ali is returning only one blow. Yet the punches to Ali's head seem not to bother him; he is swallowing the impact with his entire body. He is like a spring on the ropes. Blows seem to pass through him as if he is indeed a leaf spring built to take shock. None of his spirit is congested in his joints. Encouraged by the recognition that he can live with these blows, he begins to taunt Foreman. 'Can you hit?' he calls out. 'You can't hit. You push!' Since his head has been in range of Foreman's gloves, Foreman lunges at him. Back goes Ali's head like the carnival boy ducking baseballs. Wham to you, goes Ali, catapulting back. Bing and sting! Now Foreman is missing and Ali is hitting.

It is becoming a way to fight and even a way to live, but for Ali's corner it is a terror to watch. In the last thirty seconds of this second round, Ali hits out with straight rights from the ropes fast as jabs. Foreman's head must feel like a rivet under a riveting gun. With just a few seconds left, Foreman throws his biggest punch of the night, an express train of a left hook which leaves a spasm for the night in its passing. It has been a little too slow. Ali lets it go by in the languid unhurried fashion of Archie Moore watching a roundhouse miss his chin by a quarter of an inch. In the void of the effort, Foreman is so off balance that Ali could throw him through the ropes. 'Nothing,' says Ali through his mouthpiece. 'You have no aim.' The bell rings and Foreman looks depressed. There has been premature desperation in that left. Ali shakes his head in derision. Of course that is one of Ali's basic tricks. All through his first fight with Frazier he kept signalling to the crowd that Joe failed to impress him. All the while Ali was finding himself in more trouble.

It seems like eight rounds have passed yet we only finished two. Is it because we are trying to watch with the fighters' sense of time? Before fatigue brings boxers to the boiler rooms of the damned, they live at a height of consciousness and with a sense of detail they encounter nowhere else. In no other place is their intelligence so full, nor their sense of time able to contain so much of itself as in the long internal effort of the ring. Thirty minutes go by like three hours. Let us undertake the chance, then, that our description of the fight may be longer to read than the fight itself. We can assure ourselves: it was even longer for the fighters.

Contemplate them as they sit in their corners between the second and third rounds. The outcome of the fight is not yet determined. Not for either. Ali has an enormous problem equal to his enormous confidence. Everybody has wondered whether Ali can get through the first few rounds and take Foreman's punch. Now the problem has been refined: can he dismantle Foreman's strength before he uses up his own wit?

Foreman has another problem; he may not be as aware of it as his corner. There is no fear in his mind that he will fail to win the fight. He does not think about that any more than a lion supposes it will he unable to destroy a cheetah; no, it is just a question of catching Ali, a maddening frustration. Still the insult to his rage has to worry his corner. They can hardly tell him not to be angry. It is Foreman's rage after all which has led him to knock out so many fighters. To cut it off is to leave him cowlike. Nonetheless he must contain his anger until he catches Ali. Otherwise he is going to wear himself out.

So Sadler works on him, rubs his breasts and belly, Sadler sends his fingers into all the places where rage has congested, into the meat of the pectorals and the muscle plating beneath Foreman's chest. Sadler's touch has all the wisdom of thirty-five years of Black fingers elucidating comforts for Black flesh, sensual are his fingers as he plucks and shapes and shakes and balms, his silver bracelet shining on his Black wrist. When Sadler feels the fighter is soothed, he begins to speak, and Foreman takes on the expression of a man whose head is working slowly. He has too much to think about. He spits into the bowl held before him and nods respectfully. He looks as if he is listening to his dentist.

In Ali's corner, Dundee, with the quiet concern of a sommelier, is bringing the mouth of the adhesive-taped water bottle to Ali's lips, and does it with a forefinger under the neck so the bottle will not pour too much as he tips it up. Ali rinses and spits with his eyes off on the serious calculation of a man weighing grim but necessary alternatives.

Joe Frazier: 'George is pounding that body with shots. He's hurting the body. Ali shouldn't stay on that rope . . . If he don't move or cut George, George will walk him down. He need to move. He don't need to stay on that rope. For what reason's he on the *rope?*' Frazier sounds offended. Even the sound of the word worries him. Joe Frazier would consider himself *gone* if he had to work there. Rope is an ugly and miserable *kuntu.*

Jim Brown replies: 'Ali is punishing George Foreman even *though* he's on the rope. He's getting some tremendous blows in and' – the wisdom of the professional football player – 'at some point that can tell.'

The bell. Once more Ali comes out of the corner with a big and threatening face as if this round for certain he will bring the attack to Foreman and once again sees something wrong in the idea, profoundly wrong, shifts his plan instantly, backs up and begins to play the ropes. On comes Foreman. The fight has taken its formal pattern. Ali will go by choice to the ropes and Foreman will chase him. Now in each round Ali will work for thirty or forty seconds or for so much even as a minute with his back no more than a foot or two from the top rope, and he is on the rope as often as not. When the strength of the mood, or the logic of the clinch suggests that the virtue of one set of ropes has been used up, he will back off across the ring to use another set. He will spend on an average one-quarter of each round on each of the four sides of the ring. He might just as well be drawing conscious strength from the burial gods of the North, the West, the East and the South. Never has a major fight been so locked into one pattern of movement. It appears designed by a choreographer who knows nothing about the workings of legs and is endlessly inventive about arms. The fight goes on in exactly this fashion round after round, and yet it is hardly boring, for Ali appears in constant danger, and is, and is not. He is turning the pockets of the boxing world inside out. He is demonstrating that what for other fighters is a weakness can be for him a strength. Foreman has been trained to cut instinctively from side to side in such a way as to spoil Ali's ability to circle, Foreman has learned how to force retreat to the ropes. But Ali makes no effort to get away. He does not circle, neither does he reverse his circle. Instead he backs up. Foreman's outstretched arms become a liability. Unable to cuff at a dancing target, he must probe forward. As he does, Ali keeps popping him with straight lefts and rights fast as karate strokes. But then Ali's wife has a black belt in karate.

Sooner or later, however, Foreman is always on him, leaning on him, banging him, belting away with all the fury George knows how to bring to the heavy bag. Ali uses the ropes to absorb the bludgeoning. Standing on one's feet, it is painful to absorb a heavy body punch even when blocked with one's arms. The torso, the legs and the spine take the shock. One has to absorb the brunt of the punch. Leaning on the ropes, however, Ali can pass it along; the ropes will receive the strain. If he cannot catch Foreman's punches with his gloves, or deflect them, or bend Foreman's shoulder to spoil his move, or lean away with his head, slip to the side, or loom up to hug Foreman's head, if finally there is nothing to do but take the punch, then Ali tightens his body and conducts the shock out along the ropes, so that Foreman must feel as if he is beating on a tree trunk which is oscillating against ropes. Foreman's power seems to travel right down the line and rattle the ring posts. It fortifies Ali's sense of relaxation – he has always the last resort of composing himself for the punch. When, occasionally, a blow does hurt, he sticks Foreman back, mean and salty, using his left and right as jabs. Since his shoulders are against the ropes, he jabs as often with his right as his left. With his timing it is a great jab. He has a gift for hitting Foreman as Foreman comes in. That doubles or triples the force. Besides he is using so many right jabs Foreman must start to wonder whether he is fighting a southpaw. Then comes the left jab again. A converted southpaw? It has something of the shift of locus which comes from making love to a brunette when she is wearing a blonde wig. Of course, Ali has red wigs too. At the end of the round, Ali hits Foreman with some of the hardest punches of the fight. A right, a left, and a right startle Foreman in their combination. He may not have seen such a combination since his last street fight. Ali gives a look of contempt and they wrestle for a few seconds until the bell. For the few extra seconds it takes Foreman to go to his corner, his legs have the look of a bedridden man who has started on a tour of his room for the first time in a week. He has almost stumbled on the way to his stool.

In the aisle, Rachman Ali began to jeer at Henry Clark. 'Your man's a chump,' Rachman said. 'Ali's going to get him.' Clark had to look worried. It was hardly his night.

First his own fight had been postponed, then called off, now he was watching George from a crate in the aisle. Since he had a big bet on George, this last round offered its woes.

In the corner Sadler was massaging Foreman's right shoulder and George was gagging a bit, the inside of his lips showing a shocking frothy white like the mouth of an over-galloped horse.

Nonetheless, he looked lively as he came out for the bell. He came right across the middle of the ring to show Ali a new kind of feint, a long pawing movement of his hands accompanied by short moves of his head. It was to a different rhythm as if to say, 'I haven't begun to show what I know.'

He looked jaunty, but he was holding his right hand down by the waist. Fatigue must have lent carelessness to what he did, for Ali immediately answered with an insulting stiff right, an accelerating hook and another right so heavy to Foreman's head that he grabbed for a clinch, first time in the fight. There, holding on to Ali while vertigo collided with nausea, and bile scalded his breath, he must have been delivered into a new awareness, for George immediately started to look better. He began to get to Ali on the ropes and hit him occasionally, and for the first time in a while was not getting hit as much himself. He was even beginning to jam a number of Ali's rhythms. Up to now, whenever Ali took a punch, he was certain to come off the ropes and hit Foreman back. A couple of times in this round, however, even as Ali started his move, George would jam his forearm into Ali's neck, or wrestle him to a standstill.

All the while Ali was talking. 'Come on, George, show me something,' he would say. 'Can't you fight harder? That ain't hard. I thought you was the champion, I thought you had punches,' and Foreman working like a bricklayer running up a pyramid to set his bricks would snort and lance his arms in sudden unexpected directions and try to catch Ali bouncing on the rope, Ali who was becoming more confirmed every minute in the sinecure of the rope, but at the end of the round, Foreman caught him with the best punch he had thrown in many a minute, landing just before the bell, and as he turned to leave Ali, he said clearly, 'How's that?'

It must have encouraged him, for in the fifth round he tried to knock Ali out. Even as Ali was becoming more confident on the ropes, Foreman grew convinced he could break Ali's defence. Confidence on both sides makes for war. The round would go down in history as one of the great rounds in heavyweight boxing; indeed it was so good it forged its own frame as they battled. One could see it outlined forever in lights: *The Great Fifth Round of the Ali–Foreman fight!*

Like much of greatness, the beginnings were unremarked. Foreman ended the fourth round well, but expectation was circling ringside that a monumental upset could be shaping. Even Joe Frazier was admitting that George was 'not being calm'. It took John Daly to blurt out cheerfully to David Frost, 'Ali is winning all the way for me and I think he's going to take it within another four rounds!'

Foreman didn't think so. There had been that sniff of victory in the fourth, the good punch which landed – 'How's that?' He came out in the fifth with the conviction that if force had not prevailed against Ali up to now, more force was the answer, considerably more force than Ali had ever seen. If Foreman's face was battered to lumps and his legs were moving like wheels with a piece chipped out of the rim, if his arms were beginning to sear in the lava of exhaustion and his breath come roaring to his lungs like the blast from a bed of fire, still he was a prodigy of strength, he was *the* prodigy, he could live through states of torture and hurl his cannonade when others could not lift their arms, he had been trained for endurance even more than execution and back in Pendleton when first working for this fight had once boxed fifteen rounds with half a dozen sparring partners coming on in two-round shifts while Foreman was permitted only thirty seconds of rest between each round. He could go, he could go and go, he was tireless in the arms, yes, could knock down a forest, take it down all by himself, and he set out now to chop Ali down.

They sparred inconclusively for the first half-minute. Then the barrage began. With Ali braced on the ropes, as far back on the ropes as a deep-sea fisherman is braced back in his chair when setting the hook on a big strike, so Ali got ready and Foreman came on to blast him out. A shelling reminiscent of artillery battles in the First World War began. Neither man moved more than a few feet in the next minute and a half. Across that embattled short space Foreman threw punches in barrages of four and six and eight and nine, heavy maniacal slamming punches, heavy as the boom of oaken doors, bombs to the body, bolts to the head, punching until he could not breathe, backing off to breathe again and come in again, bomb again, blast again, drive and steam and slam the torso in front of him, wreck him in the arms, break through those arms, get to his ribs, dig him out, dig him out, put the dynamite in the earth, lift him, punch him, punch him up to heaven, take him out, stagger him – great earth-mover he must have sobbed to himself, kill this mad and bouncing goat.

And Ali, gloves to his head, elbows to his ribs, stood and swayed

and was rattled and banged and shaken like a grasshopper at the top
of a reed when the wind whips, and the ropes shook and swung like
sheets in a storm, and Foreman would lunge with his right at Ali's
chin and Ali go flying back out of reach by a half-inch, and half out
of the ring, and back in to push at Foreman's elbow and hug his own
ribs and sway, and sway just further, and lean back and come
forward from the ropes and slide off a punch and fall back into the
ropes with all the calm of a man swinging in the rigging. All the
while, he used his eyes. They looked like stars, and he feinted
Foreman out with his eyes, flashing white eyeballs of panic he did
not feel which pulled Foreman through into the trick of lurching
after him on a wrong move, Ali darting his expression in one
direction while cocking his head in another, then staring at Foreman
expression to expression, holding him in the eye, soul to soul, *muntu*
to *muntu,* hugging his head, pecking through gloves, jamming his
armpit, then taunting him on the edge of the ropes, then flying back
as Foreman dived forward, tantalising him, maddening him, looking
for all the world as cool as if he were sparring in his bathrobe, now
banishing Foreman's head with the turn of a matador sending away
a bull after five fine passes were made, and once when he seemed to
hesitate just a little too long, teasing Foreman just a little too long,
something stirred in George like that across-the-arena knowledge of
a bull when it is ready at last to gore the matador rather than the
cloth, and like a member of a *cuadrilla*, somebody in Ali's corner
screamed, 'Careful! Careful! Careful!' and Ali flew back and just in
time for as he bounced on the ropes Foreman threw six of his most
powerful left hooks in a row and then a right, it was the centre of his
fight and the heart of his best charge, a left to the belly, a left to the
head, a left to the belly, a left to the head, a left to the belly, another
to the belly and Ali blocked them all, elbow for the belly, glove for
the head, and the ropes flew like snakes. Ali was ready for the lefts.
He was not prepared for the right that followed. Foreman hit him a
powerful punch. The ring bolts screamed. Ali shouted, 'Didn't hurt a
bit.' Was it the best punch he took all night? He had to ride through
ten more after that. Foreman kept flashing his muscles up out of that
cup of desperation boiling in all determination, punches that came
towards the end of what may have been as many as forty or fifty in a
minute, any one strong enough to send water from the spine to the

knees. Something may have finally begun to go from Foreman's *n'golo*, some departure of the essence of absolute rage, and Ali reaching over the barrage would give a prod now and again to Foreman's neck like a housewife sticking a toothpick in a cake to see if it is ready. The punches got weaker and weaker, and Ali finally came off the ropes and in the last thirty seconds of the round threw his own punches, twenty at least. Almost all hit. Some of the hardest punches of the night were driven in. Four rights, a left hook and a right came in one stupendous combination. One punch turned Foreman's head through ninety degrees, a right cross of glove and forearm that slammed into the side of the jaw; double contact had to be felt; once from the glove, then from the bare arm, stunning and jarring. Walls must begin to crack inside the brain. Foreman staggered and lurched and glared at Ali and got hit again, zing-bing! two more. When it was all over, Ali caught Foreman by the neck like a big brother chastising an enormous and stupid kid brother, and looked out to someone in the audience, some enemy or was it some spiteful friend who said Foreman would win, for Ali, holding George around the neck, now stuck out one long white-coated tongue. On the other side of the ropes, Bundini was beaming at the bell.

'I really don't believe it,' said Jim Brown. 'I really don't believe it. I thought he was hurt. I thought his body was hurt. He came back. He hit Foreman with everything. And he winked at *me*.' Did he wink or stick out his tongue?

In the aisle, Rachman was screaming at Henry Clark. 'Your fighter's a chump. He's an amateur. My brother is killing him. My brother is showing him up!'

So began the third act of the fight. Not often was there a better end to a second act than Foreman's failure to destroy Ali on the ropes. But the last scenes would present another problem. How was the final curtain to be found? For if Foreman was exhausted, Ali was weary. He had hit Foreman harder than he had ever hit anyone. He had hit him often. Foreman's head must by now be equal to a piece of vulcanised rubber. Conceivably you could beat on him all night and nothing more would happen. There is a threshold to the knockout. When it comes close but is not crossed, then a man can stagger around the ring forever. He has received his terrible message and he is still standing. No more of the same woe can destroy him. He is like the victim in a dreadful marriage which no one knows how to end. So Ali was obliged to produce still one more surprise. If not, the unhappiest threat would present itself as he and Foreman stumbled through the remaining rounds. There is agony to elucidate even a small sense of the aesthetic out of boxing. Wanton waste for an artist like Ali to lose then the perfection of this fight by wandering down a monotonous half-hour to a dreary unanimous decision.

A fine ending to the fight would live in legend, but a dull victory, anticlimactic by the end, could leave him in half a legend – overblown in reputation by his friends and contested by his enemies – precisely that state which afflicted most heroes. Ali was fighting to prove other points. So he said. So Ali had to dispose of Foreman in the next few rounds and do it well, a formidable problem. He was like a torero after a great *faena* who must still face the drear potential of a protracted inept and disappointing kill. Since no pleasure is greater among athletes than to overtake the style of their opponent, Ali would look to steal Foreman's last pride. George was an executioner. Ali would do it better. But how do you execute the executioner?

The problem was revealed in all its sluggish intricacies over the next three rounds. Foreman came out for the sixth looking like an alley cat with chewed-up brows. Lumps and swellings were all over his face, his skin equal to tar that has baked in the sun. When the bell rang, however, he looked dangerous again, no longer a cat, but a bull. He lowered his head and charged across the ring. He was a total demonstration of the power of one idea even when the idea no longer works. And was immediately seized and strangled around the neck by Ali for a few valuable and pacifying seconds until Zack Clayton broke them. Afterwards, Foreman moved in to throw more punches. His power, however, seemed gone. The punches were slow and tentative. They did not reach Ali. Foreman was growing glove-shy. His fastest moves were now in a nervous defence that kept knocking Ali's punches away from his own face.

At this point Ali proceeded to bring out the classic left jab everyone had been expecting for the first round. In the next half-minute, he struck Foreman's head with ten head-ringing jabs thrown with all the speed of a good fencer's thrust, and Foreman took them in apathy to compound the existing near-apathy of his hopes. Each time his head snapped back, some communication between his mind and his nerves must have been reduced. A surgical attack.

Yet something in Foreman's response decided Ali to give it up. Perhaps no more than his own sense of moderation. It might look absurd if he kept jabbing Foreman forever. Besides, Ali needed rest. The next two minutes turned into the slowest two minutes of the fight. Foreman kept pushing Ali to the ropes out of habit, a dogged forward motion that enabled George to rest in his fashion, the only way he still knew, which was to lean on the opponent. Ali was by now so delighted with the advantages of the ropes that he fell back on them like a man returning home in quiet triumph, yes, settled in with the weary pleasure of a working man getting back into bed after a long day to be treated to a little of God's joy by his hardworking wife. He was almost tender with Foreman's labouring advance, holding him softly and kindly by the neck. Then he stung him with right and left karate shots from the shoulder. Foreman was now so arm-weary he could begin a punch only by lurching forward until his momentum encouraged a movement of the arm. He looked like a drunk, or rather a somnambulist, in a dance marathon. It would be wise to get him through the kill without ever waking him up. While it ought to be a simple matter to knock him down, there might not be enough violence left in the spirit of this ring to knock him out. So the shock of finding himself on the floor could prove a stimulant. His ego might reappear: once on the floor, he was a champion in dramatic danger of losing his title – that is an unmeasurable source of energy. Ali was now taking in the reactions of Foreman's head the way a bullfighter lines up a bull before going in over the horns for the kill. He bent to his left and, still crouched, passed his body to the right under Foreman's fists, all the while studying George's head and neck and shoulders. Since Foreman charged the move, a fair conclusion was that the bull still had an access of strength too great for the kill.

Nonetheless, Foreman's punches were hardly more than pats. They were sufficiently weak for any man in reasonable shape to absorb them. Still, Foreman came on. Sobbing for breath, leaning, almost limping, in a pat-a-pat of feeble cuffs, he was all but lying over Ali on the ropes. Yet what a problem in the strength of his stubbornness itself. Endless powers of determination had been built out of one season of silence passing into another. The bell rang the end of the sixth. Both men gave an involuntary smile of relief.

Foreman looked ready to float as he came to his corner. Sandy Saddler could not bring himself to look at him. The sorrow in Foreman's corner was now heavier than in Ali's dressing-room before the fight.

In his corner Ali looked thoughtful, and stood up abstractedly before the bell and abstractedly led a cheer in the stadium, his arm to the sky.

The cheer stirred Foreman to action. He was out of his corner and in the middle of the ring before the bell rang. Ali opened his eyes wide and stared at him in mock wonder, then in disdain as if to say, 'Now you've done it. Now you're asking for it.' He came out of his corner too, and the referee was pushing both men apart as the bell rang.

Still it was a slow round, almost as slow as the sixth. Foreman had no speed, and in return Ali boxed no faster than he had to, but kept shifting more rapidly than before from one set of ropes to another. Foreman was proving too sluggish to work with. Once, in the middle of the round, Foreman staggered past Ali, and for the first time in the fight was literally nearer the ropes. It was a startling realisation. Not since the first five seconds of the fight had Ali crossed the centre of the ring while moving forward. For seven rounds his retreating body had been between Foreman and the ropes except for the intervals when he travelled backward from one set of ropes to another. This time, seeing Foreman on the ropes instead, Ali backed up immediately and Foreman slogged after him like an infantryman looking at the ground. Foreman's best move by now might be to stand in the centre of the ring and invite Ali to come to him. If Ali refused, he would lose the lustre of his performance, and if he did come forward it would be George's turn to look for weaknesses. While Foreman waited for Ali, he could rest. Yet George must have had some unspoken fear of disaster if he shifted methods. So he would drive, thank you very much, into the grave he would determine for himself. Of course, he was not wholly without hope. He still worked with the idea that one punch could catch Ali. And with less than a minute left, he managed to drive a left hook into Ali's belly, a blow that indeed made Ali gasp. Then Foreman racked him with a right uppercut strong enough for Ali to hold on in a clinch, no, Foreman was not going to give up. Now he leaned on Ali with one extended arm and tried to whale him with the other. He looked like he was beating a rug. Foreman had begun to show the clumsiness of a street fighter at the end of a long rumble. He was reverting. It happened to all but the most cultivated fighters towards the exhausted end of a long and terrible fight. Slowly they descended from the elegance of their best style down to the knee in the groin and the overhead punch (with a rock in the fist) of forgotten street fights.

Ali, half as tired at least, was not wasting himself. He was still graceful in every move. By the end of the round he was holding Foreman's head tenderly once more in his glove. Foreman was becoming reminiscent of the computer Hal in *2001* as his units were removed one by one, malfunctions were showing and spastic lapses. All the while something of the old panache of Sadler, Saddler, and Moore inserted over those thousands of hours of training still showed in occasional moves and gestures. The weakest slaps of his gloves, however, had begun to look like entreaties. Still his arms threw punches. By the end of the seventh he could hardly stand: yet he must have thrown seventy more punches. So few were able to land. Ali had restricted himself to twenty-five – half at least must have gone to target. Foreman was fighting as slowly as a worn-out fighter in the Golden Gloves, slow as a man walking up a hill of pillows, slow as he would have looked if their first round had been rerun in slow motion, that was no slower than Foreman was fighting now, and thus exposed as in a film, he was reminiscent of the slow and curving motions of a linebacker coiling around a runner with his hands and arms in the slow-motion replay – the boxing had shifted from speed and impact to an intimacy of movement. Delicately Ali would cradle Foreman's head with his left before he smashed it with his right. Foreman looked ready to fall over from exhaustion. His face had the soft scrubbed look of a child who has just had a dirty face washed, but then they both had that gentle look boxers get when they are very tired and have fought each other very hard.

Back in the corner, Moore's hands were massaging Foreman's shoulders. Sandy Saddler was working on his legs. Dick Sadler was talking to him.

Jim Brown was saying, 'This man, Muhammad Ali, is *unreal.*' When Jim used the word, it was a compliment. Whatever was real, Jim Brown could dominate. And Frazier added his humour, 'I would say right now my man is not in the lead. I got a feeling George is not going to make it.'

On the aisle, Rachman was still calling out to Henry Clark. 'Henry, admit it, your man is through, he's a chump, he's a street fighter. Henry, admit it. Maybe I'm not a fighter, I know I'm not as good as you, but admit it, admit it, Muhammad has whipped George.' Except he hadn't. Not yet. Two rounds had gone by. The two dullest rounds of the fight. The night was hot. Now the air would become more tropical with every round. In his corner, Ali looked to be in pain as he breathed. Was it his kidneys or his ribs? Dundee was talking to him and Ali was shaking his head in disagreement. In contrast to Foreman, his expression was keen. His eyes looked as quick as the eyes, indeed, of a squirrel. The bell rang for the eighth round.

Working slowly, deliberately, backing up still one more time, he hit Foreman carefully, spacing the punches, taking aim, six good punches, lefts and rights. It was as if he had a reserve of good punches, a numbered amount like a soldier in a siege who counts his bullets, and so each punch had to carry a predetermined portion of the work.

Foreman's legs were now hitched into an ungainly prance like a horse high-stepping along a road full of rocks. Stung for the hundredth time with a cruel blow, his response was to hurl back a left hook that proved so wild he almost catapulted through the ropes. Then for an instant, his back and neck were open to Ali, who cocked a punch but did not throw it, as though to demonstrate for an instant to the world that he did not want to flaw this fight with any blow reminiscent of the thuds Foreman had sent to the back of the head of Norton and Roman and Frazier. So Ali posed with that punch, then moved away. Now for the second time in the fight he had found Foreman between himself and the ropes and had done nothing.

Well, George came off the ropes and pursued Ali like a man chasing a cat. The wild punch seemed to have refreshed him by its promise that some of his power was back. If his biggest punches were missing, at least they were big. Once again he might be his own prodigy of strength. Now there were flurries on the ropes which had an echo of the great bombardment in the fifth round. And still Ali taunted him, still the dialogue went on. 'Fight hard,' said Ali, 'I thought you had some punches. You're a weak man. You're all used up.' After a while, Foreman's punches were whistling less than his breath. For the eighteenth time Ali's corner was screaming, 'Get off the ropes. Knock him out. Take him home!' Foreman had used up the store of force he transported from the seventh to the eighth. He pawed at Ali like an infant six feet tall waving its unco-ordinated battle arm.

With twenty seconds left to the round, Ali attacked. By his own measure, by that measure of twenty years of boxing, with the knowledge of all he had learned of what could and could not be done at any instant in the ring, he chose this as the occasion and lying on the ropes, he hit Foreman with a right and left, then came off the ropes to hit him with a left and a right. Into this last right hand he put his glove and his forearm again, a head-stupefying punch that sent Foreman reeling forward. As he went by, Ali hit him on the side of the jaw with a right, and darted away from the ropes in such a way as to put Foreman next to them. For the first time in the entire fight he had cut off the ring on Foreman. Now Ali struck him a combination of punches fast as the punches of the first round, but harder and more consecutive, three capital rights in a row struck Foreman, then a left, and for an instant on Foreman's face appeared the knowledge that he was in danger and must start to look to his last protection. His opponent was attacking, and there were no ropes behind the opponent. What a dislocation: the axes of his existence were reversed! He was the man on the ropes! Then a big projectile exactly the size of a fist in a glove drove into the middle of Foreman's mind, the best punch of the startled night, the blow Ali saved for a career. Foreman's arms flew out to the side like a man with a parachute jumping out of a plane, and in this doubled-over position he tried to wander out to the centre of the ring. All the while his eyes were on Ali and he looked up with no anger as if Ali, indeed, was the man he knew best in the world and would see him on his dying day. Vertigo took George Foreman and revolved him. Still bowing from the waist in this uncomprehending position, eyes on Muhammad Ali all the way, he started to tumble and topple and fall even as he did not wish to go down. His mind was held with magnets high as his championship and his body was seeking the ground. He went over like a six-foot sixty-year-old butler who has just heard tragic news, yes, fell over all of a long collapsing two seconds, down came the champion in sections and Ali revolved with him in a close circle, hand primed to hit him one more time, and never the need, a wholly intimate escort to the floor.

The referee took Ali to a corner. He stood there, he seemed lost in thought. Now he raced his feet in a quick but strained shuffle as if to apologise for never asking his legs to dance, and looked on while Foreman tried to rouse himself.

Like a drunk hoping to get out of bed to go to work, Foreman rolled over, Foreman started the slow head-agonising lift of all that foundered bulk God somehow gave him and whether he heard the count or no, was on his feet a fraction after the count of ten and whipped, for when Zack Clayton guided him with a hand at his back, he walked in docile steps to his corner and did not resist. Moore received him. Sadler received him. Later, one learned the conversation.

'Feel all right?'

'Yeah,' said Foreman.

'Well, don't worry. It's history now.'

'Yeah.'

'You're all right,' said Sadler, 'the rest will take care of itself.'

In the ring Ali was seized by Rachman, by Gene Kilroy, by Bundini, by a host of Black friends old, new and very new, who charged up the aisles, leapt on the apron, sprang through the ropes and jumped near to touch him. Norman said to Plimpton in a tone of wonder like a dim parent who realises suddenly his child is indeed and indubitably married, 'My God, he's champion again!' as if one had trained oneself for years not to expect news so good as that.

In the ring Ali fainted.

It occurred suddenly and without warning and almost no one saw it. Angelo Dundee circling the ropes to shout happy words at reporters was unaware of what had happened. So were all the smiling faces. It was only the eight or ten men immediately around him who knew. Those eight or ten mouths which had just been open in celebration now turned to grimaces of horror. Bundini went from laughing to weeping in five seconds.

Why Ali fainted, nobody might ever know. Whether it was a warning against excessive pride in years to come – one private bolt from Allah – or whether the weakness of sudden exhaustion, who could know? Maybe it was even the spasm of a reflex he must have refined unconsciously for months – the ability to recover in seconds from total oblivion. Had he been obliged to try it out at least once on this night? He was in any case too much of a champion to allow an episode to arise, and was back on his feet before ten seconds were up. His handlers having been lifted, chastened, terrified and uplifted again, looked at him with faces of triumph and knockdown, the upturned mask of comedy and the howling mouth of tragedy next to each other in that instant in the African ring.

David Frost was crying out: 'Muhammad Ali has done it. The great man has done it. This is the most joyous scene ever seen in the history of boxing. This is an incredible scene. The place is going wild. Muhammad Ali has won.' And because the announcer before him had picked the count up late and was two seconds behind the referee and so counting eight when Clayton said ten, it looked on all the closed circuit screens of the world as if Foreman had gotten up before the count was done, and confusion was everywhere. How could it be other? The media would always sprout the seed of confusion. 'Muhammad Ali has won. By a knockdown,' said Frost in good faith. 'By a knockdown.'

Back in America everybody was already yelling that the fight was fixed. Yes. So was *The Night Watch* and *Portrait of the Artist as a Young Man.*

ROUND 9
Man of Sugar, Hands of Stone

There is a cliché that arises whenever boxing is discussed: the idea that all great fighters are the product of the gutter, that only the truly deprived, whose very existence and right to live have been challenged on a daily basis, possess that will to survive and the killer instinct essential to success in the hardboiled world of the professional ring. Like all clichés it contains at least an element of truth. Certainly in the case of Roberto Duran, the grinding poverty on the streets of Panama City helped forge the legend of the indestructible 'Hands of Stone'. In fact, his story has all the elements of the classic rags-to-riches boxing career.

In two great bouts with Sugar Ray Leonard, the world saw two conflicting sides of this complex Jekyll and Hyde character. The merciless, mocking victor on the one hand, and the inconceivable spectacle, in the second fight, of the mighty Duran quitting cold in mid-contest. It was as if the bully's bluff had been called and when he could no longer dominate, he turned his back and ran and in so doing, fell far, far short of greatness.

As for Leonard, having beaten Duran and Hagler – albeit the latter in somewhat controversial circumstances – his credentials for greatness were further enhanced by his recent ninth-round knockout of Canada's Golden Boy, Danny Lalonde, a fully fledged light heavyweight. He became the first fighter in history to hold five championship belts.

'American sportswriter Sam Toperoff here describes the two Leonard–Duran encounters, and offers a fascinating profile of the character of Roberto Duran, the man known to his fellow Panamanians as 'El Animal'.

Getting it Wrong, Getting it Right

Sam Toperoff

Jazz players love to sit around and tell Thelonius Monk stories
because the great piano stylist actually said and did the sorts of things
that characterise the spacey yet unquestionable brilliance of his music.
Comedians like to remember the things attributed to Lenny Bruce or,
in a less self-destructive mode, recount the off-screen madness of Mel
Brooks. Through such insider yarns the subject becomes a 'jazzman's
jazzman' or a 'comedian's comedian'. Boxing people like to tell tales
about Roberto Duran, the fighter's fighter.

Many of the Roberto Duran stories around the fight game hearken
back to his life as an impoverished street urchin in Panama City,
where it is said Roberto beat grown men to the cobblestones with his
bony fists. They say he was ten. They say he swam two miles across
the Canal with stolen mangoes from the other side to keep his family
alive. They say he killed sharks en route with the knife he held
between his teeth. They say he knocked down a horse with a single
blow to prove he was a heavier puncher than Antonio Cervantes.
They say he has a pet lion on his estate in Panama. There are a great
many such Roberto Duran stories.

Who knows the reality. We are speaking here of legend.
Undeniably, though, the street kid was very tough and more than
slightly manic; even after he began to confine his rage to the more
acceptable venue of a boxing ring, his hunger for violent action and
the power of his punches remained. They called him the kid with
hands of stone on the streets of Panama City; as a gloved professional
he remained 'Manos de Piedra'.

A punishing hitter, to be sure, Roberto Duran was much more,
more even than his remarkable ring record of seventy-one victories
in seventy-two bouts coming up to his challenge for Sugar Ray
Leonard's WBC welterweight title. Duran had lost just once in
thirteen years, a close decision in 1972 to Esteban DeJesus, an
opponent he knocked out twice in subsequent fights. Legend says

176

that after that loss to DeJeus, Duran pummelled the locker-room walls until his stone hands were blood-raw. Admirers sometimes persisted in calling Roberto '*El Animal*', but for some reason he didn't welcome the nickname.

Ring records can deceive gaudily; they can be pumped up as easily as silicon breasts. Not the case with Duran – he'd fought everyone willing to step in with him on his way to the lightweight championship he held for almost ten years, through twelve title defences. But Duran was considered a phenomenon not merely on the basis of KO statistics. Duran was Duran because of how he fought. A typical Duran victory usually evoked the same key words from the boxing writers, words like 'savage', 'disdainful', 'brutal', 'relentless', 'pitiless'. There were no other fighters around quite like him in the 1970s. He was a throwback in more ways than one, a mysterious, dark figure from some tropical and mythic past. Roberto Duran also looked the part.

His hair was long and blue-black; it fell behind him like a horse's mane. His moustache, goatee, and scruffy sideburns were villainous touches he cultivated and relished. The dark eyes glowed, perhaps with the same fire of the Mexican father he never remembered, enigmatically, with a vestige of the Indian blood he also surely possessed. In victory Roberto Duran was never gracious. A sneer was his typical reaction to success in the ring. He had little inclination or the time to develop an honest respect for an opponent.

As champion of the world, Duran had come a long way from the untutored street fighter, even though the apparent style of a brawler led many fans to assume that he prevailed in the ring exclusively by force of muscle and will. But this was no Rocky Graziano, say, whose crude courage and lucky punch could win him a championship for a short while. At the highest levels of professional boxing, brute force, even when linked to physical courage, is not enough to win a fighter lasting respect among his peers. Skill matters considerably. Carlos Eleta, a Panamanian millionaire and Duran's manager, understood this fact and went about hiring the best American trainers money could buy, Freddie Brown and Ray Arcel.

On the subway you'd give either one of these guys your seat. Brown, with a face like a battered car, was seventy-three, Arcel, a pugilistic professor emeritus, was eighty-two when Duran and Sugar

Ray Leonard fought for Leonard's welterweight title in Montreal in June 1980.

As unlikely a pair as you'd ever meet in boxing, they were the best in the game. Brown was assuredly one of the finest cut-men in the sport, an excellent tactician and motivator; Arcel, the master strategist. In the nine years they'd been working with Duran, he had become a very good defensive fighter, learning to pick off punches as he came in and to minimise the effect of solid blows.

Always pressing forward, willing to mix and take an opponent's best shots in order to deliver his own, there was never in him even the faintest suggestion of 'quit'. Ever. And when he sensed he'd hurt an opponent, some deep, bestial instinct, a scent for blood, a possible kill, was aroused, and Roberto Duran moved thirstily forward for the finish. 'It's a great fighter's sixth sense,' Paddy Flood, whose admiration of the Panamanian was boundless, told me. 'The man is one of the greatest finishers ever been around.'

Roberto Duran in his prime was the kind of fighter other professionals, especially lightweights, did not really want to fight, not only because it was unlikely they could win, but because they would have to pay so dearly. Duran was not a one-punch knockout artist; rather, he beat on and came forward incessantly, finally putting the other fighter away after some invisible tolerance and by bobbing his head and twisting his torso while fighting inside; he also developed his left hand as a significant weapon and to set up his devastating right. They'd helped make Roberto Duran a hell of a fighter, one boxing historians would probably be forced to consider great.

Angelo Dundee knew that, strategically speaking, he was up against the best there was in the odd couple of Arcel and Brown. Even though he could more than hold his own against them in front of the press with classic lines like, 'Those guys, they're older than water,' Angelo was going up against his own teachers. He'd carried water buckets for them decades earlier. He'd seen them work corners for fighters who constituted one wall of Boxing's Hall of Fame.

From Arcel and Brown, Angelo learned tricks of the ancient trade that had all but passed from the scene. Like the gambit he'd seen Arcel pull off over thirty years before when one of Arcel's fighters had knocked down, but not out, a tough opponent. Just as the referee picked up the count, Arcel leapt into the ring and jubilantly threw the robe over his fighter. The referee, momentarily confused by the end-of-fight celebration, concurred and hurried knockdown into knockout. Dundee admitted to using the old 'victory robe' trick with success on occasion. But no matter how sharp Angie had become over the years, compared to Brown and Arcel he'd always remain the sorcerer's apprentice. Still, he genuinely liked Sugar Ray's chances against Duran and for a variety of reasons, some of them owing to Ray's now highly developed skills as a boxer, some of them the result of vulnerabilities he saw in the Panamanian that tended to get overlooked when the Duran legends are trotted out.

There is an old truism about knockout punchers that Dundee believed would be applicable here, namely that when a KO specialist moves into a heavier weight class, his big punch becomes less effective. It's not so much a matter of the power being diminished as of the larger opponent being able to absorb the hard shots better. For whatever reason, it is the case often enough so that smart boxing people pay close attention to hitters moving up in class. Dundee felt that although Duran was a punishing lightweight, those 'Manos de Piedra' might not bowl over the muscular welterweight boxer Ray Charles Leonard had become.

Furthermore, the Leonard camp knew something that was not very widely perceived and would, in fact, take a good deal of proving even after it became known: Sugar Ray Leonard could take a hell of a punch. Because Ray never had to absorb the punishment that was Duran's modus operandi, it was widely assumed that a couple of blows from the stone hands would finally expose Leonard as the made-for-television creation he was.

However, it was not in Dundee's fight plan to have Ray prove to the world how tough he was. You go fifteen with Roberto Duran, you take some wicked shots. Sure. But you certainly don't want to get in a mugging contest with a street fighter. Duran was not Andrés Aldama, the Cuban slugger whose attack Ray smothered in this very same ring for his 1976 Olympic championship. This was the legendary Roberto Duran.

Dundee wanted Ray to move and slide, but not to hide. Conventional wisdom. He wanted more; he hoped to use the fact that Duran was a stalking fighter against him. As Duran came forward to close with Ray or to punch inside, Ray was not to be in front of him but to step quickly left or right, set, and throw punches from eleven or one o'clock, never, never, from high noon. Ray's vastly superior foot and hand speed, his defensive skills and adaptability would all have to come into play for the strategy to work. Ray's stinging offensive jab that momentarily froze most of his opponents and set up the sparkling combinations was expected to be his most important offensive weapon. It's not accurate to say that Dundee was confident going in; he did believe, though, that if Ray carried out the plan, he had precisely the style and the tools to get the job done.

Usually comparing styles, records, and ages is sufficient to enable an experienced observer to project a winner in a big fight. Occasionally, though, things unseen and unknowable hold the key; shadowy matters buried in a fighter's past or in his psyche can tip the fight one way or the other. Rarely are fights won or lost primarily because of a fighter's psychological state, as they like to show in fight movies. But this was to be the case in each of the two remarkable Leonard–Duran matches.

Psychologically speaking, Duran was worth at least a chapter in a textbook on neuroses caused by deprivation. The abject poverty that pervaded his youth had scarred the adult profoundly. He compensated by becoming the 'hungriest' fighter of his era, but his hunger was for food as well as recognition and respect, and it became insatiable as his boxing triumphs mounted. Roberto Duran literally ate himself out of the lightweight division. Between bouts, the 135-pound fighter would balloon up to 165, 170. Tales of his enormous appetite became part of the Duran legend, as did tales of the deprivation and self-punishment required to get back down to fighting weight. The debilitating effects on a fighter of such extreme weight and mood swings would surely begin to take their toll on the twenty-nine-year-old, who had been abusing his body for years.

Because he only had to make 147, the welterweight limit, for the fight with Leonard, Duran's pre-fight bloat didn't seem to be very serious; nevertheless, Freddie Brown had one hell of a job controlling Roberto's intake. With four weeks left to the opening bell, however, Duran was only six pounds over the limit; he would undoubtedly make the weight. Still, this could be the fight when the years of self-abuse conspired to transform Roberto Duran into an old fighter.

Not many students of the game were looking for chinks in Ray's psychological armour. Because he seemed incredibly well-adjusted or possibly because he'd succeeded in actually becoming the image he'd worked at projecting, most people didn't think there was a vulnerable human psyche in there. There was, and it turned out to be crucial in the outcome of the fight. One thing boxing teaches a serious student is never to assume the obvious – that's why referees wisely caution, 'Protect yourself at all times.'

There had been a slight intimation of something cooking in Ray's head at the Waldorf-Astoria's grand ballroom, where the fight was formally announced to the media and the fighters were introduced. It was at such splendiferous get-togethers that Ali first began to make his matches symphonies of hype and pizzazz. But when Sugar Ray leaned over the microphone, cast a sidewise glance at the Panamanian, and said deliberately, 'When I fight Roberto Duran, I don't just want to beat him, I want to kill him,' a breathy gasp filled the silence. The messenger and his message were totally out of character. Later, Ray tried to cover himself by saying it was just hype for the fight, something to catch the eye and ear on the six o'clock news. But the fight was a natural; it didn't require that kind of hype. Leonard's little slip was dismissed as misfired puffery. But, in fact, Ray had a bee in his bonnet, one that had a fatal sting.

Viewed purely as a financial venture, the match couldn't miss. So potentially profitable was it that Mike Trainer did the impossible – he put together a deal that attracted the antagonistic and mutually exclusive talents of boxing's heftiest promoters, Don King and Bob Arum.

Rivals in almost every respect, King and Arum grudgingly agreed to try to work together in promoting the fight because it had a chance to be the richest match in boxing history. Money is balm for deep wounds, at least temporarily. Of course you could never be certain how big a big fight will actually sell, but when all the closed-circuit and residual moneys came in, Duran was expected to earn $1.5 million, far more than he'd ever dreamed of when he was merely considered the best fighter in the world by the experts. Simply stepping into the ring with a 'star' fighter brought greater rewards than simple artistic excellence ever could. As the 'star', Leonard's lion's share guaranteed him $7.5million. Trainer had played his cards perfectly. If the world was not a fair place, the boxing world was less so.

Some promotions run smoothly from the start, some don't. This one didn't. The Quebec Olympic Installation Board bought the fight for US$3.5 million. In order to cover that nut, they scaled the arena from $500 at ringside to twenty bucks for seats in the far-distant balcony. At both extremes, sales were brisk. But tickets going for $75 to $300 didn't move well at all. A few days before the fight fewer than 30,000 tickets had been sold. Montreal's Olympic Stadium held 78,000.

The selection of the site had been a sentimental one, not a hardheaded commercial choice. This was where Sugar Ray had won the hearts and minds of fans as a sweet kid who could fight like a whirlwind. Here he announced he'd reached his goal and would retire to a less violent life. But, as Sugar Ray should have known from harsh experience at that Washington DC intersection, memory is short, allegiance even shorter. He was not the same kid, not the aspiring innocent he was made out to be in 1976. He was a hard defending champion in a hard business. Nor was there a widespread interest in the challenger, Montreal not being particularly well-known for its vast Latino population. In New York or Texas or in Southern California, the fight would have played very well. Fortunately, closed-circuit would blanket those places and most other major boxing markets in the States.

The most frightening moment for the investors and the principals came at what should have been the *pro forma* pre-fight physical about a week before the fight. Duran's electrocardiogram recorded a strange and troubling arrhythmia sometimes associated with hardening of the arteries. Four hours of tests at Montreal's Institute of Cardiology finally cleared Duran to fight. It had been touch and go for a while. This incident, too, would eventually become part of the Duran legend. Said Ray Arcel to reporters, 'They took him to the hospital to check out his heart. But everyone knows that Roberto Duran hasn't got a heart.'

Although the matter finally played no part in the fight itself, it is entirely likely that Duran had been taking pills to help him lose weight – as we discovered Ali had for his fight with Larry Holmes. Weight-loss medication could have accounted for the irregularity in Duran's cardiac exam.

When at last all the obstacles that intruded themselves with this promotion had been overcome, all the sparring and training completed, all the interviews and hype finished, all the aimless, empty hours of waiting killed off, it was time to see who could beat whom. That is, after all, the elemental purpose and attraction of the blood sport. Within such a simple objective, however, are stirred, like swirls in a marble cake, the complex variables of boxing. Courage and speed, reflex and will, strength and imagination, and unknowable, incommunicable variables as well. Between well-matched fighters such as these, you can never be certain until they punch and are punched what will unfold.

A strange thing occurred even before the bell rang. When Sugar Ray was introduced the overwhelming support he expected from the crowd was not there. Boos, in fact, could be discerned peppered in the din. Boos. Had he been perceived as too smart-alecky now that he had become television's darling?

When Carlos Padilla, the referee, called them to the centre of the ring, gave them instructions, and told them to touch gloves, Ray automatically reached out. Nothing. Duran had turned away, leaving the champ alone in the centre of the ring with his arms extended. That single small gesture of disdain by Duran, Leonard's confused and momentary humiliation, may have tipped the outcome of the fight.

Ray Leonard did not fight the fight Angelo Dundee had planned. Ray Leonard did not fight a smart fight at all that Friday night in late June. He fought according to his own lights and made an elemental mistake. Rather than taking advantage of his superior skills as a master boxer, Ray opted to brawl and maul, slug and mug with the man who had written the book on such tactics. To the consternation of his brain trust and over their urgings and objections, Ray Leonard fought Roberto Duran's fight.

Ray's irrational and uncharacteristic behaviour did have a certain logic, at least in retrospect. Unfortunately, it was the logic of losers. Ray suddenly saw very clearly his chance to bury all his critics along with their criticism. Not merely a championship to be defended and a fighter of great reputation to be defeated, the fight became for Ray Leonard a chance to prove to everyone, once and for all, that he had lots of heart. To out-tough Roberto Duran, he reasoned, would do just that. A twenty-four-year-old believes in once-and-for-all.

Perhaps Ray had been baited into the trap by Duran's constant needling, maybe that final insult in the centre of the ring had caused Ray to dismiss Dundee's best-laid plans. Depending on your point of view, it was either arrogance or ignorance that caused Leonard to spring for the obvious bait. However it was, Sugar Ray fought the wrong fight against the wrong fighter as a result.

From the opening bell, Duran bulled forward. Ray did not circle. He did not move to eleven or one o'clock; he took Duran's direct charge, an admirable tactic in college basketball but dumb as dirt when you're in with Roberto Duran. A stiff jab was Ray's strongest statement of the opening round. Just one. Duran worked inside beautifully, raking the champ along the ropes roughly, and Padilla let them fight out whenever they were momentarily entwined, a judgement that favoured Duran, the infighter supreme.

Ray was pinned in the corners for most of the second round. A left hook caught him early and put him in trouble that Duran maintained the entire round. Later Ray would say, 'I can't remember taking quite so long to recover from a punch.' For his wife, Juanita – yes, wife finally; they'd married six months earlier – watching Ray take more punishment than in any round of his career was sheer agony. She began to weep and would do so on and off until the eighth round, when she fainted dead away in the arms of Ray's sister, Sharon.

Through the middle rounds Ray seemed to get progressively stronger and, still fighting Duran's fight, began to hold his own as a rough-houser. All three judges scored the seventh and ninth rounds even. There was still time to turn the fight around if Ray Charles Leonard could reach down and find the grit and guts and staying power to quell the fury of the most furious fighter of recent decades. The thirteenth was Ray's proudest moment. It also happens to be one of the best rounds in modern boxing. Bob Waters, the late boxing-writer, realised the fact as it unfolded and filed the following in his *Newsday* story: 'If great moments were really *golden moments* then some method would be found to immortalise the thirteenth round of the contest – one of the greatest rounds of boxing, if intensity and savagery are the things by which we judge boxing then the round deserves to be etched blow by blow and saved for whatever posterity remains. . .' Fortunately, such a method does exist: on videotape the thirteenth remains as brilliant a round as it did the night it was fought.

Two of the three judges gave the round to Leonard. Of course it had been tactically wrong for Ray to try to bull a bull, but once he adjusted to Duran's *in extremis* approach to the sport, Ray sure as hell wasn't being blown away, not by a long shot. As the fight wore on the rounds were becoming increasingly difficult to score.

As he had throughout the fight, over the last two rounds Duran kept boring in; Ray managed to maintain enough room to counterpunch very well. Although they could not match thirteen for intensity, they were very up-tempo for the final rounds of an extremely rugged fight. He'd been taunting Ray in little ways throughout the early rounds. Now towards the end of the fight a confident Roberto Duran mocked his opponent brazenly by blowing kisses at him and clutching his throat disdainfully. Roberto Duran was playing Roberto Duran. This was, he said afterwards, merely his way of expressing his exuberance at having the fight won. When the bell rang at fight's end Duran thrust his fists in the air and shouted insults at Ray in Spanish. He refused to shake hands when Ray offered his. Some exuberance.

The judges gave the unanimous decision to Duran, but their scoring indicated their uncertainty. A total of nineteen rounds were scored 'even' on the three judges' cards. French judge Baldeyou scored it six-four-five even; Englishman Harry Gibbs had it six-five-four; Angelo Poletti, a son of Italy, believed he had witnessed *ten* even rounds and gave Duran three of the remaining five. More than the closeness of the fight, the scoring revealed the judges' collective incompetence. The decision belonged to Duran, I believed at the time, because he had fought a typical Roberto Duran fight and because Sugar Ray Leonard had fought a typical Roberto Duran fight too.

There was no doubt that Duran had been the busier and more aggressive fighter for most of the match, far more effective with head and elbows, shoulders and knees. But there were some writers present who believed Ray had landed the cleaner, harder punches. Bob Waters gave Ray the nod by the slightest of margins, as did Pete Bonventre, the good boxing writer for *Newsweek* and *Inside Sports*. To this day he contends, 'If you look at the replay carefully, you'll see that while Duran was mugging, Ray was doing some very effective punching. I don't believe Ray fought a smart fight, but I think he did do enough to win.'

I've looked at the fight repeatedly on a video cassette and agree, but only sort of. However, because Duran dictated the way the fight was fought – and because Ray acquiesced – it always *feels* like Duran's fight every time I watch it. A matter of the whole seeming greater than the sum of its parts.

Ray Leonard took a pretty good beating that night. His face was badly swollen, his body ached, his back had been rubbed raw along the ropes. The closed-circuit millions that were being counted even as Ray and Juanita, limp from emotional exhaustion, made their way through the darkened tunnel of Olympic Stadium were not at that moment a reasonable consolation. Slightly more satisfying, but not at all sufficient, was Ray's knowing that the courage he had shown that night would surely undercut the rap against him that he lacked 'heart'. Nothing, however, could divert him from the hard realisation that he had not only lost his championship but lost it because he fought so stupidly. Here he was, finally a doctoral candidate, given a major problem to solve, and he'd gotten it wrong. The truly galling thing, though, was that he'd known the right answer all along.

A fighter with a different temperament would have kicked his own ass for a week or so and then told his manager, 'Get me Duran again.' Financially speaking, nothing would have been easier for Mike Trainer. Ray Charles Leonard, however, when confronted with a setback or an overwhelming success, seems to yield to paralysis and malaise. Immediately after the fight Ray once again said, 'This is it. I gave it all I had, but this is it.' With Juanita supporting his inclination to retire, the next weeks had Ray bending precipitously towards quit. It was as though Ray had a deep psychological need, win or lose, to be able to say at any moment, 'Boxing is not my master,' the way a gambler or a drinker needs to be able to pass up a martini or a tip on the double.

This injury to Ray's pride hurt particularly because it was to a great extent self-inflicted. Maybe, if he had been cleanly whipped by a better fighter, he really could have walked away and stayed away. Ray didn't believe that.

The rematch was made for the Superdome in New Orleans five months later, in November.

The simplest task was Mike Trainer's. Duran–Leonard II was as easy to sell as a Japanese car. Certainly Duran, the new champ, had a right to claim the larger cut, but it would be a bigger pie than had ever been baked in boxing – a guaranteed $15 million, $8 million to Duran, $7 million to Ray.

Dave Jacobs, the man who had been in Ray's corner since the kid first walked into the Palmer Park Recreation Center in 1970, took the opportunity after the loss to Duran to drop off the team. Ever since Dundee had come aboard when Ray turned pro in 1976, Jacobs's position had become increasingly untenable. On the one hand, Janks Morton had become the fighter's ring confidant; on the other, Dundee called the shots professionally, at least until Ray decided to follow his own foolish counsel with Duran. That left Jacobs a supernumerary wrapped in a proud man's character. He'd flirted with quitting repeatedly and actually had quit once before, but he came back when Sugar Ray Leonard, Inc. sweetened his pay cheque.

The reason Jacobs offered for his resignation now was a difference of opinion with the brain trust. He didn't think Ray should step over the ropes and into a ring with Roberto Duran again without a couple of tune-ups under his waistband. A legitimate position. Let your fighter sharpen up and regain a little confidence; at the same time, let the champ get a year older, forty pounds overweight – maybe then Duran's will, if not his hands, would erode as he passed thirty. Jacobs knew how fast a fighter can become an old man.

Jacobs was overruled by economics and emotion – an overwhelming combination. Too much could happen if they waited. The interest and therefore the money were there right now. Additionally, Ray wanted to undo what he perceived as a humiliation as soon as he could. To his normal desire to prove himself as a great fighter in the ring, a thirst for personal revenge had been added. Patience might have been the wiser course; it wasn't going to be.

Normally, no one could out-patient Angelo Dundee, especially when he had the younger fighter. In this instance, though, there was a mitigating factor in addition to the lure of windfall profits. Angie was more convinced than ever that Ray could beat Duran cleanly if *he fought the proper fight*. Furthermore, word had got out weeks after the first fight that Roberto had already started eating.

Many experienced observers of the 'Battle of Montreal' believed it was Duran's dominating style that had forced Ray into his atypical, counterpunching posture. No one had ever controlled or eluded

Roberto Duran, his backers contended, and it was foolish even to try. Freddie Brown asked rhetorically in his post-fight analysis, 'Why did Leonard fight Duran's fight? It's hard to think when you're getting your brains knocked out . . . this ain't football, you know. And Duran, like Marciano, never gives you the ball.' Angelo demurred silently; he believed, as he always had, that Ray could take the ball away with lateral movement.

Since so much that had done in Ray Leonard was psychological, clearing the air, psychologically speaking, was a necessary precondition to any tactical preparations for the rematch. Ray had fought extremely well in that first fight, maybe he even deserved to win it. He'd proven to most doubters that he had gobs of heart. But that wasn't the point. He had lost. Dundee hammered away at that.

Like a sinner, Ray had first to admit and then to confess he'd fought stupidly. Rid himself of any lingering illusions and non-essentials before he was truly ready to get right what he had got wrong.

Fortunately, Angelo had learned from that first fiasco that the 'right' fight for Ray against Duran was not the artistic *tour de force* of the dancing master. It was not going to be an easy thing trying to take away a championship with footwork and a jab. But Dundee now knew that Ray could take the best Duran could give and still have something of his own to give back. 'You play checkers with a guy like this,' Dundee was fond of saying, by which he meant something quite different from a coy and clever tit-for-tat.

It's no accident that most boxing gyms of my acquaintance have a corner in which a checkers game is a constant diversion. Checkers, in Dundee's sense, is a game of angles and traps, the traps sprung successfully because the angles are so well hidden and conceived. 'You play checkers' meant that Ray would have to be able to change his position quickly and constantly and be able to strike from positions the lunging Duran did not expect. 'Everything has got to be short and timed perfectly,' Ray said; he ought to have added, 'And coming from a different place each time.' Very few fighters could carry out so new and complex a strategy.

Dundee also had Ray trying to develop quickly a very difficult manoeuvre: throwing a right-handed uppercut while pivoting on the right foot, then switching over and doing the same thing from the left side. The pivot would angle Ray automatically to one side or the other as Duran came forward; the uppercut was to be the punch the crouching Duran would not be able to avoid.

There are very few boxers a trainer would dare mess around with before an important fight, since for most boxers a style of fighting is as personal and well-defined as a thumbprint. But the artist in Ray rebelled against repetition and loved the challenge of breaking new ground – perhaps that partially explained his foolhardy and impetuous decision to become a pure slugger with Duran in the first fight. Putting in the new moves also gave the training camp a sense of intellectual challenge and immediacy that kept the idea of 'getting even' from becoming too obsessive. Revenge can easily feed on itself if you aren't careful.

Ray tried not to think too much about the first match, tried hard in interviews not to let too much of the bitterness come through. The grudge-match quality of the fight was simply there; it certainly didn't have to be hyped. As fight night approached, impatience became a problem for Ray. Certain he now owned the key to dispossessing Duran of the title and could atone for, if not erase, his only loss as a professional, Leonard became edgy waiting for the opening bell. A good sign, Dundee, Morton, and Trainer believed.

Ray dared not think about the possibility of losing again. Such an outcome, he knew, would pretty well finish any dream about becoming a boxer highly regarded by posterity, a dream that had taken centre stage in his mind. Sugar Ray Leonard would become, by losing, merely a name that enhanced the legend of Roberto Duran.

Some things about the rematch were the same as for the original fight. The seats at the Superdome were also scaled way too high – $1,000 for a prominent perch at ringside – and the live crowd would fill less than half the 80,000 seats. Nationally, however, the closed-circuit sales were excellent.

Other things were very different. Ray wore black – black trunks, shoes, and socks – for the first time in his professional career. The choice subtly announced his darker purpose – No more Mr Nice Guy'. It was as though Luke Skywalker had become Darth Vader.

In a masterly psychological touch, the national anthem was sung as a soulful blues by Sugar's namesake, Ray Charles. A hand-held television camera caught Ray the Singer in the foreground, his head bobbing unselfconsciously to the afterbeat; Ray the Fighter took the background, glowing with sweat from pre-fight exercise, his intense eyes smiling with joy. He seemed to understand the song as a personal encouragement and inspiration . . . *and the ho-ome of the brave* seemed nothing so much as a reminder from Ray to Ray of what he needed to win.

There had been salsa rhythms rolling out of Duran's supporters before and after the anthem, but from the opening bell, Leonard, the jazz fighter, dictated the tempo. He was the virtuoso, the innovator. Flicking the jab to the head, to the body, and then spinning suddenly away – these were things he hadn't done in Montreal. Halfway through the first round, Duran rushed at Leonard, who was caught off balance and standing directly in front of him. He quickly muscled Ray into the ropes – that familiar and effective Duran tactic – but Ray pivoted away and landed a nice right hand while bidding adieu. Dundee beamed. Brown and Arcel winced.

The rounds that followed, except for a lapse in the fifth, when Ray allowed himself to get caught for too long on the ropes, proved that Ray had learned his lessons very well. Almost everything he tried worked. Rarely had any boxing strategy and execution been more successful in a rematch.

In the eighth, a round that has already become an indelible part of boxing history, one that will forever tarnish the Duran legend, Ray Leonard sensed the level of Roberto Duran's frustration at not being able to have his way. Now it was Sugar's turn to taunt and mock the man with hands of stone. A payback for all the insults and humiliations in Montreal. Ray dropped his hands in mid-ring and exposed his chin, a look of teasing stupidity playing on his face. By merely twisting this way and that, he made Duran miss the too-tempting target. Frustration mounted. A few seconds later, again in the centre of the ring, Ray wound his right arm like a pantomiming softball pitcher. The so-called bolo motion is not one of boxing's classic punches, but as Duran watched the right hand winding up, Ray popped him with a quick left jab right on the schnoz. It was the sort of move my old man would have pulled on me during our first few weeks of sparring. Duran heard the crowd's derisive laughter.

With only sixteen seconds left in the round and with Ray working *him* along the ropes, Roberto Duran turned away and said to Octavio Meyran, the referee, '*No más, no más.*'

Meyran said, '*¿por qué?*'

Duran's non-answer: '*No más.*'

Roberto Duran's quitting, unhurt in mid-fight, was so big a story that Ray Leonard's strategic and technical brilliance was overlooked. His problem, Duran explained insufficiently afterwards, was stomach cramps, not Ray Leonard. Something he had drunk, something he had eaten before the fight. Other, more plausible theories emerged. He had lost too much weight too often; this time it took its toll in a sudden wave of weakness his rage could not help him overcome. There were strong rumours of mysterious drugs that had sapped his will. More logical was the theory that the macho man could handle anything except being made a fool zof in public – it had never happened during his life on the planet; now it was happening for the world to see. So he chose dishonour over humiliation.

For Sugar Ray revenge was sweet enough. He said, 'I proved to him what I could do. I *made* him quit. To make a man quit, to make a Roberto Duran quit, was better than knocking him out.'

Before the fight Duran was the hero of the boxing fraternity. They held him up as the shining example of what a professional fighter should be. After *no más, no más,* he became an instant pariah.

Still the *¿por qué?* remains. For a while I subscribed to the macho-humiliation theory. And I still do to a certain extent. But there was more.

I recalled reading a remarkable profile Gay Talese wrote on Floyd Patterson for *Esquire* in 1964. When I dug it out of the attic it fell open to a dog-eared page. Patterson had been trying to explain why he brought false whiskers and a moustache to wear as a disguise after fights he feared he might lose. Admittedly, not your conventional manner for preparing to cope with defeat. After his first fight with Sonny Liston, in which he was KO'ed in 2:06 of the first round, Patterson put on his disguise and drove from Chicago to New York. In New York he continued directly to the airport, still incognito.

Patterson confessed, 'I had on this beard, moustache, glasses, and hat – and I also limped to make myself look older. I was alone. I didn't care what plane I boarded. I just looked up and saw this sign at the terminal reading, "Madrid", and so I got on that flight after buying a ticket. When I got to Madrid I registered at a hotel under the name Aaron Watson. I stayed in Madrid about four or five days.'

Talese was a wise enough writer not to mention his own reaction to what the former heavyweight champion of the world was telling him. But when I first read those words, and as I read them again, my mouth fell open in disbelief.

Almost to fill the silence Talese had left, Patterson added, 'You must wonder what makes a man do things like this. Well, I wonder too. And the answer is, I don't know . . . but I think that within me, within every human being, there is a certain weakness. It is a weakness that expresses itself more when you're alone. And I have figured out that part of the reason I do the things I do . . . is because . . . I am a coward . . . My fighting has little to do with the fact, though. I mean you can be a fighter – and a winning fighter – and still be a coward . . .'

After a while Talese asked, 'How does one see this cowardice you speak of ?'

'You see it when a fighter loses,

'Could Liston be a coward?'

'That remains to be seen,' Floyd said. 'We'll find out what he's like after somebody beats him, how he takes it. It's easy to do anything in victory. It's in defeat that a man reveals himself . . .'

Patterson's remarkable insights are stunning in their implications. Of course it takes a certain kind of bravery for a man even to step into the ring, but Patterson believed that courage in the face of defeat was the acid test. Sugar Ray had his mettle tested in Montreal: then, after struggling mightily within himself, he survived his dark night of the soul. When it was Duran's turn to lose, he simply could not cope. Roberto Duran was, that night in the Superdome, at least in Floyd Patterson's sense of the term, a coward.

Just in case anyone thinks that is a smug judgement of Roberto Duran, let me remind myself and whoever else is interested that in time we will all have to confront certain defeat – it comes automatically with our mortality. Only then can each of us know what we are in our deepest, most private selves.

Fighters simply get to explore these frightening places sooner than the rest of us. From them are kept few secrets of the human heart.

ROUND 10

For Whom the Bell Tolls

Death in the ring. Thankfully, it is a very rare occurrence, but none the less tragic in its very public and shocking effect. Boxing, like all physical contact sports, has its dangers but it must be said that nowadays everything possible is done to minimise the risk of injury or death.

After all, boxing is a young man's game and young men will always court danger. There are many sports which are infinitely more dangerous, but which do not have the high-profile immediacy that inevitably attends a boxing fatality. There are many who would ban the sport of boxing, who would like to present its rare casualties as victims. But the sport's fatalities deserve better.

It is to three such fallen ring warriors, Johnny Owen, Young Ali and Benny Paret, that the following chapter is respectfully dedicated.

Onward Virgin Soldier

Hugh McIlvanney

It can be no consolation to those in South Wales and in Los Angeles who are red-eyed with anxiety about Johnny Owen to know that the extreme depth of his own courage did as much as anything else to take him to the edge of death. This calamitous experience could only have happened to an exceptionally brave fighter because Lupe Pintor, the powerful Mexican who was defending his World Boxing Council bantamweight championship against Owen, had landed enough brutal punches before the twelfth and devastatingly conclusive round to break the nerve and resistance of an ordinary challenger. The young Welshman was, sadly, too extraordinary for his own good in the Olympic Auditorium.

In the street, in a hotel lounge or even in his family's home on a Merthyr Tydfil housing estate, he is so reticent as to be almost unreachable, so desperately shy that he has turned twenty-four without ever having had a genuine date with a girl. But in the ring he has always been transformed, possessed by a furious aggression that has driven his alarmingly thin and unmuscular body through the heaviest fire and into the swarming, crowding attacks that gave him a record before Friday night of twenty-four victories, one defeat (avenged) and one draw in twenty-six professional matches. That record was built up in Europe and its reward was the European bantamweight championship and acceptance as a contender for the world title. Given the basic harshness of boxing as a way of earning a living, no one could blame Owen or his father or his manager, Dai Gardiner, for going after the biggest prize available to them, but some of us always felt that the right to challenge Pintor in Los Angeles was a questionable privilege. Making some notes about the background to the fight on Friday morning, I found myself writing: 'Feel physical sickness at the thought of what might happen, the fear that this story might take us to a hospital room.' This scribble was not meant to imply any severe criticism of a match which, on the basis of the relevant statistics, could not be condemned as outrageous. Indeed, the apprehension might have been illogically excessive to anyone who set Pintor's career figures of forty-one wins, seven losses and a draw against the fact that Owen's one defeat had been a blatant case of larceny in Spain and the further, impressive fact that he had never been knocked off his feet as a professional boxer.

Yet it is the simple truth that for weeks a quiet terror had been gathering in me about this fight. Perhaps its principal basis was no more than a dread that the frailty that the boy's performances had hitherto dismissed as illusory would, some bad time in some bad place, prove to be terribly real. There is something about his pale face, with its large nose, jutting ears and uneven teeth, all set above that long, skeletal frame, that takes hold of the heart and makes unbearable the thought of him being badly hurt. And, to my mind, there was an ominous possibility that he would be badly hurt against Pintor, a Mexican who had already stopped thirty-three opponents and would be going to work in front of a screaming mob of his countrymen, whose lust for blood gives the grubby Olympic Auditorium the atmosphere of a Guadalajara cockfight, multiplied a hundred times.

No fighters in the world are more dedicated to the raw violence of the business than Mexicans. Pintor comes out of a gym in Mexico City where more than 100 boxers work out regularly and others queue for a chance to show that what they can do in the alleys they can do in the ring. A man who rises to the top of such a seething concentration of hostility is likely to have little interest in points-scoring as a means of winning verdicts. So it was hard to share the noisy optimism of the 100-odd Welsh supporters who made themselves conspicuous in the sweaty clamour of the hall and brought a few beer cups filled with urine down on their heads. But they seemed to be entitled to their high spirits in the early rounds as Owen carried the fight to Pintor, boring in on the shorter, dark-skinned champion and using his spidery arms to flail home light but aggravatingly persistent flurries of punches.

The first round was probably about even. Owen might have edged the second on a British score card and he certainly took the third, but already Pintor's right hooks and uppercuts were making occasional dramatic interventions, sending a nervous chill through the challenger's friends around the ring.

It was in the fourth round that Pintor's right hand first struck with a hint of the force that was to be so overwhelming subsequently, but this time it was thrown overarm and long and Owen weathered it readily enough. He was seen to be bleeding from the inside of his lower lip in the fifth (the injury may have been inflicted earlier) but, since both Pintor's eyebrows were receiving attention from his seconds by then, the bloodshed seemed to be reasonably shared. In fact the laceration in the mouth was serious and soon the challenger was swallowing blood. He was being caught with more shots to the head, too, but refused to be discouraged and an American voice behind the press seats said incredulously: 'I don't believe this guy.'

Pintor was heaving for breath at the end of the fifth but in the sixth he mounted a surge, punished Owen and began to take control of the contest. The official doctor, Bernhard Schwartz, checked the lip for the second time before the start of the seventh. Pintor dominated that one but Owen revived heroically in the eighth, which made the abrupt disaster of the ninth all the more painful.

Pintor smashed in damaging hooks early in the ninth but their threat appeared to have passed as the round moved to its close. Then, without a trace of warning, Pintor dropped a shattering right hook over Owen's bony left shoulder. The blow hurled him to the floor and it was here that his courage began to be a double-edged virtue. He rose after a couple of seconds, although clearly in a bad condition. There was a mandatory eight count but even at the end of it he was hopelessly vulnerable to more hooks to the head and it took the bell to save him.

By the tenth there was unmistakable evidence that the strength had drained out of every part of Owen's body except his heart. He was too tired and weak now to stay really close to Pintor, skin against skin, denying the puncher leverage. As that weariness gradually created a space between them, Pintor filled it with cruel, stiff-armed hooks. Every time Owen was hit solidly in the eleventh the thin body shuddered. We knew the end had to be near but could not foresee how awful it would be.

There were just forty seconds of the twelfth round left when the horror story started to take shape. Owen was trying to press in on

Pintor near the ropes, failed to prevent that deadly space from developing again and was dropped on his knees by a short right. After rising at three and taking another mandatory count, he was moved by the action to the other side of the ring and it was there that a ferocious right hook threw him on to his back. He was unconscious before he hit the canvas and his relaxed neck muscles allowed his head to thud against the boards. Dai Gardiner and the boxer's father were in the ring long before the count could be completed and they were quickly joined by Dr Schwartz, who called for oxygen. Perhaps the oxygen might have come rather more swiftly than it did but only if it had been on hand at the ringside. Obviously that would be a sensible precaution, just as it might be sensible to have a stretcher immediately available. It is no easy job to bring such equipment through the jostling mass of spectators at an arena like the Auditorium, where Pintor's supporters were mainly concerned about cheering its arrival as a symbol of how comprehensive their man's victory had been. The outward journey to the dressing-room, with poor Johnny Owen deep in a sinister unconsciousness, was no simpler and the indifference of many among the crowd was emphasised when one of the stretcher-bearers had his pocket picked.

There have been complaints in some quarters about the delay in providing an ambulance but, in the circumstances, these may be difficult to justify. Dr Ferdie Pacheco, who was for years Muhammad Ali's doctor and is now a boxing consultant with NBC in the United States, insists that the company lay on an ambulance wherever they cover fights but no such arrangements exist at the Auditorium and the experienced paramedics of the Los Angeles Fire Department made good time once they received the emergency call. Certainly it was grief and not blame that was occupying the sick boy's father as he stood weeping in the corridor of the California Hospital, a mile from the scene of the knockout. A few hours before, I had sat by the swimming pool at their motel in downtown Los Angeles and listened to them joke about the calls Johnny's mother had been making from Merthyr Tydfil on the telephone they had recently installed. The call that was made to Mrs Owen from the waiting-room of the California Hospital shortly before 7 a.m. Saturday, Merthyr time (11 p.m. Friday in Los Angeles) had a painfully different tone. It was made by Byron Board, a publican and close friend of the family, and he found her already in tears because she had heard that Johnny had been knocked out. The nightmare that had been threatening her for years had become reality.

She can scarcely avoid being bitter against boxing now and many who have not suffered such personal agony because of the hardest of sports will be asking once again if the game is worth the candle. Quite a few of us who have been involved with it most of our lives share the doubts. But our reactions are bound to be complicated by the knowledge that it was boxing that gave Johnny Owen his one positive means of self-expression. Outside the ring he was an inaudible and almost invisible personality. Inside, he became astonishingly positive and self-assured. He seemed to be more at home there than anywhere else. It is his tragedy that he found himself articulate in such a dangerous language.

(The doctors' struggle to rescue Johnny Owen from deep coma proved to be hopeless and he died in the first week of November 1980. His body was brought home to be buried in Merthyr Tydfil.)

This Sporting Life

Jim Sheridan

Meanwhile Barry had to go to London to fight the West African bantamweight champion Young Ali. Close by the Grosvenor House Hotel in Park Lane there is a statue to an Irishman, Arthur Wellesley, Duke of Wellington. Achilles stands, an imposing figure, every part of his body down to his esteemed ankles cast from melted-down cannon used at various wars throughout the nineteenth century. On 6 June 1982 Barry McGuigan drove past Achilles, stopped at the door to the Grosvenor House Hotel and entered the lobby. Just inside on the left-hand-side wall is a painting commemorating one of the most auspicious occasions ever witnessed in the hotel. In it the painter is seated conveniently behind the Prince of Wales as he watches an ice-show. The skaters are dressed in motley and some are even dancing on stilts. The Prince appears to be having a good time.

He and his entourage are smoking large cigars, and the rest of the company seem contented enough with the ice-show. The room in which all this is taking place is the Great Room. The Prince is seated on the lower balcony, surrounded by royalty. On the upper balcony sit the Lords, Ladies and Peers of the Realm.

The room as it stands today is almost the same as it was on that auspicious occasion in 1932 except that the lone chandelier has been replaced by no less than eight spectacular cousins that look like illuminated wedding dresses when the light is switched on. The floor in the centre of the room rises to make a natural arena.

This was not the Ulster Hall. This was fashionable London in June. The fight had been organised by the World Sporting Club. Membership of the Club was an honour. When the Club organised an event they did it well. The food matched the surroundings, which were first class. The atmosphere would be a thousand miles from that in the little Belfast hall. Displays of partisanship were frowned upon here. One did not cheer either one's champion or his opponent . . . that was not fair play. At the end of the round you clapped, depending on the level of expertise manifested by the two fighters.

It was a black-tie affair. As Barry came towards the ring he would have noticed more white coats than was normal at a fight. These were not stewards, however; they were waiters bringing drinks to the tables. Dinner had been served and now everybody was relaxing as the contests began. McGuigan got into the ring to a good round of applause. Young Ali came out. He only spoke a few words of English. He too got a round of applause. It must have spurred Ali on because that night he fought with the heart of a lion. The bell rang for the first round. The fighters teased each other out. It is impossible to know what went through Young Ali's head that night. Here was a poor fighter from Africa in the most plush surroundings of his life, fighting a white man, watched by white men – and nobody was shouting McGuigan on. It must have had the quality of a dream. In the following rounds it would turn into a nightmare.

McGuigan for the first time in ages could actually hear what was going on in the other corner. In broken English Young Ali kept telling his corner, 'Too strong, too strong.' As if to indicate what he meant, he kept holding his gloves up to his jaw. The African's heart proved bigger and stronger than his body. In the fourth and fifth rounds McGuigan was surprised by the level of aggression Ali could mount. At the end of each round the knowledgeable crowd applauded enthusiastically. On the second balcony looking down, Alfie McLean, a lifelong friend of Barney Eastwood, sat uncomfortably in his tuxedo. He felt sure he would be able to get out of it soon.

At the start of the sixth round McGuigan was amazed that Ali was still in there, considering the amount of punishment he had taken. Whether through resilience or tiredness, he had stopped protesting to his corner. McGuigan will never forget the sixth round. 'I hit him round the temples a lot. He was tired. The damage always occurs when a man is fatigued. I hit him with a punch right between the eyes. The eyes spun round in his head like the numbers on a slot machine. He fell. I stood back and he fell straight to the floor. I looked over at Mr Eastwood and he made a quick motion as if to say, "It's all over", but there was a worried look on his face. He pointed to a neutral corner and I went there, all the time looking at Young Ali.'

Up on the balcony the Belfast contingent were having a hard time behaving like gentlemen. Brian Eastwood turned to Big Alfie in euphoria. 'He'll never get up,' said Brian, not understanding the full import of what he was saying. Big Alfie was looking at the figure on the floor below him lying quiet and silent, the only motion disturbing the unnecessary count being that of the cigar smoke from a hundred private tables. Big Alfie repeated Brian's words and added, 'That's right. He'll never get up. He's dead.'

Like McGuigan, Big Alfie underestimated the resilience of the bantamweight champion of West Africa. He rose to his feet with some assistance from his corner. McGuigan went to see how he was but was brusquely pushed away. Eastwood took him upstairs. The mood in the dressing-room was sombre. Downstairs Young Ali was walking unassisted from the ring to warm applause. He fell a second time. This time he wouldn't get up. An ambulance was called. His corner-men improvised as best they knew how. They laid him out on one of the dining tables and wrapped a tablecloth around him for comfort. After about fifteen minutes he was carried from the Grosvenor House out into the night air and rushed to hospital. Sean Kilfeather was reporting another McGuigan victory back to his head office in Dublin when he heard an unusual sound. 'I heard this sound and I looked around and they were taking Young Ali out on a stretcher. He was totally inert but there was a strange noise in his throat. It was an eerie sound. I suppose it was the death rattle.' Young Ali wouldn't succumb. He hung on in a coma for dear life.*

Don Dunphy at Ringside

Don Dunphy

The Griffith persona seemed to dominate the 1960–64 period in boxing. In April of 1961, he captured the welterweight crown by knocking out Benny 'Kid' Paret in thirteen rounds in Miami Beach. In June he KO'ed tough Gaspar Ortega in Los Angeles and in September lost the crown back to Paret in New York. It was a controversial decision and I agreed with those who felt that Griffith should have been declared the winner and still champion.

Paret and Griffith were matched again for the title on 12 March 1962. It was an exciting week. On Monday I was asked to come to the ABC-TV studios. There I learned that a videotape replay had been developed and that I was invited to take part in a demonstration for a great many important ABC executives and members of the press. Jim McKay, the host of ABC's *Wide World of Sports*, was also there. A ring had been set up and two boxers were there ready to trade punches. They fought a one-round exhibition and, with the videotape cameras rolling, I described the action as I would in a real fight. When the round was over, it was replayed again and again for the studio audience and pronounced a success. The new system was ready to make its début at the Paret–Griffith fight the following Saturday night.

---

*Young Ali hung on to life for some months, but died without regaining consciousness. Ironically, McGuigan received the news on the day of his wedding anniversary. When Barry subsequently won the world title from Eusebio Pedroza, he dedicated his victory to the memory of his fallen rival, Young Ali. It was a sincere and emotional tribute, and altogether typical of the man.

It turned out to be a tragic beginning. The fight was a bruising one. The men had faced each other twice and knew each other's style. In the sixth round Griffith backed Paret into the ropes in a corner and was really working him over. Paret had a habit of playing possum and letting Griffith pour punches on him. Ruby Goldstein, the referee, was about to move in to get them out to the centre of the ring when suddenly Paret opened up with a blistering attack, stunned Griffith and floored him. Griffith beat the count but was in bad shape. The bell probably saved him. Clancy, Griffith's co-manager (with Howard Albert) and trainer, told me later that he thought if the round had lasted much longer Griffith might have been knocked out.

Emile was in superb condition and the minute's rest revived him. The bout continued with blistering action into the twelfth round. In the sixth round, Paret had backed into Griffith's corner on my right. Now in the twelfth, he backed into the neutral corner on my left. Again Griffith rained punches on him. For a split second I wondered if Paret might be playing possum again. I don't know what Goldstein's thoughts were as he bounced around the ring. Could he also have thought the champion was playing possum? He wasn't. Griffith continued to rain punches on him. Paret made no return. As Goldstein rushed in to part them, Paret sagged to the canvas. The commission doctors rushed in to try to revive him. They couldn't. A stretcher was brought in and he was taken to the hospital.

All this was now on videotape. The replays went on the air and showed the beating Paret was taking. Again and again they were repeated. I heard later that the ratings for the post-fight show were more than for the fight itself. Apparently people were calling friends and telling them to tune in, that a guy was getting beaten to death on the television.

Paret never regained consciousness. He died in the hospital on 3 April.

❦There was bad blood between us at the weigh-in [for the third fight] because he was put up to this, and by him being put up he called me names. I don't believe in buying publicity like that. He called me *"maricón"*. *Maricón* means in English "faggot". Then he was nude on the scale and he was right up on me, if I step back a little bit my body would touch his. I didn't go for that, I was ready to punch him, and Gil yelled don't fight now, wait till the fight. So we had a big argument in the place anyway, I just walk away and forget it, because if you get angry the way I was that day and try to go in the ring and fight with anger in you, you can't fight.

He knocked me down in that fight, he put his hand on his hip, he looked at me from his corner, he started laughing. I got up, went to my corner, Gil smacked me. He says to me the next time I get him hurt, keep punching until the referee step in, and that's all I remember. It's been ten long years but still I'm sensitive about that time. I have gone on to be quite a heck of a fighter since then, too. I've never stopped anybody since then really, either. People tell me it wasn't my fault but I felt that I fought the man and I felt responsible about what happened to him. I'll tell you the truth, the only thing I remember in that whole fight was what Gil said to me, "If you hurt the man, keep punching." I try to see in my mind, but after ten years I still can't seem to put it together. Maybe it's best that way, I don't remember it.❡

Emile Griffith (from *In this Corner* by Peter Heller)

ROUND 11

Only the Ring was Square

The infiltration of gangsters and/or organised crime into professional boxing has long been a subject of rumour and innuendo. Many a boxer has acquired a reputation, deservedly or otherwise, as a 'mob' fighter.

One of the most notorious cases of its kind centred on a famous encounter between 'Kid' Gavilan and Billy Graham, with Gavilan getting a dubious decision which caused a near riot. In the first of these articles Teddy Brenner, a legendary figure in US boxing circles and for twenty years the matchmaker at Madison Square Garden, recalls the inside story of that remarkable event. It is a fascinating tale and, like all good stories, there is an unexpected ending.

Probably the most scandalous example of exploitation in American boxing history concerned the giant Italian heavyweight Primo Carnera. A manufactured fighter, totally unskilled and with a jaw as fragile as a piece of Dresden china, he was robbed and cheated at every turn. In the second article Paul Gallico recounts the sad and shameful story of this gentle giant.

The Night the 'Fix' was In

Teddy Brenner and *Barney Nagler*

I gave the shirt off my back to get into boxing. What I mean is that I went from selling shirts for a company on Fifth Avenue to selling left hooks. One thing I know, if a guy can sell one item, he can sell anything. Like when I was a kid, living in Brooklyn in an apartment in Borough Park, I used to sell newspapers on the subway.

It was not easy in those days, not for my family anyway. My father was a skilled cutter of leather for fine women's shoes and handbags, but it was the Great Depression which made things rough. We lived one step ahead of the landlord. What helped was that things were so tough, landlords had to give new tenants concessions, which meant the first two months you lived in a flat rent-free. After the first two months you looked around for another apartment. We moved a lot.

I was going to James Madison High School in Brooklyn, but nights I made a few dollars selling newspapers. I sold the *American,* the *News,* and the *Mirror.* The *Times* and the *Herald-Tribune* were too heavy. They were those regular-size eight-column papers and when you carried twenty-five or fifty of them you could hardly move. I sold tabloids. They did not weigh so much.

I was in the open and I got to know the people who bought my papers, and one of them was a gangster named Frankie Yale. He was a big-shot who would give me twenty-five cents for a two-cent paper. He was the first mobster I ever knew. Later, in boxing, I got to know others.

The night I remember from the time I was selling papers was 12 May 1932. That night I sold 1,000 copies of the *Daily News* and 1,000 copies of the *Daily Mirror.* That was because the headline said: 'Baby Dead!' – the Lindbergh baby, murdered by his kidnapper. It was a big story – sad, too – but what it meant to me was that I sold 2,000 papers that night.

After a while I had no more time for selling papers. I was playing a lot of playground basketball and made the varsity team in James

Madison High School. But in my senior year I quit school and got a job with a company selling women's corsets. Now, when I think of it, it was funny, but in the Depression just having a job was a serious matter.

It was about this time that I really got interested in boxing. I stalled going to the Young Men's Hebrew Association – they called it the 'Bensonhurst Y' – and that is where I met Irving Cohen. He was the boxing instructor there, but later he got his name in the papers a lot because he was the manager of Rocky Graziano and Billy Graham, and other real good fighters.

Dan Parker used to write that 'butter wouldn't melt' in Irving Cohen's mouth. Parker was the sports editor of the *Daily Mirror* in New York, which died a few years ago. So did Parker. When he was writing, he was a real knocker. He kept boxing people on their toes, because he had more spies than the CIA. The informers got good treatment in his column. Irving was a problem for Parker. What can you say about a man who ran a lingerie shop and had a good family and spoke so softly, you had to listen carefully to get his words?

Though he had to deal with at least one gangster in boxing, Irving kept his name clean. Not even Parker went after him when it became public that he was associated with Eddie Coco in the management of Rocky Graziano.

Coco was a small man with a big reputation in the mob. He had a police record as long as your income tax form and some years ago he was convicted in Florida of shooting a man to death. Before Coco was sentenced to prison for a long term, Al Weill, who was Rocky Marciano's manager, wrote to the judge and said, 'I've known Eddie Coco for twenty-five years and I've always found him to be a straight shooter.' Could be the judge didn't have a sense of humour. He threw the book at Coco, and it wasn't *The Ring Record Book* either.

By the time Cohen became associated with Coco he had been in boxing for many years. His first fighter was Marty Pomerantz, but by the time I got to know him he was handling a welterweight named Eddie Alzek. I started to go around to boxing with Cohen. Monday nights it was the St Nicholas Arena, Tuesday nights it was either the Bronx Coliseum or the Broadway Arena in Brooklyn. Madison Square Garden ran on Friday nights and on Saturday there were fights at the Ridgewood Grove on the Brooklyn–Queens borderline.

One night in 1938, I went over to Garfield, NJ, with Irving. He had Alzek working on percentage in an eight-round bout with Freddie (Red) Cochrane. Six years later, Cochrane won the world welterweight championship by upsetting Fritzie Zivic in fifteen rounds, but in 1938 he was just another fighter from Elizabeth, NJ.

The fight was held in an outdoor arena in Garfield, and because the weather was overcast, a small crowd paid their way in. While the fighters were still in their corners awaiting the opening bell, the referee came to Cochrane's corner and greeted Willie Gilzenberg, Cochrane's manager.

'What's in it for me?' the referee asked Gilzenberg, a hardbitten man who was called 'The Beard' because five minutes after he shaved, he looked as if he needed another shave.

'What's in it for you?' Gilzenberg snarled. 'Look at the house. We're on a percentage and we'll be lucky to get peanuts. Go take a walk.'

The referee scowled and turned away. Crossing the ring, he approached Cohen and repeated the question: 'What's in it for me?'

Cohen turned his baby-blue eyes on the referee. He had the countenance of a cherub and when he was embarrassed his face assumed the form of a newborn infant whose bottom had been spanked for the first time. His eyes had the expression of scared rabbits.

'Aw, gee,' Irving Cohen said, 'look at the house. We're hardly going to make expenses. I'm sorry but there's nothing in it for you.'

By now the referee realised that neither side was going to stake him. In New Jersey in those days, the decision in a fight was solely in the hands of the referee; there were no judges at ringside.

Alzek and Cochrane hit each other with everything but the referee's score card and when the fight was over, they were so tired they could hardly make their way to their corners. Alzek clearly deserved the decision.

Now it was time for the referee to announce his decision. He called both fighters to the centre of the ring and just as calmly as a man sitting down to Sunday breakfast, he raised both of their hands. Both corners screamed, but the referee had the last laugh. 'No tickee, no washee,' I thought. Right then and there I decided that boxing was going to be my game. I had a vision of big things happening to me in it. As we drove back to Brooklyn, Irving said, 'What a rotten game this is.'

Irving Cohen was a dead honest guy, which, for me, he proved when he was managing Billy Graham. In 1951, Graham was signed to fight 'Kid' Gavilan for the world welterweight championship in Madison Square Garden. A few days before the fight, Irving got word that Frankie Carbo wanted to see him. When Carbo called, people answered. He was described by the newspapers as the underworld's overlord of boxing.

I said Irving was honest; I didn't say he was brave or foolish. He went to see Carbo at the bar in the old Forrest Hotel on 49th Street, down the block from the Garden.

'You want your boy should be the champ?' Carbo said. 'You give me twenty per cent of him and you get the title.'

Irving's baby-blue eyes got old suddenly. 'Frank, I can't give you twenty per cent,' the manager said. 'I got a piece and there's Jack Reilly, who brought Billy to me. He's got a piece. There ain't room for you.'

Carbo said, 'Talk to the fighter. He's the one that's got the say.'

So Irving talked to Graham and Graham didn't go for it. 'Listen, if I have to turn on my friend Reilly I'd rather not have the title,' the fighter said. 'A guy wants to be champ, but he don't have to be a louse to get it.'

Billy Graham was that kind. In fifteen years he had 126 fights and was never off his feet. Everybody knew he was a professional, an artist in the trade, and he could do more with gloves on than anybody, maybe up to Sugar Ray Robinson. I used to tell Billy, 'You're such a good boxer, you always make it look easy. That's why you don't excite people.'

When Cohen told Carbo there was no deal, Carbo said, 'Does the kid know he ain't going to win?'

'He knows,' Irving said.

'He's got a lot to learn about life,' Carbo said.

In two fights before their title bout, Graham won the first, Gavilan the second. Gavilan was a flashy puncher. He grew up in Cuba and learned a bolo punch, which was really an uppercut. Graham was a New York kid, an East Sider who had all the moves, which he got as a kid at the Catholic Boys' Club on the East Side of Manhattan.

The title fight with Gavilan went fifteen rounds, all of them close, and when it was over, I had Billy the winner. What Graham did was to wait for Gavilan's leads and if it was a jab he would pick it off. What he could always do was to turn from the other guy's rights and step inside the long punches. He won it ten rounds to five, but as

Johnny Addie announced the decision a great roar came down from the balconies. The people were angry and around ringside the big spenders were screaming at the officials.

In New York State referees and judges use both round-by-round scoring and point scoring. If a fight ends with both fighters having scored the same number of rounds, then points count. The points are scored on a scale of one to four in each round.

The referee, Mark Conn, had it seven rounds for Graham, seven rounds for Gavilan, with one even, but gave the decision to Gavilan, ten points to seven. One of the two judges, Frank Forbes, had the same round score, but voted for Graham, eleven points to ten. The second judge, Artie Schwartz, called it nine rounds for Gavilan to six for Graham. Gavilan got a split decision.

I remember the way Graham stood in the centre of the ring, dumbfounded as his supporters came out of their seats into the aisles, waving their fists towards the ring, screaming threats at Conn and Schwartz. Security men kept the angry crowd from storming the ring.

What else I remember is what Irving Cohen told me about Artie Schwartz, the judge who had a lopsided card in favour of Gavilan. Many years later, as Schwartz lay dying in a New York hospital, he sent a message to Irving to come and see him. When Irving went into the hospital room, he wished Schwartz well, which was like Irving. He was the softest, kindest man I ever knew. Irving said Schwartz looked up at him from his bed and said, 'You know, Irving, I got to get this off my mind because you are a very decent fellow. When I voted for Gavilan against Graham I had to do it. I want you to know this. The boys ordered me to do it. I couldn't help myself and it's bothered me ever since. I'm sorry, Irving, for what I did to you and Graham.'

When Irving told me the story later, he said, 'Poor guy. I know what he meant. The boys order you to do something, you do it, if you want to live. At least Schwartz got it off his chest. He died in peace, I hope.'*

---

*In 1984, the New York State Athletic Commission under José Torres announced it would carry out an inquiry into the Gavilan–Graham decision – and reverse it if any evidence of wrongdoing could be substantiated. However, the Commission was unable to come up with the necessary proof and Billy Graham never did get his belt.

Pity the Poor Giant

Paul Gallico

There is probably no more scandalous, pitiful, incredible story in all the record of these last mad sports years than the tale of the living giant, a creature out of the legends of antiquity, who was made into a prizefighter. He was taught and trained by a wise, scheming little French boxing manager who had an Oxford University degree, and he was later acquired and developed into the heavyweight champion of the world by a group of American gangsters and mob men; then finally, when his usefulness as a meal ticket was outlived, he was discarded in the most shameful chapter in all boxing.

This unfortunate pituitary case, who might have been Angoulaffre, or Balan, or Fierabras, Gogmagog, or Gargantua himself, was a poor simple-minded peasant by the name of Primo Carnera, the first son of a stone-cutter of Sequals, Italy. He stood 6 feet 7 inches in height, and weighed 268 pounds. He became the heavyweight champion, yet never in all his life was he ever anything more than a freak and a fourth-rater at prizefighting. He must have grossed more than $2 million during the years that he was being exhibited, and he hasn't a cent to show for it today.

There is no room here for more than a brief and hasty glance back over the implications of the tragedy of Primo Carnera. And yet I could not seem to take my leave from sports without it. The scene and the story still fascinate me, the sheer impudence of the men who handled the giant, their conscienceless cruelty, their complete depravity towards another human being, the sure, cool manner in which they hoaxed hundreds of thousands of people. Poor Primo! A giant in stature and strength, a terrible figure of a man, with the might of ten men, he was a helpless lamb among wolves who used him until there was nothing more left to use, until the last possible penny had been squeezed from his big carcass, and then abandoned him. His last days in the United States were spent alone in a hospital. One leg was paralysed, the result of beatings taken around the head.

None of the carrion birds who had picked him clean ever came back to see him or to help him.

No one who was present in Madison Square Garden the night that Primo Carnera was first introduced to American audiences will ever forget him as he came bounding down the aisle from the dressing-room and climbed into the ring. It was a masterpiece of stage management.

He wore black fighting trunks on the side of which was embroidered the head of a wild boar in red silk. He disdained the usual fighter's bathrobe and instead wore a sleeveless vest of a particularly hideous shade of green, and on his head a cap of the same shade, several sizes too large for him and with an enormous visor that made him look even larger than he was. Leon See, the Frenchman, then his manager, was a small man. The bucket-carriers and sponge-wielders were chosen for size too – diminutive men; everything was done to increase the impression of Primo's size.

Carnera was the only giant I have ever seen who was well proportioned throughout his body for his height. His legs were massive and he was truly thewed like an oak. His waist was comparatively small and clean, but from it rose a torso like a Spanish hogshead from which sprouted two tremendous arms, the biceps of which stood out like grapefruit. His hands were like Virginia hams, and his fingers were ten thick red sausages.

His head was large, even for the size of his body, and looking at him you were immediately struck with his dreadful gummy mouth and sharp, irregular, snaggle teeth. His lips were inclined to be loose and flabby. He had a good nose and fine, kind brown eyes. But his legs looked even more enormous and tree-like than they were, owing to the great blue bulging varicose veins that wandered down them on both sides and stuck out far enough so that you could have knocked them off with a baseball bat. His skin was brown and glistening and he invariably smelled of garlic.

This was the horror that came into the Madison Square Garden ring and sent a sincere shudder through the packed house. That is to say, he was horrible until he commenced to fight, when he became merely pitiful and an object demanding sympathy. Behind what passed for the wild battle blaze in his eyes and the dreadful gummy leer, emphasised by the size of the red rubber mouthpiece (tooth-protector) with which they provided him, there was nothing but bewilderment and complete helplessness. The truth was that, handicapped by rules and regulations, a sport he did not understand and was not temperamentally fitted for, and those silly brown leather bags laced to his fingers, never at any time could he fight a lick. His entire record, with a few exceptions, must be thrown out as one gigantic falsehood, staged and engineered, planned and executed by the men who had him in tow and who were building him up for the public as a man-killer and an invincible fighter.

But I think the most dreadful part of the story is that the poor floundering giant was duped along with the spectators. He was permitted, in fact encouraged, to believe that his silly pawings and pushings, when they connected, sent men staggering into unconsciousness and defeat. It was not until late in his career, when in spite of himself he learnt something through sheer experience and number of fights, that he ever knocked anyone out on the level. But he never could fight, and never will. In spite of his great size and strength and his well-proportioned body, he remained nothing but a glandular freak who should have remained with the small French travelling circus from which Leon See took him.

This big, good-natured, docile man was exhibiting himself in a small wandering *cirque* in the south of France as a strongman and Greco-Roman wrestler, engaging all comers and local talent in the nightly show, having found that it paid him more and offered a better life than that of his chosen profession of mosaic-worker. Here he was discovered by a former French boxing champion who signed him up and apprenticed him to one Monsieur Leon See to be taught the rudiments of *la boxe*. It is highly probable that the time spent as a wrestler set his muscles and prevented him from ever becoming a knockout puncher. But Monsieur Leon See was taking no chances. He taught and trained Carnera strictly as a defensive boxer.

Now, it must be understood that Leon See was one of the most intelligent, smart and wily men that ever turned a fighter loose from his corner. He was not much more scrupulous than the bevy of public enemies who eventually took Carnera away from him simply by muscling him, but he was much more far-seeing and he had certain well-thought-out notions and theories about the ridiculous game of boxing. Among them was the excellent and sensible thought that the human head was never intended by nature to be punched, and that secondly, from the manner of its construction out of hundreds of tiny, delicately articulated bones, the closed fist was never meant to be one of man's most effective weapons. In this last idea, Monsieur See was not alone. The coterie of tough guys and mobsters who eventually relieved him of his interest in Carnera rarely used the fist, reckoning it, as did See, an inefficient weapon. The boys always favoured the pistol or Roscoe, also known as the Difference, the Equaliser, the Rod, and the Heat.

See was a keen student of the human body – for a prizefight manager – and he knew something about men. He was aware that abnormalities of size were usually compensated for by weaknesses elsewhere. He found out – exactly how is not known – that Primo Carnera would never be able to absorb a hard punch to the chin. He may have had some secret rehearsal in a gymnasium somewhere in Paris and, having ordered some workaday heavyweight to clout Primo one just to see what would happen, saw that the giant came all undone, wobbled and collapsed. Be that as it may, Monsieur See knew. And never at any time while he was connected with Carnera would he permit anyone to punch Primo in the head – neither his sparring partners nor his opponents. Since both received their pay from practically the same source, this was not so difficult to arrange as might be imagined. But See also had something else. He was a Frenchman and so he had a heart. He loved big Carnera.

Years later See proved to be right. When Carnera through exigent circumstances was forced to fight without benefit of pre-arrangement, and the heavyweights began to sight along that big, protruding jaw of his and nail him for direct hits, he was slaughtered. He was brave and game and apparently could take punches to the body all the night long. But one hard, true tap on the chin and he fell down goggle-eyed. For a long time during the early years, however, nobody was permitted to hit him there, and Carnera himself began to think he was invincible.

Primo's first trip to the United States was arranged through an American contact man and importer of foreign fighting talent, a character from Tin Ear Alley named Walter Friedman or, as Damon Runyon nicknamed him, Walter (Good-Time Charley) Friedman. See was smart enough to know that without an American 'in', without cutting in an American manager, he would not get very far in America. What he was not quite smart enough to know was how deep his 'in' took him, that the ramifications of Friedman's business and other connections were to lead through some very tough and rapacious parties.

Carnera's first fight in New York involved him with a lanky Swede named 'Big Boy' Peterson. In this fight poor Carnera was hardly able to get out of his own way and caused his opponent the most frightful embarrassment through not being able to strike a blow that looked sufficiently hard to enable him to keep his end of the bargain, if there was one. Eventually Peterson succumbed to a push as Carnera lumbered and floundered past him, and to make assurance doubly sure, the Swede hit himself a punch on the jaw as he went down. Someone had to hit him.

Now, this was a shameless swindle from start to finish, one way or another. If Peterson was making an honest effort to fight he never should have been permitted to enter the ring. The press unanimously announced beforehand that it would probably be a sell and a fake, and when it was over, suggested strongly that it had been. But it said so in a gay and light-hearted manner as though the whole thing were pretty funny (as indeed it was), and there was no one on the New York State Athletic Commission either sufficiently intelligent or courageous enough to throw Primo and his handlers and fixers right out of the ring and from there out of the country. The Peterson fight in Madison Square Garden, the stronghold of professional boxing, was a sort of test case by the Carnera crowd to see how much they could get away with. On that score it was a cleancut success. They found out that they could get away with anything. And so they proceeded to do just that. Primo's first American tour was organised, a tour that grossed something like $700,000, of which handsome piece of money Carnera received practically nothing. He was barnstormed across the country in the most cold-blooded, graceless, shameful series of fixed, bought, coerced, or plain out-and-out tank acts ever. If one of them was contested on its merits it was only because the opponent by no possible stretch of the imagination, or his own efforts, could harm Carnera or even hit him.

Where the fight could not be bought – that is to say, where the fighter was unwilling to succumb to a tap on the elbow for a price –

guns were produced by sinister strangers to threaten him, and where neither threats nor money were sufficient to bag the fight, he was crossed or tricked, as in the case of Bombo Chevalier, a big California Negro who was fascinated by the size of Carnera's chin, and nothing would do but he was going to hit it, just to see what would happen. Between rounds, one of Chevalier's own attendants rubbed red pepper or some other inflammatory substance into his eyes so that he lost all interest in tapping anybody's chin.

In Newark, New Jersey, a Negro was visited in his dressing-room before the bout by an unknown party not necessarily connected with Carnera's management, and was asked to inspect shooting irons, and in Philadelphia another Negro, Ace Clark, was amusing himself readying up Carnera for a knockout – he had already completely closed one of Primo's eyes – when somebody suggested he look down and see what the stranger beneath his corner was holding under his coat, and what calibre it was.

Every known build-up fighter was lined up for this tour, including faithful old hands like K.O. Christner, Chuck Wiggens, and poor Farmer Lodge. Political and gangster friends in the cities visited volunteered with their private heavyweights for quick splashes that might look well on the record books. It was all for the cause. The more money Carnera made, the more the boys would have to cut up amongst themselves. It was all just one big happy family. It seemed almost as though every scamp in the boxing game contributed his bit somehow to that Carnera build-up.

Friedman, as has been indicated, was the go-between, and although Leon See was quite capable of all the planning necessary to keep Carnera in the victory columns, nevertheless it would have been considered bad form, and downright dangerous, if See had not cut the local boys in. And, at that, I suspect the said local boys showed the amiable and gifted Frog a few things about building up a potential heavyweight champion that made the two Stribling fights arranged by Monsieur See, one in Paris and the other in London and both ending in fouls, look like Holy Gospel.

As adviser and co-director of this tour, Broadway Bill Duffy was cut in. Bill was then in the nightclub and fight-managing business, but in his youth he had been convicted of a little alfresco burgling and had been sent away for a spell. He was still to achieve the highest pinnacle of fame that can come to an American – to be named a Public Enemy. It is a curious commentary upon the conduct of boxing around New York that Duffy was allowed to operate as a manager and a second when there was a rule on the books of the State Athletic Commission, if indeed it was not written directly into the boxing law, that no one ever convicted of a felony was to be eligible for any kind of a licence.

Duffy usually split even on things with his dearest friend, Owen Madden, better known as Owney, who had also been away for a time in connection with the demise of a policeman. Owney was out on parole at the time – he was sent back later – making beer (and very good beer it was, too) and acting as silent partner in the operation of a number of prizefighters. Also in this crowd was a charming but tough individual known as Big Frenchy De Mange who made news one evening by getting himself snatched and held for ransom by Mad-Dog Vincent Coll. The Mad Dog was subsequently rubbed out in a West Side drugstore telephone booth. But the subject, after all, is Primo Carnera and not gangsters and racket men, though pretty soon it was all one subject and all one sweet and fragrant mess. The boys had their connections in every town. The Philadelphia underworld collaborated through the medium of the always friendly and helpful Maximilian Boo-Boo Hoff, and the same courtesies were extended all the way through to the Pacific Coast, where occurred the Bombo Chevalier incident, which was too nauseous even for the local commission there to stomach. There was an investigation resulting in the suspension of a few unimportant people. But Carnera and his swindle went merrily onwards.

And it continued until he won the heavyweight championship of the world by ostensibly knocking out Jack Sharkey, then world's champion, in the sixth round, with a right uppercut. I say ostensibly because nothing will ever convince me that that was an honest prizefight, contested on its merits.

Sharkey's reputation and the reputation of Fat John Buckley, his manager, were bad. Both had been involved in some curious ring encounters. The reputation of the Carnera entourage by the time the Sharkey fight came along, in 1933, was notorious, and the training camps of both gladiators were simply festering with mobsters and tough guys. Duffy, Madden, et Cie., were spread out all over

Carnera's training quarters at Dr Bier's Health Farm at Pompton Lakes, New Jersey. A travelling chapter of Detroit's famous Purple Gang hung out at Gus Wilson's for a while during Sharkey's rehearsals. Part of their business there was to muscle in on the concession of the fight pictures.

If that fight was on the level, it wasn't like either of the companies operating the two pugs. If it was honest, the only explanation was that the boys were going sissy. As far as Primo knew, the right uppercut with which he tagged Sharkey in the sixth round was enough to kill a steer. He had knocked out many men with the same punch. Now he was the heavyweight champion of the world, and even if he didn't have any money to show for it, Italy and Mussolini were going to be very pleased. I have often wondered how long he remained innocent, how long it was before he began to catch on.

For instance, it must have been a terrible surprise and considerable of an eye-opener to Carnera the night he fought Tommy Loughran in Miami as heavyweight champion of the world. It was a no-decision match and a bad one for the gang to make, but they had to do something because they were desperate for money at the time. If the Sharkey fight was crooked, it is probable that the entire end of Primo's purse had to be paid over for the fix.

The Loughran fight had to go on the level because no one had ever managed to tamper with Loughran, and neither he nor his manager was afraid of guns. And Tommy had another curious and valuable protection. He was a good Catholic, and many priests were his friends. The gunmen were a little shy of those padres, who might usually be found in twos and threes at Tommy's home or his training camps. But the mob figured that with a 100-pound advantage in weight Carnera could take care of Loughran, who was little more than a light heavyweight and never was a hard hitter. During the fight Carnera hit Loughran more than a dozen of the same uppercuts that had stretched Sharkey twitching on the canvas, and never even reddened Tommy's face. Loughran was a cream-puff puncher and yet he staggered Carnera several times with right hands and was himself never in any kind of danger from a punch. He merely got tired from having Carnera leaning on him for half an hour. If nothing else, that fight beneath the Miami moon exposed how incompetent Carnera was as a bruiser, and how utterly false were the stories about his invincibility, besides casting fresh suspicion upon his knockout of Sharkey. We had all seen Loughran put on the floor by a 175-pounder. If a man weighing around 280 pounds, as Primo did for that fight, hit him flush on the jaw and couldn't drop him, and yet had knocked out one of the cleverest heavyweights in the business, it wasn't hard to arrive at a conclusion. It was obvious that he was a phoney and the first stiff-punching heavyweight who was levelling would knock him out.

Max Baer did it the very next summer. The following summer Joe Louis did it again, and then an almost unknown Negro heavyweight by the name of Leroy Haynes accomplished the feat for the third time. And that was the beginning of the end of Primo.

His lucrative campaigns and the winning of the heavyweight championship had enriched everyone connected with him except poor Primo, who saw very little of the money he earned. There were too many silent partners and 'boys' who had little pieces of him. Monsieur See had long since been dispensed with and shipped back to France for his health; he had served his purpose. But it was an evil day for Carnera when they chased Leon back to Paris, for Leon never would have permitted anyone to belt Carnera on his vulnerable chin. As suggested, the little Frenchman had a love for the big fellow whom he had taught and trained and watched over so carefully. The Duffy crowd had no love for anything. Fighters' chins were made to be smacked and they might just as well get used to taking the punches there.

It seemed as though their power was beginning to lose some of its effectiveness, exhausted perhaps by its own virus and viciousness, shortly after they had made Carnera champion. Primo escaped to Italy with his title and nothing else and later returned here for the disastrous fight with Loughran under the guidance of a little Italian banker by the name of Luigi Soresi, who appeared to be genuinely trying to get and keep for poor Carnera some of the money he was making.

The by-products of the Miami affair were typical and pathetic. Duffy and company were living over a Miami nightclub in style and spending money like water – Primo's money. Carnera was relegated to a cheap cottage back of the town with a trainer. No one really looked after him. No one cared particularly whether he trained or not. He came into the ring against Loughran twenty pounds overweight. Shortly after that, Duffy was clapped into the jug for a spell for some boyish pranks with his income tax, and from the cooler he wrote pleading letters at the time that Carnera was preparing to defend his title against Baer, maintaining that he was needed to guide, advise, and teach Primo, to prime him for the first serious defence of his title, and that he should be given furlough from quod to attend to this matter. Carnera vigorously denied that he needed him. He was only too delighted to have Duffy held in durance vile. Of course what was really killing Uncle Will was that he was where, for the first time, he couldn't get his fingers on a nice big slice of the sugar that big, stupid wop would make for boxing Baer.

It is difficult to bag or fix a heavyweight championship prizefight, though it has been done. But in the post-war sports renaissance there was so much money at stake in a heavyweight championship fight that it took more cash than most could produce to purchase either champion or challenger. It stood to reason that if the champion figured to make $1 million or more out of his title he wasn't going to sell out for any less. Too, the power of the gangs was weakening. Repeal dealt them a terrible blow and took away their chief source of revenue. Three or four years before, Carnera's title would have been safe because his handlers would not have accepted any challenger for the title unless he agreed to preserve the state of the champion's health throughout the encounter. And there were always ways and means of keeping a challenger from double-crossing.

But Duffy was in the sneezer, as the boys sometimes quaintly called the jailhouse, Carnera was broke and needed money. He could only get it by fighting Baer. And the Baer fight could not be fixed. Baer's reputation was good; at least, he had not been caught out in any shady fights. He was a powerful hitter and it was apparent that now at last the rest of us were going to be made privy to what it was that happened when Carnera was struck forcefully on the chin. We didn't have to wait long. He was knocked down three times in the first round, and lost his championship in the eleventh round on a technical knockout when he was helpless, having been knocked down a total of thirteen times during the ten and a half rounds.

Not, however, until he fought and was knocked out by Joe Louis was it apparent what a dreadful thing had been done to this great hulk of a man. Strange to feel pity and sympathy excited for one so gross and enormous and strong. But the outsizes of the world are not the happy men, and their bulk is often of little use or help to them. If anything, it is a handicap when up against the speed and timing and balance of a normal man. Carnera's great strength was practically useless to him in the ring. The hardest blow he could strike was little more than a push. True, if he caught you in a corner he could club you insensible, but no smart fighter is caught in corners, and the big man was never fast enough anyway to catch anyone but out-and-out tramps.

When he fought Joe Louis he was defensive but little better than he was the first time I saw him, which, as it happened, was not in Madison Square Garden, but in the smoky, stuffy, subterranean Salle Wagram, a little fight club in Paris where I happened to be one evening when Jeff Dickson was promoting a fight between Primo Carnera, who had then been fighting a little less than a year, and one Moise Bouquillon, a light heavyweight who weighed 174 pounds. Monsieur See was experimenting a little with his giant. It was obvious that Bouquillon was going to be unable to hurt him very much, but what I noted that evening and never forgot was that the giant was likewise unable to hurt the little Frenchman. Curiously, that fight was almost an exact duplicate of the one that Carnera as champion later fought with Loughran. Walter (Good-Time Charley) Friedman was there too. Many years later he told me quite frankly: 'Boy, was that a lousy break for us that you come walking into that Salle Wagram that night and see that the big guy can't punch! Just that night you hadda be there. Leon wanted to see if he could go ten rounds without falling down. And you hadda be there. We coulda got away with a lot more if you don't walk in there and write stories about how he can't punch.'

Joe Louis slugged Carnera into bleating submission, cruelly and brutally. Handsome Uncle Will Duffy was back in his corner again, jawing angrily at him when he was led trembling and quivering back to his chair after the referee had saved him again, one side of his mouth smashed in, dazed and dripping blood. The very first right-hand punch Louis hit him broke Carnera's mouth and hurt him dreadfully.

Here, then, was the complete sell. He had nothing. His title was gone, his money squandered by the gang. And the one thing he thought he had, an unbeatable skill in defence and an irresistible crushing power in attack that no man living could withstand, never existed. It was a fable as legendary as the great giants of mythology that he resembled. The carrion birds that had fed upon this poor, big, dumb man had picked him clean. They had left him nothing, not even his pride and his self-respect, and that probably was the cruellest thing of all.

In his last fight, the one with Haynes, he was again severely beaten about the head. One of his legs refused to function. The fight was stopped. While he lay in the hospital in New York for treatment, as I have said, he lay alone.

I often wonder what that hulk of a man thinks today as he looks back over the manner in which he was swindled, tricked and cheated at every turn, as he recalls the great sums of money that he earned, all of it gone beyond recall. The world has no place for him, not even as a freak in a circus, from where he emerged and where he might happily have spent his life and become prosperous. Because as a giant, a terror and a horror, he stands exposed as a poor, unwilling fraud who was no man-killer at all, but a rather helpless, sad creature who, when slugged by a 185-pound mortal, either toppled stricken to the floor or staggered about or bled or had to be saved from annihilation by a third man who obligingly stepped between him and his tormentors.

He was born far, far too late. He belonged to the twelfth or thirteenth century, when he would have been a man-at-arms and a famous fellow with mace and halberd, pike or bill. At least he would have fought nobly and to the limit of his great strength, properly armed, because Carnera was a courageous fellow to the limit of his endurance, game and a willing fighter when aroused. In those days he would have won honour afield and would have got himself decently killed or, surviving, would have been retired by his feudal lord to round out his days and talk over the old brave fights.

Today there is nothing left for this man but reflection upon his humiliations. He was just a big sucker whom the wiseguys took and trimmed. What an epitaph for one who came from the ancient and noble race of giants.

All this took place in our country, Anno Domini 1930–1935.

ROUND 12

A Funny Thing Happened on the Way to the Garden

Boxing is not without its humorous side, though the humour is often tinged with that underlying bitter-sweet taste of adversity. The three pieces which follow epitomise in their different ways the essence of that defiant laughter. Firstly, a fictional account of a hilarious bare-knuckle contest, by William Kennedy, from Quinn's Book, *one of the famous 'Albany Trilogy'. Next, a true incident recalled by Jerry Izenberg from his book* How Many Miles to Camelot? *A funny story, but with an underlying pathos. Finally, from his collection of short stories entitled* Men without Women *comes an extract from Ernest Hemingway's 'Fifty Grand' in which an ageing boxer, Jack Brennan, is visited in his training camp by two shady characters. Tired of the hard graft, and yearning for wife and home, he agrees to 'throw' the fight and earn himself a retirement bonus in the process. But, as in all deadly serious pursuits, whether they be love, war, politics or competitive sport, things seldom work out exactly as planned.*

John the Brawn

William Kennedy

John never gambled when I first knew him, preferring to store up his savings for drink. But we find new targets for our vices as we move, and when he knocked down Hennessey, the champion of the world entirely, John's life entered an upward spiral that took him into bare-knuckle battles in Watervliet, Troy, the Boston Corner, White Plains, Toronto, and home again to Albany. I wrote John's ongoing story for the *Albany Chronicle* until the Toronto bout, Will Canaday then deciding not to finance expeditions quite so distant. I grew audacious enough to tell Will he was erring in news judgement, for John McGee and his fists had excited the people of Albany and environs like no sportsman in modern memory.

'Sportsman? Nonsense,' said Will. 'The man is loutish. No good can come of celebrating such brutes.'

It is true that John's brawling was legendary by this time, his right hand a dangerous weapon. He knocked over one after the other in his early battles and in between times decided to open a saloon in Albany to stabilise his income. He set it up in the Lumber District, an Irish entrenchment along the canal, and called the place Blue Heaven. Over the bar he hung a sign that read: 'All the fighting done in this place I do . . . [signed] . . . John McGee.'

A brute of a kind John was. Nevertheless, he was a presence to be understood, as even Will Canaday perceived when John fought at Toronto. In that fight, ballyhooed as Englishman against Irishman, John knocked down, and out, in the twenty-eighth round, a British navvy who was Canada's pride. John escaped an angry crowd, bent on stomping his arrogance into the turf, only with the help of the fists, power, and guile of the man who had been his sparring mate, and whose talent for escaping hostile pursuants was also legendary. I speak of Joshua.

And so it thereafter came to pass that John the Brawn was, at the age of thirty years, polarised as the heroic Irish champion of the

United States, and matched against Arthur (Yankee) Barker, the pride of native Americans. The fight took place on a summer afternoon in 1854 at the Bull's Head Tavern on the Troy road out of Albany, a hostel for wayward predilections of all manner and scope, where, as they say, cocks, dogs, rats, badgers, women, and niggers were baited in blood, and where Butter McCall, panjandrum of life at the Bull's Head, held the purse of $10,000, five from each combatant, and employed a line of battlers of his own to keep excitable partisans in the crowd from joining the fight, and whose wife, Sugar, kept the scrapbook in which one might, even today, read an account of the historic fight taken from the *Albany Telescope,* a sporting newspaper, and written by none other than Butter himself, an impresario first, perhaps, but also a bare-knuckle bard, a fistic philosopher, a poet of the poke.

> Wasn't it a grand day [Butter wrote], when we all 20,000 of us gathered in the Bull's Head pasture to witness the greatest fight boxiana has ever known? It was a regular apocalypse of steam and stew, blood and brew that twinned John (the Brawn) McGee, also known as John of the Skiff and John of the Water (from his days on the river), and Arthur (Yankee) Barker, also known as the Pet of Poughkeepsie and the True American – twinned and twined the pair in mortalising conflict over who was to be bare-knuckle champion of this godly land.
>
> John came to the pasture like Zeus on a wheel, tossed his hat with the Kelly-green plume into the ring, and then bounded in after it like a deer diving into the lakes of Killarney. His second bounced in after him, Mick the Rat, a stout Ethiopian who, they say, all but broke the nozzle of the God of Water in a sparring meet. The Mick tied the Water's colours to the post as the Yank trundled in, no hat on this one, just the flag itself, Old Glory over his shoulders.
>
> Peeling commenced and the seconds took their stations while the flag was wrapped around the Patriot's stake. Referees and umpires were appointed, the titans shook hands, and yo-ho-ho, off they went. The odds were even at first salvo, but the grand bank of Erin was offering three-to-two on the Water.

ROUND ONE

Both stood up well but the Pet in decidedly the handsomest position. Hi-ho with the left, he cocks the Skiffman amidships and crosses fast with a right to his knowledge box, but oh, now, didn't he get one back full in the domino case and down.

ROUND TWO

The Pet didn't like it a bit. He charged with his right brigade and hooked his man over the listener, which the Brawn threw off like a cat's sneeze and countered with a tremendous smasher to the Patriot's frontispiece, reducing him to his honkies. Said Mick the Rat from the corner, 'Dat flag am comin' unfurled.'

ROUND THREE

The Patriot came to his work this time with anger at the Mick's funny saying, rushed like a hornet on ice at the Waterman, firing pell-mell, lefts, rights, and whizzers at the Water's nasal organ. Water comes back bing-bing, and we see the claret running free from the Brawn's nostrilations. First blood has been declared for the Pet, which raised the clamour of three-to-one on Patriotism and plenty of takers, including Brawny Boy himself, who ordered the Rat to take a cud of the old green from his jacket and offplay the action. The Water let his bottleman second him while the Rat did his duty at the bank.

ROUND FOUR

The boys came up to scratch, the Pet again for business with vigour from Yankee heaven, pinning the Water boy on the ropes and hitting him at will. What happened to yer brawn, Johnny boy? Oh, it was fearful, and the claret thick as pea soup. Was he gone from us? Hardly. The skiffer outs with an ungodly roger up from the decks of Satan's scow; evil was that punch and it hit the True One in his breadbasket, loosing the crumbs it did, for a great noise came out of the Patriot's bung and he went flat as Dutch strudel.

ROUND FIVE

The Brawn lost blood, all right, but he's a game one. Up for mischief again, he levelled a terrible cob on the Pet's left ogle, leaving Pet's daylights anything but mates, and the blood of the Patriot gushed out like the spout on a he-goat. The Skiffer grabbed the Pet's head of cabbage around the throttle and used every exertion to destroy the Patriot's vocal talent, which we thought a pity, for the Patriot loves to sing duets with his sweetpea, that lovely tune, 'I won't be a nun, I shan't be a nun, I'm too fond of Arthur to be a nun.' The seconds separated the battlers and it was called a round.

ROUND SIX

Oh, the punishment. The Yankee Pet came up to scratch, erect on his pins, and lit out at the Skiffer's cabbage bag, but an uppercut sent him sliding like a chicken in a blizzard. The Brawn follows with the lefties and righties to the ogles, the smeller, and the domino case, but the Pet won't go down. Tough he was and tough he stayed, but dear God the blood. No quarter now from the God of Water, who goes after the Pet's chinchopper and schnotzblauer, which is a bleeding picture, and one of Erin's poets in the crowd observes, 'Don't our John do lovely sculpture?'

ROUND SEVEN

The Patriot came to the scratch in a wobble of gore, both eyes swollen and all but closed, his cheek slit as if by a cutlass, the blood of life dripping down his chest and he spitting up from his good innards. Was ever a man bloodier in battle? I think not. Yet the Pet of Patriotism, a flag himself now – red, white, and blue, and seeing the stars and stripes – moved at the Skiffman, who had contusions of his own, but none the worse for them. And the Skiff let go with a snobber to the conk that put the Pet to patriotic sleep. Old Gory went down like a duck and laid there like a side of blue mutton. A sad day for the Natives, and Green rises to the top like the cream of Purgatory.

We would judge the victory a popular one in this pasture, city, state, nation, and hemisphere, opinions to the contrary notwithstanding. John McGee proved himself a man of grain and grit, and the True Yankee now knows the measure of his own head. For those who wanted more fight, well, more there was – and plenty, too, which the Yankees found to their liking, loving punishment as they do.

A good time was had by all, nobody got killed that we know of, and the nigger carried off John the King on his shoulders.

John McGee, the black man's burden, retired after this fight, claiming the American championship, and rightly so. He left his Blue Heaven only for occasional trips to Boston, New York, and other centres of manly vice to box with Joshua and a few select sparring mates in exhibitions for the sporting crowd. He was heroised everywhere and he approved of such. But in New York (he once told Joshua) he felt kin to all that he saw: the ant-like mob of Irish, the Irish political radicals, the city politicians, the gamblers, the brawlers, the drinkers, and oh, those lovely women.

John always said he retired from fighting for the sake of his nose. 'No sensible woman,' he said, 'wants a man whose nose is twice as wide as itself, or that travels down his face in two or three assorted directions.'

The power that our hero manifested in galvanising the attention and loyalty of other men, the magic of his name and fists, generated wisdom of the moment in Manhattan's Democratic politicians. And so they hired John to round up a few lads and fend off the gangs hired by politicians of the Native American stripe, the most vicious and fearsome of these headed by Bill (The Butcher) Platt, whose method was directness itself: invade the polling places in Democratic strongholds and destroy the ballot boxes. But the presence of the newly fearsome John McGee was a countervailing influence, which by dint of bludgeons, brickbats, and bloody knuckles proved the superiority of several Democratic candidates for public office in the great city.

(from *Quinn's Book*)

Greatest Crawford

Jerry Izenberg

I once knew a man named Greatest Crawford. Most people never get to make claims like that, but I can, because one of the fringe benefits of this business is that you get to deal with people who have names like Cheerful Norman, the Emperor Jones, Evil Eye Finkel, Willie the Beard, and Hymie the Mink. Once I even met a bookmaker who stood behind the first tee at the US Open and handled action on the golfers right under the United States Golf Association's blue-blooded nose. I mention him here only because in civilian life he worked for Hertz Rent-A-Car and was therefore known as U-Drive Willie.

Greatest Crawford, of course, was a fighter. With a name like that on his birth certificate, he had damned well better know how to fight. I will remember Greatest forever. The reason I will remember goes back to a sweltering July night at Shea Stadium when a light heavyweight named Irish Wayne Thornton (whom I will remember no longer than it takes to write these lines) was matched with José Torres in a colossal mismatch.

In the very first round José hit Wayne Thornton with a vicious left hook, lifting him straight off the ground like a Minneapolis housewife picking up a pair of sweat socks which had frozen on her December wash line. José hit him many times, and with just about everything except the ring post. It was exhausting for José and exhausting for the onlookers, and it couldn't have been too invigorating for Irish Wayne either. After that everyone collapsed.

Irish Wayne couldn't fight. José was so exhausted, he wouldn't. And the promoters, well, in a sense they are what this is about. They had selected Shea Stadium on the forlorn hope that José Torres, who spent his formative years in boxing selling himself at Spanish movie-houses and Puerto Rican wakes, and who became a champion, was going to turn the evening into a bilingual bonanza. In anticipation of this, they had priced the bottom seat at five bucks, forgetting the cardinal rule of people who stage prizefights by selling tickets to poor people: 100 per cent of two bucks is worth a great deal more than 100 per cent of five bucks when the few people in the five-bucks seats have sneaked into the joint in the first place. Virtually everybody who was anybody wasn't there.

It was a dreadful fight, and it bankrupted the promoters. As the principals left the ring, Greatest Crawford passed them. Greatest was supposed to fight a six-rounder after the main event. He moved towards the ring with great dignity, considering the fact that you could hear the screams from the lifeboats as the promoters tried to abandon ship in a sea of red ink. To save money on the electric bill – or at least in order to owe less – they told the referee to cut Greatest's fight to four rounds.

When they came to the centre of the ring before a small intimate crowd which by then numbered perhaps 126 – the rest had already raced out to beat the muggers to the subway before the main event ended – the referee told Greatest Crawford the news.

Greatest stood there with his plain, dark robe draped across his shoulders against the wind that was now blowing in from Flushing Bay, looked at the referee, and said in quiet dignity: 'What you say?'

'I said,' the referee repeated, 'that the promoter wants to cut the fight to four rounds to save some money.'

'Fuck him,' Greatest said with great deliberation. 'Fuck him,' repeated Greatest, who had sparred with champions and who headlined mediocre cards in Holyoke and Worcester and even Philadelphia. 'Fuck him,' he said a third time, although he needed the money. 'I ain't no four-round fighter.' And then he walked slowly out of the ring, down the steps, and away from an easy pay night. I have never seen a prouder man.

Fifty Grand

Ernest Hemingway

Up at the hotel Jack took off his shoes and his coat and lay down for a while. I wrote a letter. I looked over a couple of times and Jack wasn't sleeping. He was lying perfectly still but every once in a while his eyes would open. Finally he sits up.

'Want to play some cribbage, Jerry?' he says.

'Sure,' I said.

He went over to his suitcase and got out the cards and the cribbage board. We played cribbage and he won three dollars off me. John knocked at the door and came in.

'Want to play some cribbage, John?' Jack asked him.

John put his kelly down on the table. It was all wet. His coat was wet too.

'Is it raining?' Jack asks.

'It's pouring,' John says. 'The taxi I had, got tied up in the traffic and I got out and walked.'

'Come on, play some cribbage,' Jack says.

'You ought to go and eat.'

'No,' says Jack. 'I don't want to eat yet.'

So they played cribbage for about half an hour and Jack won a dollar and a half off him.

'Well, I suppose we got to go eat,' Jack says. He went to the window and looked out.

'Is it still raining?'

'Yes.'

'Let's eat in the hotel,' John says.

'All right,' Jack says, 'I'll play you once more to see who pays for the meal.'

After a little while Jack gets up and says, 'You buy the meal, John,' and we went downstairs and ate in the big dining-room.

After we ate we went upstairs and Jack played cribbage with John again and won two dollars and a half off him. Jack was feeling pretty good. John had a bag with him with all his stuff in it. Jack took off his shirt and collar and put on a jersey and a sweater, so he wouldn't catch cold when he came out, and put his ring clothes and bathrobe in a bag.

'You all ready?' John asks him. 'I'll call up and have them get a taxi.'

Pretty soon the telephone rang and they said the taxi was waiting.

We rode down in the elevator and went out through the lobby, and got in a taxi and rode around to the Garden. It was raining hard but there was a lot of people outside on the streets. The Garden was sold out. As we came in on our way to the dressing-room I saw how full it was. It looked like half a mile down to the ring. It was all dark. Just the lights over the ring.

'It's a good thing, with this rain, they didn't try to pull this fight in the ball park,' John said.

'They got a good crowd,' Jack says.

'This is a fight that would draw a lot more than the Garden could hold.'

'You can't tell about the weather,' Jack says.

John came to the door of the dressing-room and poked his head in. Jack was sitting there with his bathrobe on, he had his arms folded and was looking at the floor. John had a couple of handlers with him. They looked over his shoulder. Jack looked up.

'Is he in?' he asked.

'He's just gone down,' John said.

We started down. Walcott was just getting into the ring. The crowd gave him a big hand. He climbed through between the ropes and put his two fists together and smiled, and shook them at the crowd, first at one side of the ring, then at the other, and then sat down. Jack got a good hand coming down through the crowd. Jack is Irish and the Irish always get a pretty good hand. An Irishman don't draw in New York like a Jew or an Italian, but they always get a good hand. Jack climbed up and bent down to go through the ropes and Walcott came over from his corner and pushed the rope down for Jack to go through. The crowd thought that was wonderful. Walcott put his hand on Jack's shoulder and they stood there just for a second.

'So you're going to be one of these popular champions,' Jack says to him. 'Take your goddam hand off my shoulder.'

'Be yourself,' Walcott says.

This is all great for the crowd. How gentlemanly the boys are before the fight! How they wish each other luck!

Solly Freedman came over to our corner while Jack is bandaging his hands and John is over in Walcott's corner. Jack puts his thumb through the slit in the bandage and then wrapped his hand nice and smooth. I taped it around the wrist and twice across the knuckles.

'Hey,' Freedman says. 'Where do you get all that tape?'

'Feel of it,' Jack says. 'It's soft, ain't it? Don't be a hick.'

Freedman stands there all the time while Jack bandages the other hand, and one of the boys that's going to handle him brings the gloves and I pull them on and work them around.

'Say, Freedman,' Jack asks, 'what nationality is this Walcott?'

'I don't know,' Solly says. 'He's some sort of a Dane.'

'He's a Bohemian,' the lad who brought the gloves said.

The referee called them out to the centre of the ring and Jack walks out. Walcott comes out smiling. They met and the referee put his arm on each of their shoulders.

'Hello, popularity,' Jack says to Walcott.

'Be yourself.'

'Listen – ' says the referee, and he gives them the same old line. Once Walcott interrupts him. He grabs Jack's arm and says, 'Can I hit when he's got me like this?'

'Keep your hands off me,' Jack says. 'There ain't no moving-pictures of this.'

They went back to their corners. I lifted the bathrobe off Jack and he leant on the ropes and flexed his knees a couple of times and scuffed his shoes in the resin. The gong rang and Jack turned quick and went out. Walcott came towards him and they touched gloves and as soon as Walcott dropped his hands Jack jumped his left into his face twice. There wasn't anybody ever boxed better than Jack. Walcott was after him, going forward all the time with his chin on his chest. He's a hooker and he carries his hands pretty low. All he knows is to get in there and sock. But every time he gets in there close, Jack has the left hand in his face. It's just as though it's automatic. Jack just raises the left hand up and it's in Walcott's face. Three or four times Jack brings the right over but Walcott gets it on the shoulder or high up on the head. He's just like all these hookers. The only thing he's afraid of is another one of the same kind. He's covered everywhere you can hurt him. He don't care about a left hand in his face.

After about four rounds Jack has him bleeding bad and his face all cut up, but every time Walcott's got in close he's socked so hard he's got two big red patches on both sides just below Jack's ribs. Every time he gets in close, Jack ties him up, then gets one hand loose and uppercuts him, but when Walcott gets his hands loose he socks Jack in the body so they can hear it outside in the street. He's a socker.

It goes along like that for three rounds more. They don't talk any. They're working all the time. We worked over Jack plenty too, in between the rounds. He don't look good at all but he never does much work in the ring. He don't move around much and that left hand is just automatic. It's just like it was connected with Walcott's face and Jack just had to wish it in every time. Jack is always calm in close and he doesn't waste any juice. He knows everything about working in close too and he's getting away with a lot of stuff. While they were in our corner I watched him tie Walcott up, get his right hand loose, turn it and come up with an uppercut that got Walcott's nose with the heel of the glove. Walcott was bleeding bad and leaned his nose on Jack's shoulder so as to give Jack some of it too, and Jack sort of lifted his shoulder sharp and caught him against the nose, and then brought down the right hand and did the same thing again.

Walcott was sore as hell. By the time they'd gone five rounds he hated Jack's guts. Jack wasn't sore; that is, he wasn't any sorer than he always was. He certainly did used to make the fellows he fought hate boxing. That was why he hated 'Kid' Lewis so. He never got 'Kid's goat. 'Kid' Lewis always had about three new dirty things Jack couldn't do. Jack was as safe as a church all the time he was in there, as long as he was strong. He certainly was treating Walcott rough. The funny thing was it looked as though Jack was an open classic boxer. That was because he had all that stuff too.

After the seventh round Jack says, 'My left's getting heavy.'

From then he started to take a beating. It didn't show at first. But instead of him running the fight it was Walcott was running it, instead of being safe all the time now he was in trouble. He couldn't keep him out with the left hand now. It looked as though it was the same as ever, only now instead of Walcott's punches just missing him they were just hitting him. He took an awful beating in the body.

'What's the round?' Jack asked.

'The eleventh.'

'I can't stay,' Jack says. 'My legs are going bad.'

Walcott had been just hitting him for a long time. It was like a baseball catcher pulls the ball and takes some of the shock off. From now on Walcott commenced to land solid. He certainly was a socking-machine. Jack was just trying to block everything now. It didn't show what an awful beating he was taking. In between the rounds I worked on his legs. The muscles would flutter under my hands all the time I was rubbing them. He was sick as hell.

'How's it go?' he asked John, turning around, his face all swollen.

'It's his fight.'

'I think I can last,' Jack says. 'I don't want this bohunk to stop me.'

It was going just the way he thought it would. He knew he couldn't beat Walcott. He wasn't strong any more. He was all right though. His money was all right and now he wanted to finish it off right to please himself. He didn't want to be knocked out.

The gong rang and we pushed him out. He went out slow. Walcott came right out after him. Jack put the left in his face and Walcott took it, came in under it and started working on Jack's body. Jack tried to tie him up and it was just like trying to hold on to a buzz-saw. Jack broke away from it and missed with the right. Walcott clipped him with a left hook and Jack went down. He went down on his hands and knees and looked at us. The referee started counting. Jack was watching us and shaking his head. At eight John motioned to him. You couldn't hear on account of the crowd. Jack got up. The referee had been holding Walcott back with one arm while he counted.

When Jack was on his feet Walcott started towards him.

'Watch yourself, Jimmy,' I heard Solly Freedman yell to him.

Walcott came up to Jack looking at him. Jack stuck the left hand at him. Walcott just shook his head. He backed Jack up against the ropes, measured him and then hooked the left very light to the side of Jack's head and socked the right into the body as hard as he could sock, just as low as he could get it. He must have hit him five inches below the belt. I thought the eyes would come out of Jack's head. They stuck way out. His mouth came open.

The referee grabbed Walcott. Jack stepped forward. If he went down there went fifty thousand bucks. He walked as though all his insides were going to fall out.

'It wasn't low,' he said. 'It was an accident.'

The crowd were yelling so you couldn't hear anything.

'I'm all right,' Jack says. They were right in front of us. The referee looks at John and then he shakes his head.

'Come on, you polak son-of-a-bitch,' Jack says to Walcott.

John was hanging on to the ropes. He had the towel ready to chuck in. Jack was standing just a little way out from the ropes. He took a step forward. I saw the sweat come out on his face like somebody had squeezed it and a big drop went down his nose.

'Come on and fight,' Jack says to Walcott.

The referee looked at John and waved Walcott on.

'Go in there, you slob,' he says.

Walcott went in. He didn't know what to do either. He never thought Jack could have stood it. Jack put the left in his face. There was such a hell of a lot of yelling going on. They were right in front of us. Walcott hit him twice. Jack's face was the worst thing I ever saw – the look on it! He was holding himself and all his body together and it all showed on his face. All the time he was thinking and holding his body in where it was busted.

Then he started to sock. His face looked awful all the time. He started to sock with his hands low down by his side, swinging at Walcott. Walcott covered up and Jack was swinging wild at Walcott's head. Then he swung the left and it hit Walcott in the groin and the right hit Walcott right bang where he'd hit Jack. Way low below the belt. Walcott went down and grabbed himself there and rolled and twisted around.

The referee grabbed Jack and pushed him towards his corner. John jumps into the ring. There was all this yelling going on. The referee was talking with the judges and then the announcer got into the ring with the megaphone and says, 'Walcott on a foul.'

The referee is talking to John and he says, 'What could I do? Jack wouldn't take the foul. Then when he's groggy he fouls him.'

'He'd lost it anyway,' John says.

Jack's sitting on the chair. I've got his gloves off and he's holding himself in down there with both hands. When he's got something supporting it his face doesn't look so bad.

'Go over and say you're sorry,' John says into his ear. 'It'll look good.'

Jack stands up and the sweat comes out all over his face. I put the bathrobe around him and he holds himself in with one hand under the bathrobe and goes across the ring. They've picked Walcott up and they're working on him. There're a lot of people in Walcott's corner. Nobody speaks to Jack. He leans over Walcott.

'I'm sorry,' Jack says. 'I didn't mean to foul you.'

Walcott doesn't say anything. He looks too damned sick.

'Well, you're the champion now,' Jack says to him. 'I hope you get a hell of a lot of fun out of it.'

'Leave the kid alone,' Solly Freedman says.

'Hello, Solly,' Jack says. 'I'm sorry I fouled your boy.'

Freedman just looks at him.

Jack went to his corner walking that funny jerky way and we got him down through the ropes and through the reporters' tables and out down the aisle. A lot of people want to slap Jack on the back. He goes out through all that mob in his bathrobe to the dressing-room. It's a popular win for Walcott. That's the way the money was bet in the Garden.

Once we got inside the dressing-room, Jack lay down and shut his eyes.

'We want to get to the hotel and get a doctor,' John says.

'I'm all busted inside,' Jack says.

'I'm sorry as hell, Jack,' John says.

'It's all right,' Jack says.

He lies there with his eyes shut.

'They certainly tried a nice double-cross,' John said.

'Your friends Morgan and Steinfelt,' Jack said. 'You got nice friends.'

He lies there, his eyes are open now. His face has still got that awful drawn look.

'It's funny how fast you can think when it means that much money,' Jack says.

'You're some boy, Jack,' John says.

'No,' Jack says. 'It was nothing.'

ROUND 13

Hard Luck Stories

The stigma that surrounds the number thirteen is a fairly universal one. In the glory days of boxing, when all major bouts ran to fifteen rounds, that ominous thirteen must have loomed large in the fighter's mind, and strangely enough many a crucial upset or 'turn around' seems to have centred on that ill-omened round.

We have already seen one outstanding example of this in the Joe Louis–Billy Conn encounter. Here are two more classic examples of the same jinx at work. Both were contests where the eventual loser appeared to have the battle won, but come the fateful thirteenth and the apparent loser snatched victory from the jaws of defeat, leaving his opponent to ponder forever on the unexpected outcome of that 'hard luck' round.

The late great A.J. Leibling, scholar, gourmet, bon vivant, and doyen of all boxing writers, here recalls the fascinating details of two great boxing upsets.

New Champ

A.J. Leibling

Before Marciano fought and beat Louis, Charlie Goldman told me that Rocky was in what he called 'an improving phase'. 'He's still six months – maybe a year – away,' Goldman told me. Almost a year passed before Marciano was matched to meet Jersey Joe Walcott for the heavyweight championship. 'The great thing about this kid is he's got leverage,' Goldman kept saying in the time between. 'He takes a good punch and he's got the equaliser.' By this last, he meant that Marciano had the ability to equalise – or cancel out with one solid punch – the advantage in points piled up by a more skilful opponent in the rounds preceding equalisation.

Marciano knocked Louis out in the eighth round after wearing the older man down. But there was a trace of intellection in the way he finished off the former champion. His right hand had received all the advance publicity, and during the fight he threw it so often, usually missing, that Louis paid less and less attention to the left. Then, in the eighth, Marciano knocked him out with three left hooks and an almost redundant right. The progress of an education, whether that of a candidate for the presidency or that of a candidate for the heavyweight championship, always interests me. So when I read in a newspaper that Marciano had been matched to fight Jersey Joe Walcott for the title in the Philadelphia Municipal Stadium on the night of 23 September 1952, I went.

A boxer solidly constructed, intelligently directed, and soundly motivated is bound to go a long way. I had not seen Marciano since the Louis bout, but I knew that in the interim he had knocked out several lesser heavyweights to keep his hand in. In the first of these bouts, against Lee Savold, he had seemed to some of the experts to be regressing. I ran into Goldman after that one, and he said, 'Yeah, we let him lay off a couple months after Louis, and he went back. He's the kind you got to keep working. We won't make that mistake again.' Mr Goldman added, 'After all, they call him crude because he misses a lot of those punches, but it's his style. I could teach him to punch short – across his chest – but to tell the truth it wouldn't be very effective. So let him throw them old Suzi-Qs.' In his subsequent fights. Marciano, I noted in the newspapers, finished his chaps off in fast time, winding up with a fellow named Harry Matthews, a clever sort, whom he knocked out in the second round. Matthews's manager, Jack Hurley, had predicted a contrary result, basing his forecast on a mysterious strategy he said he had imparted to his fighter. 'Hurley wanted to be a Svengali but the strings broke,' Al Weill said to me later.

As soon as I learned that Rocky had been made with Jersey Joe, I went in quest of Weill, to hear how his fighter's education was getting on. Weill's office then was on the third floor of the Strand Theatre Building, and he had worked out of it for nearly thirty years, retaining it even when he was the Garden matchmaker, as if he knew he would be back there some day. It was impregnated with the smell of the cigars he smokes and decorated with framed photographs and cartoons of boxers he has managed at one time or another. The wide window across the front of the room looked out on Broadway, a street fraught with temptations for fighters to spend money. For this reason, Weill kept his boxers as far from it as possible, usually within earshot of Goldman. He knew he could resist the temptations all right himself. Also, a fighter learns more when sufficiently secluded. Out of sheer boredom, he may listen to some of the pearls of wisdom Goldman casts in his direction, such as, 'If you're ever knocked down, don't be no hero and jump right up. Take a count,' or, 'Always finish up with a left hook, because that brings you into position to start another series of punches.' Goldman frequently voices less technical advice, too, such as, 'Never play a guy at his own game; nobody makes up a game in order to get beat at it,' and, 'Never buy anything on the street, especially diamonds.' Weill now has an office in the Hotel Lexington, on the more fashionable East Side, as befits the manager of the heavyweight champion of the world, but it doesn't smell right yet. It takes a heap of smoking to give a hotel suite the atmosphere of a humidor.

On the morning of my call, I found Weill looking out the window and smoking a cigar while waiting for, he at once informed me, telephone calls from Pittsburgh, Providence, Honolulu, and Salt Lake

City. A prizefight manager will never admit he is waiting for a telephone call that costs less than a dollar. 'People all over the country are going crazy about this fight, and everybody expects me to get them a good seat,' he said. 'I already sold fifteen thousand dollars' worth personally.' Looking like a kind of grey-haired Napoleon, he wore a white-on-white shirt, fresh that morning – an evidence of prosperity – while his chief assistant was in not-so-white-on-not-so-white, out at the elbows. A prizefight manager's assistants assist him in waiting for telephone calls, especially when he goes out for a cup of coffee. Sometimes they inherit his shirts.

Mr Weill, aware that I don't smoke, offered me a cigar and then said, with a romantic intonation, 'You know, this fight means a lot to me. I've had three champions – a feather, a lightweight, and a welter – but never a heavyweight champion. I had Godoy, who fought Louis twice, and gave him a lot of trouble, but he didn't make it. And I had a good young prospect named Marty Fox, but he went wrong. He was fighting Unknown Winston in Hartford, and he was stabbing Unknown to death. The referee waves to him to go in and fight, because they were stinking out the joint, and you know what the damn fool done? He done what the referee told him. Winston knocked him cold. When I heard what he done, I told him, "You are too dumb to be a fighter." So I retired him.'

The manager threw to the floor a cigar only four-fifths smoked, for him an evidence of great emotion, and ground the stub with his right heel, as if obliterating an evil memory. 'I can't fight for them,' he said. 'They got to help me.' But he brightened when I asked about Marciano. 'He come a long way since you seen him,' he said. 'You wouldn't know him. I got him up at Grossinger's.' Grossinger's is a legendary and dietary resort hotel in the Catskills. With its attached golf courses and airfield, it is only slightly inferior in area to the King Ranch, in Texas. A prizefighter training for a big match is one of the attractions at Grossinger's, giving the guests something to talk about between meals and getting the hotel publicity every time a fight-writer files a dispatch datelined Grossinger, New York. It was a mark of Rocky's advancement that in the course of one year he had come to be considered an attraction of Grossinger magnitude.

I flew up to Grossinger's on the Tuesday just two weeks before the fight, in a plane chartered by the IBC, which had arranged the match, and freighted mainly with photographers going up to take pictures of the challenger posing with Jack Dempsey, the old heavyweight champion and restaurateur, who was scheduled to watch him spar and then make the customary Delphic prediction. On the next day, Dempsey and the photographers were booked to visit Walcott, in Atlantic City. I found Rocky and Charlie Goldman and the rest of the camp, including Rocky's father, sprawled on cots in the sun in front of the training quarters, which were on the rim of the airfield, a couple of miles from the hotel and its potential distractions. The fighter and his faction had a rather large cottage and an annexe to live in, and an old airplane hangar had been fitted up as a gymnasium, with benches for spectators, who paid a dollar a head to watch workouts. The airfield is used only by occasional small planes, and at night the quiet is mountainous. In between Rocky and Charlie was Al Columbo, the fighter's friend, contemporary, and assistant trainer, who is from his home town. All three were wearing blue-and-yellow checked peaked caps with red pompons; it is part of a trainer's role to provide small sources of amusement for his fighter, and Goldman thinks there is something particularly funny about headgear. (In town, he usually wears either a bowler or a beret. 'It takes a handsome man to carry them off,' he says.)

Marciano isn't a hard man to keep in a good humour; he doesn't go in for the rough practical jokes with which some fighters both enliven their camps and get rid of their apprehensions. His outline has a squareness and his skin a terracotta tint that make you think of an Etruscan figurine. His body has no Grecian grace; he has big calves, forearms, wrists, and fingers, and a neck so thick that it minimises the span of his shoulders. He is neither tall nor heavy for a heavyweight – he weighs around 185 in fighting trim – but he gives the impression of bigness when you are close to him. His face, like his body, is craggy – big jaw, big nose (already askew from punching), high cheekbones – and almost always, when he is outside the ring, has a pleasant asymmetrical grin on it. It is the grin of a shy fellow happy to be recognised, at last, as a member of the gang in good standing. His speech doesn't fit the typecaster's idea of what a prizefighter's should be; he speaks with that southern New England accent in which the 'a' in 'far' is sounded as New Yorkers sound the 'a' in 'hat' and the 'a' in 'half' is sounded as we sound the 'a' in 'far'.

Grammatical constructions are more carefully worked out there than in most parts of the country, and Marciano (whose name in this dialect becomes 'Masiano', with two short 'a's) sometimes sounds more like former Senator Lodge than like one of his own professional colleagues working on the New York–Chicago–California axis. He is, in fact, as much of an exotic, in his way, as was Luis Angel Firpo, the man in the celluloid collar. Weill, mindful of the pitfalls of Broadway, is anxious to keep him that way. Marciano goes back to Brockton after every fight. Each expedition into the outside world has for him the charm of an overnight trip with the Brockton High School football team, on which he once played centre, and, like the team, he is accompanied by hundreds of home-town rooters. When I asked him, for lack of a more original question, how he felt, he replied, with an accent I remembered from my days on the *Providence Journal*, 'Peufict'. He is not exactly gabby.

The workout in the hangar that day was not spectacular. Marciano boxed two rounds with a coloured light heavyweight from California named Tommy Harrison, a fast, shifty fellow who kept stabbing and going away while Rocky slid along after him. It was logical to expect evasive action from Walcott, a celebrated cutie who had never, as far as anyone could remember, made a stand-up fight with any opponent. Against Rocky, who was notoriously slow afoot, the champion might be expected to circle and move in and out even more than usual. But the test was inconclusive, since Harrison, who weighed 170 and was in his early twenties, was certainly faster than Walcott, who was by his own admission thirty-eight and weighed nearly 200. And Rocky would have fifteen rounds, not two, in which to catch up with the old fellow.

Then Marciano did two rounds with Keene Simmons, a coloured heavyweight every bit as big and rugged as Walcott, and much younger. Simmons had once given Marciano a pretty good fight in public. His imitation of Walcott was good – he would throw quick sneak punches, some of them right-hand leads, and slide away. When he didn't slide away, he clinched. He even did the kind of jig-step shuffle Walcott uses to disconcert his opponents, although there is no particular reason it should. Marciano, I noticed, wasn't throwing as many long, looping punches as he threw the previous year. He couldn't afford to be caught off balance by a sharpshooter like Walcott, who could move in fast on any mistake. But I remembered what Goldman had said about Rocky's ineffectiveness with short punches. I wondered what he would use against Walcott in place of 'them Suzi-Qs'. His boxing had improved vastly – from terrible to mediocre – but I couldn't imagine him outpointing Walcott. He would have to keep crowding – pushing him around until the spring went out of the old man's legs and arms and it was safe to revert to the Suzi-Q.

After the workout, a fellow drove Rocky back to the house – a distance of a few hundred yards – and Goldman and Columbo and I followed on foot. When we got there, the boxer was already lying on a bed in a second-floor room, warmly covered to keep him sweating. 'This is the best part of boxing,' he said. Goldman talked to him about old fighters; I noticed that, unlike veterans, who want to talk about anything but boxing, Marciano was intensely interested. He seemed to be trying to build up background for the position he felt he had been called to. When Marciano went downstairs for his shower, Columbo told me how they had come out of the army together when they were both twenty-two, and how Rocky had started boxing in amateur tournaments in New England. 'He was crude, but there was one move he would wait for the other fellow to make, and when he made it, Rocky would swing and knock him out,' Columbo said.

'He must have knocked out a hundred. Half the time he would hit them on top of the head. One time he broke his right thumb on a bird with a hard head, and they laid him off at the shoe factory where he worked. So he knew he would have to make up his mind – either give up boxing or the shoe factory. By that time, Weill had seen him, and he offered to carry him along for the first year or so if he would turn pro, until he started to earn real money. So he turned.'

The fighter came back and Goldman rubbed him down. I asked him again how he felt, and he said, 'Peufict'.

Rocky's father, addressed as Pop by the trainers and sparring partners, ate supper with us, at five-thirty. His name is Pietro – or, affectionately, Pietrone – Marchegiano. ('Marciano' is a contraction adopted for the convenience of fight announcers.) He is a small, thin man, gravely polite, with a heavy Italian accent and a most un-Italian reserve. From the day of his arrival in America until recently, he cobbled shoes in his own one-man shop in Brockton. Only in his large, strong hands does he resemble his son. While we ate – a good-sized steak apiece, with bread and butter, string beans, and potatoes – the telephone rang almost continuously. Most of the callers were well-wishers in Massachusetts and Rhode Island, asking for blocks of good tickets to sell to friends. One said the Mayor of Brockton was coming to the fight and was bringing the Governor of Massachusetts and Adlai Stevenson as his guests.

While waiting for an automobile to pick me up – the plane had long since gone back to New York with the photographers and their undeveloped plates – I stood on the lawn for a moment with Charlie Goldman. 'The shoe factory that laid him off sends him a new pair of boxing shoes before every bout,' he said. 'They done it for his last ten bouts, and every pair has his name inside. Everybody rides with a winner.' The little man looked up at me and said, 'You know, there are two kinds of friends – the ones who are with you when you are winning and the ones who stick when you are losing. I prefer the second kind. But you got to take advantage of the others while you got them. Because they won't be with you long.'

A fortnight later I boarded the five o'clock train to Philadelphia at Pennsylvania Station with a $25 ticket in my wallet and a small but good pair of binoculars in my pocket. There were six Brocktonians across the aisle from me. They made no secret of their civic identity. Florid men with small, merry eyes, all in clothes slightly tight for them – probably, like trees, they added a circumferential ring each year – they might have been either union officials or downtown businessmen, types hard to distinguish between in their part of the world. They were organising a two-dollar pool among themselves on which round Rocky would win in. One, addressed by the others as Mac, caused indignation, which I judged to be not entirely feigned, by saying that for his two dollars he would take Walcott by decision.

'Then we'll be laying you 5-to-1,' one of his townsmen said.

'You don't think Walcott has a chance, do you?' Mac asked. 'I'm doing you a favour.' I could see he had raised a doubt in their minds, and at the same moment he saw he was losing popularity. 'I just said it for laughs,' he added lamely.

But their journey to Philadelphia had been spoiled. Mac had opened up a possibility they had shoved resolutely into the back of their minds. In forty-two fights, Rocky had never even been knocked from his feet.

On arrival, I took a subway to the centre of town and walked about for a while, looking for Lew Tendler's restaurant. Tendler is an old Philadelphia fighter who has remained a Philadelphia idol because, I think, he embodies the city's sense of being eternally put upon. He once had Benny Leonard beaten when Leonard was lightweight champion; Leonard was on the floor but got up before 'ten', and it was a no-decision bout. I thought I knew where Lew's restaurant was, and wouldn't ask anybody the way. I soon got tired of walking, though, and ate in a place called Mike Banana's. A minute after I had finished and left, I found Tendler's, but I saw I couldn't have eaten there anyway. I couldn't even have got as far as the bar, it was so packed. The sidewalk on Broad Street in front of the restaurant was jammed right out to the kerb, and gentlemen with embossed ears were struggling to keep from being pushed under taxicabs. Everybody (I use the word in its Ward McAllister sense) who goes to Philadelphia for a fight meets at Tendler's and tries to put the lug on somebody for a free ticket. On the night of 23 September, the people with the free tickets had apparently sold them to scalpers. Some, in their enthusiasm, had even sold their own seats, and were now looking for friends to put the lug on. It was a scene of great confusion. Joe Walcott, in a car preceded by a police escort, passed by on his way to the fight. The main bout would not go on until ten-thirty, but he wanted to get there in plenty of time. Walcott is from Camden, New Jersey, across the river from Philadelphia, and the crowd in the street cheered. I had thought I could put the lug on somebody for a ride to the stadium, but the only acquaintance I met who had a car had to wait for somebody who had promised him a ticket. I was lucky to get a seat in a taxi.

The Municipal Stadium, situated in a kind of Gobi Desert at the end of all transportation lines, can, it is said, seat 100,000. The crowd of 40,000 in attendance filled one end of the oval grandstand and, of course, a great carpet of 'ringside' seats on the grass inside the running track. I found that my fifteen inches of concrete in the stand afforded a good view, with the aid of binoculars, except for a minute segment of the ring that was masked by one of a number of tall steel masts that were disposed around its circumference. I suppose they had something to do with the public address system, since they all had capitals of entwined horns, like morning-glories. However, I had an aisle seat, and by stretching far out, like a runner with a lead off base, I could take this obstacle in enfilade in a matter of seconds. The preliminaries gave me a chance to adjust my lenses and perfect my moves to the right and the left of the post. They had no other interest for me.

When the main-bout fighters entered the ring with their factions, I saw that Weill had decided to act as Marciano's chief second. He had four subordinates, of whom the smallest, and consequently the hardest to see, was Goldman. One of Weill's strongest points of resemblance to Napoleon – or, for that matter, to Mr Pickwick – is what he calls his 'built'. He worked from a standing but bending position directly in front of his seated fighter and facing him. As Marciano was in the corner diagonally across from my perch, my only memory of what happened there between rounds centres on the scat of my old friend's white flannel pants. All I could see of Walcott was the back of his head.

The fight was, as you probably read, one of the stubbornest matches ever fought by heavyweights. When all the lights except those over the ring went out and the bout started, I began to be aware there had been a mistake, and I soon recognised what it was. Walcott, a great, earthen-hued man, mature but sprightly, has a cylindrical torso and a smaller cylinder of a head rising directly out of it. He weighed 196 pounds, twelve more than Rocky. And the mistake was that he was not imitating Keene Simmons' imitation of him. Instead he was walking forward, hitting at Marciano and moving him back. In just about a minute he landed a beautiful left hook to the jaw, and the hope of Brockton went down on his left side. Walcott started to walk away, assuming, I suppose, that anything human so hit would take the longest permissible count – nine seconds. But Rocky jumped up at three. (This was the only thing Marciano did all night that Goldman complained of after the fight.) Walcott turned, unable to believe his good fortune, but didn't get back to him soon enough. The way Marciano came up made me think the hope of Brockton was out of his head. I learned afterwards that what had made him bounce was a combination of indignation and inexperience. The remainder of the round was not reassuring to the Brockton rooters, and when the old fellow continued to batter Charlie's pupil in the second, I was reminded of the remark of a trotting-horse man I know, made in similar circumstances: 'The cow got loose and killed the butcher.'

There was a coloured man to my right, entirely surrounded by whites. I could hear him yelling, and what he was yelling hardly sounded sensible – though, come to think of it, it may have been. 'Don't get mad, Joe!' he was hollering. '*Please* don't get mad!' But Walcott continued to act mad, walking right out to meet Marciano in the third. Half a minute later it was Marciano who was shaking the champion, knocking him back with body blows and punches that did not land clean on the jaw but hit him on the side or the back of his bobbing head. The old fellow gave way slowly, hitting all the time, not breaking away and circling, as he had in other fights. Pierce Egan would have called his tactic 'milling in retreat'. The match now seemed to be following the script more closely. Rocky was slowing him down. The old man would go in a couple more rounds. If he started running he might last a little longer. The young fellow kept pounding in the fourth and fifth. At the end of several rounds they continued after the bell, and Marciano usually got in the last punch. At the end of the fifth I couldn't understand how Walcott stood up.

Then, in the sixth, there was blood all over Walcott's white trunks and Marciano's matted chest. It didn't show on Marciano's trunks, which were black, or Walcott's torso, which was nearly so. Walcott, I could see with the glasses, had a cut over his left eye. Marciano was bleeding, too, but from an unlikely place – the top of his head. You could figure how head and eye must have come together. Marciano, an inch or so shorter than Walcott, accentuated the difference by fighting out of a crouch; his game was to get his head in against the bigger man's chest, where Walcott couldn't hit it, and then punch up, and when he stepped back out of one clinch, his head had come up hard. This accident, the crowd thought, would hasten Walcott's end. In the seventh, though, it was, unaccountably, Marciano who began to flounder. He wavered and almost pawed the air, although he had not been hit by any one particular big punch. He seemed to be coming unstuck, and in the eighth it was the same. Walcott's seconds had closed his cut after the sixth round, using one of those mysterious astringent solutions trainers treasure. And Marciano's corner had closed the wound on his scalp. But now Marciano's right eye had been cut by a punch. (Late that night, or early next morning, at a party given by a man called Jimmy Tomato, who had won a good bet on Marciano, I was told by Weill and Goldman that Rocky, nestling his brow against Walcott's chest early in the seventh round, had got a liquid in both eyes that blinded him. They did not know whether it was some of the astringent solution, dripping from the cut above Walcott's eye, or just liniment, well spiked with capsicum, which Walcott's seconds had sloshed on their man as a form of chemical warfare. 'He fought four rounds that he couldn't see the guy,' Weill said. I thought this an exaggeration, because in the ninth Marciano had recaptured the lead, which was pretty good going for a blind man.)

In nine rounds the lead changed hands three times – Walcott to Marciano in the third round, Marciano to Walcott in the seventh, Walcott to Marciano in the ninth. You don't see many fights like that. In the tenth, which was the hardest-fought round of all, Marciano stayed on top. But somehow the calculations had gone awry; the old fellow looked further from collapse now than he had six rounds earlier. It might go to a decision, after all. I thought with pity of my Brocktonians on the train. If it was close, I felt, Walcott would get the decision. It is traditional not to take a championship away on a close one, and Philadelphia was virtually his home.

Then Walcott, as if bolstered by the certainty that he could last, came out for the eleventh and had his best round of the fight, except for the opener, when he had floored Rocky. It was the fourth switch in the plot. In the twelfth, he looked not only more effective but stronger than the challenger. Up to then I had had the feeling that if Marciano did land flush on the jaw, he could take the champion with one punch. Now his arms and legs seemed a trifle rubbery. He was swinging wildly, and missing by absurd margins. At the end of the twelfth, Walcott was well ahead and looked stronger than ever.

In the thirteenth the fighters disappeared momentarily from my view behind that steel mast. They were doing nothing particularly exciting. Walcott was giving ground slowly, backing towards the ropes, as he had done repeatedly. Whenever he reached the ropes, he would start a rally; it was a habitual tactic of his. Marciano was following – hopelessly, it seemed. He had to keep moving in, because if he stayed away, Walcott, who had a much longer reach, could hit him without return. I wasn't as quick going into my own crouch with the binoculars as I had been in the early rounds; perhaps I was feeling slightly rubbery myself. Then I heard one of those immeasurable shouts that follow a ball over the fence in a World Series. And I could see Walcott's legs protruding to the right of the mast. The fellow next to me, who thought he had seen what happened, yelled, 'I can't believe it! He knocked him cold with a left hook. Who said he could hit with a left?' This miserable creature, who by sheer luck had been looking when I wasn't, invited my contempt, and I shouted back, 'Who said he couldn't? He knocked Louis crazy with lefts! He belted Matthews cold with a left!' Actually, as I learned later, Rocky had knocked Walcott out with a right that travelled at most twelve inches, straight across his chest to the champion's jaw. The guy next to me hadn't seen the punch at all; Marciano had had his back towards our side of the ring. But Marciano had grazed Walcott with a left hook as the champion fell, already dead to the world. 'He trun it for insurance,' a fellow who had been in his corner told me later. The fan could be excused, of course. The sportswriter of the Philadelphia *Inquirer,* sitting at ringside, wrote that Rocky had hit Joe with a 'roundhouse right, swung from his hip and his heart.' The punch was the antithesis of a roundhouse; it was a model of pugilistic concision. The newsreel film of the fight shows that both men started right leads for the head at the same moment. Walcott, the sharp, fast puncher, figured to get there first in such an exchange. But Marciano hit sharper, faster, and, according to old-timers, about as hard as anybody ever hit anybody. Walcott, the film shows, flowed down like flour out of a chute. He didn't seem to have a bone in his body. And so, after old Jersey Joe had piled up a lead by fighting the way he wasn't supposed to, Rocky knocked him out with the kind of punch he wasn't supposed to know how to use. 'In other words,' Charlie Goldman said to me at Jimmy Tomato's party in the Hotel Warwick after the fight, 'he equalised.' Mr Tomato, whose real name few of his acquaintances remember, is a businessman and patron of the arts who has been known to bet on Marciano. From the scale of the party it was safe to conclude his investment had been more than nominal.

When the referee, a Pennsylvanian named Charlie Daggert, had counted Walcott out – a hollow formality – all the ringside seat holders from Brockton, Swansea, Taunton, New Bedford, Attleboro, Seekonk, Pawtucket, Woonsocket, East Providence, Providence, and even Hopkinton, Hope Valley, and Wakefield climbed over the shoulders of the sportswriters, kicked them under the typewriter benches, stamped on their typewriters, and got up into the ring to shake hands with Rocky. It seemed that they might pluck his arms off like petals from a daisy, but somehow he escaped and came shooting through the crowd, propelled by the long line of admirers pushing along behind him. A group of police cleared the way and the fellows from his corner locked arms behind him to keep the jubilious from pawing him over. He disappeared under the stand almost at a dead run. As for Walcott, I can't even remember seeing him leave.

The Melting Middleweight

A.J. Leibling

The division of boxers into weight classes is based on the premise that if two men are equally talented practitioners of the Sweet Science, then the heavier man has a decided advantage. This is true, of course, only if both men are trained down hard, since a pound of beer is of no use in a boxing match. If the difference amounts to no more than a couple of pounds, it can be offset by a number of other factors, including luck, but when it goes up to five or six or seven, it takes a lot of beating. The span between the top limit of one weight class and the next represents the margin that history has proved is almost impossible to overcome. Between middleweight and light heavyweight, for example, that gap is fifteen pounds. A middleweight champion may weigh, at the most, 160, and a light heavy 175. But some champions are more skilful than others, and every now and then one comes along who feels he can beat the titleholder in the class above him. That was what made it interesting to anticipate the match between Sugar Ray Robinson, the middleweight champion, and Joey Maxim, the champion of the light heavyweights, in June 1952. As soon as I heard the match had been arranged, I resolved to attend it. I had seen Robinson in four fights, not including television, and knew that he was a very good fighter. I had heard that Maxim, whom I had never seen, was merely pretty good. But there was that fifteen pounds. It was the smaller man who appealed to the public's imagination, and to mine. Goliath would not have been a popular champion even if he had flattened David in the first round. Robinson is such a combination of skill and grace that I had a feeling he could do the trick. For exactly the same reason, the London fancy, back in 1821, made Tom Hickman, the Gas-Light Man, who weighed 165, a strong favourite over Bill Neat, at 189. The Gas-Light Man, according to Egan, was 'a host within himself – his fist possessing the knocking-down force of the forge-hammer – his brow contemptuously smiling at defeat – *to surrender* not within the range of his ideas, even to the extremity of perspective – and VICTORY, proud victory, only operating as a beacon to all his achievements.' Neat was a mere plugger, but he 'turned out the Gas'.

One man who did not share the public's sentimental regard for Robinson was an old-time prizefighter, saloon-keeper, and manufacturer of fire extinguishers named Jack Kearns. This was not surprising, because Kearns, who in more glorious eras managed Jack Dempsey (the Manassa Mauler) and Mickey Walker (the Toy Bulldog) now happens to be the manager of Maxim. Not even Kearns hinted that Maxim was a great champion, but he said he had a kind nature. 'All he lacks is the killer instinct,' Jack maintained. 'But he takes a good punch. When he's knocked down he always gets up.' He once told a group of fight-writers, 'Maxim is as good a fighter as Dempsey, except he can't hit.' Since that was all Dempsey could do, Kearns wasn't handing his new man much.

Kearns is as rutilant a personality as Maxim apparently isn't, and from many of the newspaper stories that appeared in the weeks leading up to the fight one would have thought that Kearns, not Maxim, was signed to fight Robinson. This was an impression Kearns seemed to share when I met him six days before the date set for the fight, in the large, well-refrigerated Broadway restaurant operated by his former associate Dempsey. The old champion and his manager quarrelled spectacularly back in the 1920s, but are now friendly. 'This is my big chance,' Kearns said, buying me a drink and ordering a cup of coffee for himself. He was one of the big speakeasy spenders but says he has been on the wagon for eight years. 'Up to now, I had to stuff myself up and fight heavyweights,' he said. 'Me, the only white guy with a title. But now I got somebody I can bull around.' By this he meant, I gathered, that, in order to obtain what he considered sufficiently remunerative employment in the past for Maxim, he had had to overfeed the poor fellow and spread the rumour that he had grown into a full-sized heavyweight. Then, after fattening him to 180, he had exposed him to the assault of more genuine giants, who had nearly killed him. But now, he implied, Maxim had an opponent he could shove around and control in the clinches. I said I hoped it would be a good fight to watch, and he said, 'I got to be good. I can't afford to lay back. I got to keep moving him, moving him.' As he said this, he picked off imaginary punches – Robinson's hooks, no doubt – with both hands and shoved straight out into space, to show how he would put on the pressure.

Most managers say 'we' will lick So-and-So when they mean their man will try to, but Kearns does not allow his fighter even a share in the pronoun. He is a manager of the old school. His old-school tie, on the day I met him, was Columbia blue covered with sharps and flats in black, green, and cerise. The weaver of his shirt had imprisoned in it the texture as well as the colour of pistachio ice cream. It was a wonder children hadn't eaten it off his back in the street, with the weather the way it was outside. He was wearing a pale grey suit and skewbald shoes, and his eyes, of a confiding baby blue, were so bright that they seemed a part of the ensemble. He has a long, narrow, pink face that widens only at the cheekbones and at the mouth, which is fronted with wide, friendly looking incisors, habitually exposed in an ingenuous smile. The big ears folded back against the sides of his head are not cauliflowered. They are evidence that in his boxing days he was never a catcher. Kearns is slim and active, and could pass for a spry fifty-five if the record books didn't show that he was knocked out by a welterweight champion named Honey Mellody in 1901, when he must have been at least full-grown.

In the course of his boxing career, which was not otherwise distinguished, Kearns had the fortune to meet the two fighters who in my opinion had the best ring names of all time – Honey Mellody and Mysterious Billy Smith. Smith was also a welterweight champion. 'He was always doing something mysterious,' Kearns says. 'Like he would step on your foot, and when you looked down, he would bite you in the ear. If I had a fighter like that now, I could lick heavyweights. But we are living in a bad period all around. The writers are always crabbing about the fighters we got now, but look at the writers you got now themselves. All they think about is home to wife and children, instead of laying around saloons soaking up information.'

He told me in Dempsey's that he played nine holes of golf every day to keep his legs in shape. Since Kearns was obviously in such good condition, I saw no point in taking the three-hour ride to Grossinger's, in the Catskill Mountains, to see Maxim train.

I did go out to look at Robinson next day, however. He was training at Pompton Lakes, New Jersey, which is only an hour's drive from town. I got a free ride in one of the limousines chartered by the International Boxing Club, which was promoting the fight. There were four newspapermen with me, including a fellow named Frank Butler, from the *News of the World,* of London, who had seen both Robinson and Maxim fight in England and said Maxim could bash a bit when he liked. 'He took all Freddie Mills' front teeth out with one uppercut,' he said. 'I rather think he'll do Robinson.'

Any effect Mr Butler's prediction might have had on me was dissipated by the atmosphere of the camp. When we arrived, a crowd had already gathered around George Gainford, Robinson's immense, impressive manager, on the lawn between the sleeping quarters and the press building. It was a mass interview. The topic of discussion was what Robinson was going to do with *two* championships after he whipped Maxim. Since Robinson would indubitably weigh under 175 pounds for the fight, the light heavyweight title would be his if he won. But since Maxim would certainly weigh more than 160, he could not take the middleweight championship, no matter what he did to Robinson. The chairman of the New York State Athletic Commission, someone said to Gainford, had announced that if Robinson won the heavier championship, he would have to abandon the lighter one. It sounded to me like the kind of hypothetical problem harried publicity men so often cook up as fight day approaches. But Gainford, a vast ebony man, broad between the eyes, played it straight. 'The Commission do not make a champion,' he intoned. 'Neither may the Supreme Court name him. The people of the world name him; that is democracy. And if Robinson emerge victorious, he will be champion in both classes until somebody defeat him.'

'How about the welterweight championship?' somebody asked. Robinson was the welterweight champion (147 pounds) until he entered the middleweight class. He was never beaten at that weight.

'I do not want to make that weight,' Gainford said majestically, using the first person singular as if he were Jack Kearns. He must weigh 240.

While Gainford propounded, the fighter and three campmates were sitting around a table, unperturbed by the jostling visitors. They were playing hearts, and all shouting simultaneously that they were being cheated. Robinson put an end to the game by standing up and saying he had better get ready for his workout. He was wearing a green-and-white straw cap and a red-and-white Basque shirt and cinnamon slacks, and he looked as relaxed and confident as a large Siamese tomcat. Sam Taub, the IBC press agent at the camp, led him into the press shack to be interviewed by 'just the bona-fide newspapermen', and he sprawled gracefully on a narrow typewriter shelf, one leg straight out and the other dangling. Robinson is about six feet in length, very tall for a middleweight, and on casual inspection he seems more like a loose-limbed dancer than a boxer. A long, thin neck, the customary complement of long arms and legs, is a disadvantage to a boxer, because a man with his head attached that way doesn't take a good punch. The great layer of muscle on the back of Robinson's neck is the outward indication of his persistence. It is the kind that can be developed only by endless years of exercise – the sort of exercise no shiftless man will stick with.

'Have you ever fought a man that heavy?' a newspaperman asked him.

'Never a *champion* that heavy,' Robinson said, smiling.

'Do you think you can hurt him?' the man asked.

'I can hurt anybody,' the boxer said. 'Can I hurt him enough is the question. I'll be hitting at him, all right.'

'Have you a plan for the battle?' another fellow asked.

'If you have a plan, the other fellow is liable to do just the opposite,' Robinson said.

'How are your legs?' somebody else asked.

'I hope they all right,' Robinson said. 'This would sure be a bad time for them to go wrong.'

The interview broke up and the fighter went along to get into his ring togs. He worked four easy rounds with two partners, who didn't seem to want to irritate him. They sparred outdoors, in a ring on a kind of bandstand under the trees. Around the ring were bleachers, occupied by a couple of hundred spectators – Harlem people and visiting prizefighters and a busload of boys brought out from the city by the Police Athletic League. 'We had 300 paid admissions at a buck here last Sunday,' Taub told me. 'Sugar gave a dinner for sixty-five. "My friends and relatives," he said. They ate fifty-five chickens.'

The newspapermen agreed that tepid sparring was all right, since Sugar Ray was as sharp as a tack already, and this was almost the end of his training. The thing about Robinson that gets you is the way he moves, even when shadow-boxing. He finished off with a good long session of jumping rope, which he enjoys. Most fighters jump rope as children do, but infinitely faster. Robinson just swings a length of rope in his right fist and jumps in time to a fast tune whistled by his trainer. He jumps high in the air, and twists his joined knees at the top of every bound. When he jumps in double time to 'I'm Just Wild About Harry', it's really something to see.

On the way back to town we all said he had never looked better.

The fight itself, as you have probably read, was memorable, but chiefly for meteorological reasons. It was postponed from the night of Monday, 23 June to that of Wednesday, 25 June because of rain. Wednesday was the hottest 25 June in the history of the New York City Weather Bureau. I rode the subway up to the Yankee Stadium, where the fight was to be held, and the men slumped in the seats and hanging to the straps weren't talking excitedly or making jokes, as fight fans generally do. They were just gasping gently, like fish that had been caught two hours earlier. Most of those who had been wearing neckties had removed them, but rings of red and green remained around collars and throats to show the colour of the ties that had been there. Shirts stuck to the folds of bellies, and even the floor was wet with sweat.

My seat was in a mezzanine box on the first-base line, and I felt a mountain climber's exhaustion by the time I had ascended the three gentle inclines that lead to the top of the grandstand, from which I had to descend to my seat. A fellow in a party behind me, trying to cheer his companions, said, 'And you can tell your grandsons about this fight and how hot it was.' The preliminaries were on when I arrived, and two wretched forms were hacking away at each other under the lights that beat down on the ring. I could see the high shine on the wringing-wet bodies, and imagined that each man must be praying to be knocked out as speedily as possible. They were too inept; the bout went the full distance of six rounds, and then both men collapsed in their corners, indifferent to the decision. A miasma of cigarette smoke hung over the 'ringside' seats on the baseball diamond, producing something of the effect you get when you fly over a cloud bank. There was no breeze to dispel it, and the American flags on the four posts at the corners of the ring drooped straight down. It was 104 degrees Fahrenheit in there, we were to learn from the newspapers next morning.

I missed the next two preliminaries because I was up at the top of the stand, waiting in line for a can of beer. The vendors who usually swarm all over the place, obstructing your vision at crucial moments in a fight, had disappeared, on the one night when their presence would have been welcome. So the customers had to queue up – a death march to get to a bar tended by exactly two men. Meanwhile, the fights were invisible, but once one was locked in the line, the thought of giving up one's place unslaked became intolerable. Our line inched along towards a kind of storm-trooper with a head like a pink egg. Rivulets of sweat poured from the watershed of his cranium, and his face appeared behind a spray, like a bronze Triton's in a fountain. At every third customer, he would stop the line and threaten to pack up and call it a day. We would look at him beseechingly, too thirsty even to protest, and after enjoying our humiliation for a while he would consent to sell more beer.

By the time I got back to my seat, Robinson and Maxim were in the ring and the announcer was proceeding with the usual tiresome introductions of somebodies who were going to fight somebody elses somewhere. Each boy, after being introduced, would walk over and touch the gloved right paw of each principal. The last one in was old Jersey Joe Walcott, the heavyweight champion, and the crowd evidenced torpid goodwill. I could see the vast Gainford in Robinson's corner, over towards third base, and, with the aid of binoculars, could discern that his face still wore the portentous, noncommittal expression of a turbaned bishop in a store-front church. Kearns had his back to me, but I could tell him by his ears. He was clad in a white T-shirt with 'Joey Maxim' in dark letters on the back, and he seemed brisker than anybody else in the ring. Maxim had his back to me, too. When he stood up, I could see how much thicker and broader through the chest he was than Robinson. His skin was a reddish bronze; Sugar Ray's was mocha chocolate.

Fighting middleweights, Robinson had always had a superiority over his foes in height and reach, together with equality in weight. Against Maxim he had equality in height and reach but the weight was all against him. His was announced as 157.5 and Maxim's as 173. The first ten rounds of the fight weren't much to watch. Maxim would keep walking in and poking a straight left at Robinson's face. Robinson would either take or slip it, according to his fortune, belt Maxim a couple of punches, and grab his arms. Then they would contend, with varying success, in close. Some of the fans would cry that Robinson wasn't hurting Maxim at all in these interludes, others that Maxim wasn't hurting Robinson at all. There seemed to be some correlation between their eyesight and where they had placed their money. Because of the nature of the combat, most of the work fell upon the referee, Ruby Goldstein, a former welterweight then in his forties, who had to pull the men apart. In consequence, he was the first of the three to collapse; he had to leave the ring after the tenth round. I have never seen this happen in a prizefight before. Old-time photographs show referees on their feet at the end of twenty-five-round fights, and wearing waistcoats and stiff collars. It is a bad period all around.

Robinson had been hitting Maxim much more frequently than Maxim had been hitting him but neither man seemed hurt, and both were slowing down from a pace that had never been brisk. Now the relief referee Ray Miller, a snub-nosed little man with reddish hair, entered the ring, bringing with him more bounce than either of the contestants possessed. He must have been sitting on dry ice. Miller, also an old fighter, enjoined the fighters to get going. The crowd had begun clapping and stamping, midway in the fight, to manifest its boredom. Miller broke clinches so expeditiously in the eleventh and twelfth that the pace increased slightly, to the neighbourhood of a fast creep. Up to then, it had been even worse than the first ten rounds of the previous year's fight between Sugar Ray and Randy Turpin, the milling cove. But that fight had ended in one wildly exciting round that made the fancy forget how dull the prelude had been.

This fight was to produce excitement, too, but of a fantastically different kind. In the eleventh round, Robinson hit Maxim precisely the same kind of looping right to the jaw that had started Turpin on the way out. The blow knocked the light heavy clear across the ring, but he didn't fall, and Robinson's legs, those miracles, apparently couldn't move Ray fast enough to take advantage of the situation. It may have been as good a punch as the one of the year before, but it landed on a man fifteen pounds heavier. Maxim shook his head and went right on fighting, in his somnambulistic way. Now all Sugar Ray had to do was finish the fight on his feet and he would win on points. But when he came out for the thirteenth, he walked as if he had the gout in both feet and dreaded putting them down. When he punched, which was infrequently, he was as late, and as wild, as an amateur, and when he wasn't punching, his arms hung at his sides. He had, quite simply, collapsed from exhaustion, like a marathon runner on a hot day. Maxim – at first, apparently, unable to believe his good fortune – began, after a period of ratiocination, to hit after him. He landed one or two fairly good shots, I thought from where I sat. Kearns must have been yelling to Maxim.

And then Robinson, the almost flawless boxer, the epitome of ring grace, swung, wildly and from far back of his shoulder, like a child, missed his man completely, and fell hard on his face. When he got up, Maxim backed him against the ropes and hit him a couple of times. The round ended, and Robinson's seconds half dragged, half carried him to his corner. He couldn't get off the stool at the end of the one-minute interval, and Maxim was declared the winner by a knockout in the fourteenth, because the bell had rung for the beginning of that round.

Sugar Ray, according to the press, was pretty well cut up over his defeat, and in his dressing-room, after enough water had been sloshed on him to bring him to, he raved that divine intervention had prevented his victory. This refusal to accept the event is also an old story in the ring, but in the words of John Bee, a rival of Egan, it is 'a species of feeling which soon wears out, and dies away, like weak astonishment at a nine days' wonder'. On the day after the fight many of the sportswriters took the line that Robinson had been beaten by the heat alone, and some of them even sentimentally averred that he had been making one of the most brilliant fights of his life right up to the moment when his legs gave out. They tried to reconcile this with their assertions that Maxim was a hopelessly bad fighter and had made a miserable showing until his unbelievable stroke of luck. It would have required no brilliance on anyone's part to outpoint the Maxim they described. But Goliath never would have been popular anyway.

The heat was the same for both men. This much is sure, though: whenever a man weighing 157 has to pull and haul against a man weighing 173, he has to handle sixteen pounds more than his own weight. The other fellow has to handle sixteen pounds less than his. And when you multiply this by the number of seconds the men struggle during thirty-nine minutes of a bout like this, you get a pretty good idea of why they weigh prizefighters. The multiplication is more than arithmetical, of course; a man who boxes four rounds is more than four times as tired as if he had boxed one. I had no idea, from watching the fight, whether Maxim was pacing himself slowly, like Conn McCreary, the jockey who likes to come from behind, or whether he just couldn't get going any faster, like even Arcaro when his horse won't run. But I talked to Kearns a couple of days after the fight, and he left no doubt in my mind about what he wanted me to believe had happened. The nine holes of golf a day, he said, had kept him personally in such condition that he could exercise all the natural alacrity of his perceptions during the conflict. 'The heat talk is an alibi and an excuse,' he said. 'Robinson was nailed good in the belly in the tenth round, and again in the twelfth, and he got a left hook and a right to the head at the end of the thirteenth, when he was on the ropes. If the bell hadn't a rang, he'd be dead. I didn't move Maxim until the twelfth round. I didn't have to. I knew I could win in any round when I got ready. The only reason I shoved Maxim in at all was because I wanted to win with a one-punch knockout. Robinson escaped by luck.'

I paused to commit this to memory, and then asked Dr Kearns, who seemed in high good humour, to what he attributed his victory. 'Oh, I don't know,' he said modestly. 'Anybody who was around those old-time fights we used to have in the hot sun on the fourth of July knew you had to rate any athlete according to what the heat was. Robinson figured he had any one of fifteen rounds in which to win. He was going to try for a knockout in every round he fought. But I just told Maxim, "Just keep this fellow moving, moving. Then he'll have to clinch and hang on." After that, it just depended how quick I decided to move Maxim. It was up to me to pick the round. Next time I'll knock him out quicker.'

'And who do you want next?' I inquired.

'I'd like that Walcott or Marciano,' Dr Kearns replied bravely. 'I'll fight anybody in the world.'

Since then Robinson has come back, at least as far as being middleweight champion again. After the Maxim fight he retired, and a fellow named Bobo Olson won the title after an elimination tournament among the inept leftovers. Robinson returned to the ring and stopped Mr Olson in two rounds at Chicago, which was nice going, and the Cadillacs are back at his door. One fight writer, reporting the victory, said Olson was a 'burned-out hollow shell', which is like merging Pelion and Ossa, or Ford and General Motors, in the cliché business. He must have meant the shell of a broiled lobster after a shore dinner.

Maxim lost his title to a great man, named Archie Moore, but Dr Kearns did not say after the bout, 'Moore licked me.' He said, 'Moore licked Maxim.'

ROUND 14
The Rumble of Dissent

While the brouhaha and acrimony surrounding the Leonard–Hagler fight still reverberates like the insistent clanging of the ringside bell, it is interesting to note that even the experts cannot agree as to the justice or otherwise of the final decision.

Of the many correspondents present on that night, two of the most prominent publicly disagree. On the one hand, US sportswriter George Kimball maintains that Leonard won the decision fair and square. In the opposite corner, no less a figure than Scotland's Hugh McIlvanney profoundly disagrees.

Leonard–Hagler: The Fight and Its Aftermath

George Kimball

For an event that continues to weigh so heavily on the national consciousness (survey the contents of any saloon in America and you're more likely to find a consensus about the Vietnam War than over who really won history's biggest prizefight on 6 April 1987), it seems odd that the more vivid vestigial images took place outside the ring.

More than any one punch thrown over the course of forty-eight minutes, for instance, there is the recollection of the round-card girl during one of the preliminary fights – this one between Lupe Aquino and Davey Moore – climbing under the ring ropes only to have her left breast flop fully out of her skimpy dress top. The spontaneous ovation greeting that exposure was overshadowed a round later by the chorus of boos with which the Caesars Palace crowd pelted the ring when one of her colleagues climbed into the ring a round later and her boobs did not fall out.

A spirited exchange between promoter Bob Arum and his arch-rival Don King that took place shortly after the final bell is also indelibly etched in memory, more so than any single minute of fighting that took place in the preceding twelve rounds. This one took place right in front of me at ringside: King, correctly anticipating that Ray Charles Leonard was about to be named the winner, thereby casting the middleweight title on to the open market for the first time in a decade, began to climb into the ring to join the celebration. Arum, the smaller by far and apparently unmindful of King's track record in *mano a mano* fights (King's enthusiasm in winning one of these bought him a stretch for manslaughter) leapt on to his back, initiating a wrestling match in which he ripped one of the pockets from King's expensive jacket. This one was ultimately quelled in Arum's favour by a large Caesars security guard, who escorted King from the ring as the latter addressed him as 'a lousy black motherfucker.'

And, much later that evening, as Marvin Hagler slowly made his way through the deserted and litter-strewn lot beside the Caesars tennis courts that had served as a makeshift stadium, there was the image of Hagler coming across two vendors loading a truck with unconsumed Budweiser. The Hollywood glitterati and Vegas high-rollers had long since departed in celebratory swarms in the direction of the casino tables when Hagler stopped and asked 'Hey, how 'bout a six-pack?'

One of the concessionaires looked up and recognised him. 'You're the champ, Marvin,' he grinned and handed over two cases of beer. Hagler took them back to his room. No one would be surprised if he drank them all that night.

But the fight itself? Sure, you remember the southpaw champion opening up with an orthodox, right-handed attack, and stubbornly pursuing this course of action long after its ineffectiveness had become apparent. You remember the final round and Leonard calling to his corner 'How much time?', and when he was told 'One minute!' Ray raised his glove in celebratory triumph as he danced away, secure in the knowledge that at least on this night Marvin Hagler wasn't going to get him. And a snarling, huffing Hagler, realising the same thing, mockingly hoisted his own glove aloft as he vainly chased Leonard through the final seconds.

You think you remember Goody Petronelli in the corner, repeatedly dispatching advice to Hagler: 'Rough him up inside!' But it dawns on you later that you couldn't possibly have heard that at ringside; Hagler's corner was clear across the ring, so the memory is a faulty one, inspired instead from the countless viewings of the fight on videotape. The image is no less valid, though: the tone of the voice clearly implies 'Keep roughing him up inside,' although Leonard did not have a mark on him.

That night at ringside it was similarly difficult to discern what Leonard retrospectively labelled the turning-point of the fight. When Hagler finally turned nasty in the fifth round he might have turned the tide himself: in his round-by-round for the Associated Press, Fast Eddie Schuyler summarised the concluding moments: 'Hagler got in a left to the head, then a hook to the body. Hagler landed a short left to the face. Leonard landed a left to the face. Hagler got in a good left to the head in Leonard's corner. Hagler got a good right and left to the head with 30 seconds left. They were fighting the range. Hagler had Leonard against the ropes. Hagler landed a right at the bell.' My own equally cryptic version of the round's conclusion did note that 'as the bell sounded ending that round Leonard woozily eyed Hagler and then stumbled – no, staggered – back to his stool.'

It was months later that Ray Leonard recapitulated the moment. 'I was definitely in trouble. I thought I was gone. But then I looked Marvin in the eye and I realised "He doesn't even know I'm hurt. He doesn't know it!" I knew then I had him.'

The odd part of this is that Leonard had won the first four rounds on the score cards of two judges (as well as my own), yet it was the first round he decisively lost that he continues to regard as pivotal. My own hastily composed description of what happened that night read: 'Any delusions that the corner had been turned were quickly laid to rest the next round. As Hagler pressed the attack, Leonard was a veritable will o' the wisp, dancing about as Hagler's mighty blows flew harmlessly all around him, pausing long enough to land an effective flurry of his own just before the bell.

'Although Hagler came back to win the next three rounds – win them everywhere, in any case, but on the score card of Mexican judge Jo Jo Guerra, who wound up scoring the bout a lopsided 118–110 in Leonard's favour – he was clearly in for a fight; just when Leonard was looking shaky at the end of the ninth, he rallied and stood toe to toe with Hagler as the bell rang. There would be more of these confrontations in the fight's final stages. Leonard was landing more punches, but seemingly getting the worse of the exchanges. (As Hagler moved in for one bit of infighting, Leonard's trainer Angelo Dundee was shouting "Watch that bald-headed sucker's head!" to referee Richard Steele.)'

If the evening's events for the most part remain a blur, the nebulous spectre of Leonard playing the master toreador to Hagler's raging bull continue to dominate. Pick almost any round and it is the same: Ray landing more punches, albeit ones of dubious usefulness, Hagler missing but eliciting more pain when he did manage to land.

The debate rages over who won the fight. Two judges, Lou Filippo and Dave Moretti, saw it 115–113, but had different winners.

Guerra, who will probably never score a major fight again, gave Leonard all but two rounds. Having covered all of Hagler's title fights dating back to that rainy night in London when he won the championship from Alan Minter, I went into this bout plainly disposed towards the champion, but scored the fight 116–114 (six-four-two) in Leonard's favour. A subsequent viewing of the tape caused me to alter one of the even rounds, and I scored it seven-four-one, Leonard, the second time around.

Clearly, there is room for philosophical argument on both sides: Leonard's punches never did any real damage, other than to pile up points, while Hagler's were clearly more lethal – when they managed to connect. In terms of 'Clean Punches' the fight was no better than a wash. 'Aggression?' Hagler was obviously the aggressor for most of the night; but the operative word in this category is supposed to be effective aggression. And it seemed to me that Leonard's mastery of another category of supposedly equal importance, 'Defence', was at least sufficient to offset any supposed edge Hagler might have built up here.

With the first three criteria more or less a push, then, it seemed and seems to me that in the fourth – 'Ring Generalship' – there was a clearcut dominance on the part of Leonard. It was Leonard who dictated the terms under which this battle was waged. It was Ray who was able to lead Marvin around by the nose, forcing him to fight Leonard's fight rather than his own. Leonard did what he wanted to do and denied Hagler what he wanted to do for the better part of the evening.

There are persuasive arguments to be made in the other direction, none more eloquent than the case Hugh McIlvanney, the Boxing Bard of Scotland, made in a *Sports Illustrated* retrospective a few weeks later. But not even Marvin Hagler was arguing that he had dominated the fight. At least not that night he wasn't. Even after claiming that the fight had been 'stolen' from him, Hagler privately offered that he thought the fight should have been a split decision, only in his favour.

'A split decision should go to the champion,' he complained. 'I've never seen a split decision go to the other guy . . . He should have had to beat me more decisively. He never knocked me down. It was the same as the first Antuofermo fight [which, with Hagler the challenger, ended in a draw]. It's the second tie in my life. That's Las

Vegas – a gambling town. I've done a lot for boxing and I wish they didn't take it away like that.' As Hagler headed off in search of the six-pack that would grow to eight of them before he reached his room, his wife Bertha murmured 'He was afraid this was going to happen. And I know he's mad right now. Mad and hurt.'

Gracious in defeat, Leonard proclaimed in the ring that Hagler 'is still a champion to me'. Hagler would later take this to claim that Leonard believed he had lost the fight. The name-calling had only just begun.

'He called me a sissy,' reported Leonard.

'He fought like a girl,' claimed Marvin.

Although each fighter had insisted for months beforehand that this fight would be his last, the controversy seemed to cry out for a rematch. In his post-fight commentary, Hagler had even suggested that the decision had been a means of forcing one: 'I believe the boxing world wants me back, and the only way they can keep me here is with a rematch,' he complained somewhat illogically.

But despite a year of talking, a rematch seems further away than ever. The seeds of discontent that were sown that night had already begun to sprout the next morning. 'I'm not taking anything away from Ray Leonard,' said Pat Petronelli the next morning, 'but this guy Jo Jo Guerra is a disgrace. He ought to be put in jail. Ask Leonard if *he* thought Marvin Hagler only won two rounds.'

The perfect irony of this response was that Guerra had not been included on the initially proposed slate of ringside officials for the big fight. The original panel – comprised of Moretti, Filippo, and Great Britain's Harry Gibbs, along with that of referee Steele – had been submitted to representatives of both fighters beforehand by the WBC. The Petronellis had objected to Gibbs.

Despite 'philosophical' differences they would later voice, the reason for the prejudice was plain and simple: Gibbs was an Englishman. And the memory of the night seven years earlier when Hagler had stopped Alan Minter in London's Wembley Arena to capture the middleweight title, only to be driven from the ring by a fusillade of beer cans at the moment he should have been awarded the championship belt, was one that had never left them. For Pat and Goody Petronelli, if not for Marvin Hagler himself, it was reason enough to hate a whole country.

So they hemmed and hawed for a while about the supposed inclination of British fight officials to penalise infighting and then made their peremptory challenge to Gibbs. Then, at the pre-fight rules meeting, they went one further. 'We want a Mexican judge,' they demanded. So they got one. Harry Gibbs flew home to England and didn't even watch the fight. Two weeks later he got the chance to see it on British television tape-delay. He scored the fight eight-four-one for Hagler.

The complaints about Guerra's scoring hardly precipitated the bitter post-fight breach, though. Even Angelo Dundee was able to shrug the next day and admit that 'unfortunately, one of the judges wasn't with us last night.' But then, just ten days later, a Boston television sportscaster went on the air with an uncorroborated rumour that an investigation was underway in Nevada following reports that an unidentified gambler who had bet a massive amount on Leonard had improperly influenced one of the judges to swing the fight to the challenger.

As it turned out, an investigation was not underway, but following the widespread circulation of John Dennis's story, Nevada officials were forced to initiate one. In order to avoid potential conflict of interest charges, Nevada commissioner Duane Ford turned the matter over to a special investigator representing the state attorney general's department.

It did not require the services of Sherlock Holmes to discern that the gambler in question was sometime fight manager Billy Baxter, and that the judge whose ethics had been called into question was not Guerra, but Moretti. After an investigation lasting several months both men were completely exonerated.

Neither Leonard nor his handlers ever accused the Hagler camp of complicity in the bogus 'fix' story, but it scarcely helped to smooth things over. Dennis had in the past been close to Hagler and the Petronellis, who were not above using him as a conduit when they wanted to leak a story – and the mere fact that they took no steps to refute or deny it only exacerbated matters. Others suspected that the 'fix' story might have been initiated by Arum himself since, had sufficient evidence been found to warrant the mandating of a rematch, Arum would have got that fight, too. The promoter vociferously denied any role in the proceedings.

'What gets me,' complained Leonard's attorney and manager Mike Trainer, 'is that Ray never uttered a peep after he lost the first fight to Duran, one that in our minds was equally disputable. All this belly-aching, all this complaining, all these excuses, it's made Ray very disappointed in Marvin. He hasn't been a very good sport about the whole thing.'

Indeed, even as Hagler continued to grouse about a rematch, another Leonard confidant suggested that had Hagler come out of the ring and simply said 'Well, I thought I won, but I guess the judges saw it differently. Let's do it again,' Ray might have said 'Sure.' As it was, everything Hagler and his people did over the next several months only soured Ray on the idea of fighting again. Or at least fighting Marvin again. But this whole sour grapes attitude they've had since the moment they stepped out of the ring is not going to have its desired effect, I can tell you that. 'If they really wanted to fight Ray again, the last things they should have been doing is running around telling people they got robbed and the fight was fixed and all that bullshit like that.'

At a packed press conference in Washington six weeks later, Leonard announced his retirement. 'Why should we believe you this time?' he was asked. 'You're retired now, but will you ever fight again?'

'No,' he insisted, just before adding with a twinkle, 'but you guys know me!'

By late June Hagler was back in the news, this time as the recipient of a court order obtained by his wife Bertha, who had charged him with, among other things, assault. Newspapers – particularly those in London, where I happened to be at the time – were quick to label him a wife-beater. Only later did it develop that the 'assault' in question consisted of Marvin throwing rocks at his wife's car, his way of expressing his disapproval over the fact that she had returned to the family home at something like three in the morning.

It was a painful episode for Marvin Hagler who valued his relationship with his children above all else. Suddenly he found himself visiting them only at the pleasure of the court. Taking up a reclusive residency in downtown Boston, he only rarely ventured out. His only public sightings became late-night visits to the discos and nightclubs of Boston, while his attorneys attempted to smooth things out with his wife, who had by now retained Marvin Mitchelson.

There was certainly no indication that he ever intended to fight again, although Arum, with the likely connivance of the Petronellis, managed to tease Thomas Hearns and his manager Emanuel Steward.

Hagler emerged from his shell in order to serve as television commentator for the broadcasts of the very fights that divided up his old domain – or at least the two of them that Arum was promoting. He was in Italy with ESPN to watch Sumbu Kalambay outpoint Iran Barkley for the WBA version of the middleweight title last October. In the same country five years earlier Kalambay had played a supporting role in one of Hagler's defences, struggling to beat Marvin's then sparring partner Buster Drayton on the undercard of Hagler's second knockout of Fulgencio Obelmejias in San Remo.

From there Hagler flew straight to Vegas to watch Hearns annex the WBC crown by knocking out Juan Roldan. Hagler had to sit at ringside and deliver the closed-circuit commentary on a 'title' fight whose participants consisted of two men he himself had already knocked out. Leonard was also present.

Much later that night the two chanced to land in the men's room of a Las Vegas meat market-cum-disco called Botany's at precisely the same moment. Leonard made one last stab at offering the olive branch.

'Some fight, huh?' he chirped to Hagler as he sidled up alongside him at the urinal. In response he got an icy stare of silence.

As Hagler started away Leonard accosted him. 'Hey, I'm not here to make friends,' spat Leonard. The two have not spoken since.

Months later, very possibly as his resentment grew, Leonard's interest began to revive. In January he allowed that he 'wouldn't consider fighting again unless Marvin sat down and talked with me first,' which seemed to open the door.

'I wish I could tell you I can read him all the time, but I can't,' admitted Trainer. 'Sometimes I don't know what he's thinking. Sometimes I'm not sure he does himself. But I do know that he's wanted to sit down with Marvin one-on-one for a long time. I'm sure that every time he sits down to watch a big fight, the juices start flowing and he gets to thinking about fighting again. But if you get him to sit down for a beer a few hours later when he's thinking about the commitment that entails, I'm not sure he's ready to do that.'

With no response from Hagler, Leonard turned up the volume a few weeks later. In an interview with a Washington television station he said 'If Marvin wants to fight me he has to come to me and talk about it first.' The week after that, while guesting on the syndicated *Oprah Winfrey Show,* he took off the gloves for real: 'Hagler never gave me credit,' groused Leonard. 'I beat him fair and square. He made allegations that some of the officials in Nevada were corrupt and what have you. I think it's unprofessional, and I want to beat him up.'

This managed to wake Marvin up, even though Hagler seemed uneager to agree to a rematch with no title at stake. 'Let him go get another belt first,' the former champion huffed in response. 'If he really wanted to fight again, why did he give up the title?'

Leonard's latest stance is that 'all Marvin has to do is call me up.'

'If I ever do call him,' says Hagler, 'it'll be collect.'

Which is where the rift stands today. It seems tragic in several respects. Hagler is left surrounded by shattered dreams, while Leonard seems genuinely wounded by the dissolution of what he had once considered a warm friendship – even though Hagler insists 'we were never really friends.' Maybe so, but they were and are both friends of mine, to the extent that before they fought I had publicly gone on record urging each of them to retire – Ray out of consideration for his eyesight, and Marvin after the John Mugabi fight had unmasked the very erosion of skills that Leonard would exploit a year later. And if I didn't think they should fight the first time, I can hardly countenance a rematch; even if it were something both wanted.

Meanwhile, the alternative seems to be listening to them call each other names for a few more years. I don't much look forward to that either.

How Hagler Won that Fight

Hugh McIlvanney

Over here in the owning-up corner, it seems right to start with two basic statements: (1) What Sugar Ray Leonard did after his long, eroding absence from boxing was almost miraculous. (2) What he couldn't quite do was beat Marvin Hagler. Such a rejection of the official result, coming from someone who so hugely underestimated Leonard's capacity to warp time with the obsessive strength of his will, may strike many as an example of how judgement can be embittered and distorted by chewing on too many sour grapes.

All I can say is that I am ready to take my lumps for refusing to believe that a welterweight who had fought only nine memorably unimpressive rounds in five years which also included surgery for a detached retina could give sustained and serious trouble to as true a middleweight champion as Hagler, even a Hagler noticeably in decline. Put in a comparable predicament tomorrow, I am afraid I'd just have to go the same route and risk walking into logic's booby-trap again.

But who could be soured by the sight of a great spirit so boldly challenging every lesson handed down by the history of the fight game? The embarrassment of a bad call means little alongside such excitement. Ray Leonard was a marvel in Las Vegas last Monday night and the large body of us who were astonished by how much of his old impudent brilliance he was able to resurrect could surely take nothing but pleasure from his achievement. Yet it is true that for me and many others the final effect of Sugar Ray's unforgettably spectacular return to boxing was tinged with profound sadness created when an outstanding and honourable performer is subjected to the kind of injustice that will haunt him for the rest of his days.

There can be no doubt that the irrational scoring which deprived Hagler of the world middleweight championship he had held since beating Alan Minter in London in 1980, and inflicted on him his first defeat in more than eleven years, will darken his future to that extent. When Leonard approached him in the turmoil of immediate reactions to the verdict and said, 'Marvin, I hope we're still friends,' the subdued pain and utter simplicity of the response were indelibly moving.

'It's unfair, man, it's unfair,' said Hagler and as he went on to repeat the same low-key, almost gentle complaint his eyes filled with a dejection deeper than sport should bring. Those who point out that he has earnings of perhaps $15 million to case his hurt are entitled to their jibe, but if they believe even that pile of money will allow Hagler to make light of his sense of being abused they don't know the man.

With some justification, he is convinced that he, unlike Leonard, has never been truly fortune's child. Even when removal to New England and a career in boxing lifted him far above the grimness of his early years in a Newark (New Jersey) ghetto ravaged by race riots, he found the world unwilling to grant him an easy passage.

He was made to endure a frustrating wait for his chance to win the world championship, then a much longer wait for the opportunity to collect a share of the monster purses prevalent in the modern game. And although he contrived to turn his identification as a blue-collar fighter into a source of self-contained strength (making a habit to this day of carrying his own bag to training and keeping his entourage to a tiny group of close and relevant allies) he was bound to resent the Rolls-Royce glide to riches enjoyed by Leonard, who moved straight from Olympic gold medallist to highly paid television hero while Hagler, already a veteran, was still hustling for modest pay in the hard rings of north-eastern towns like Philadelphia, Providence and Hartford.

All of that resentment flooded back in the open-air arena behind Caesars Palace Hotel as he listened to the announcement of scores which once again confirmed that the genuinely considerable but sometimes undramatic qualities he brings to his trade are always in danger of being undervalued when he is compared with opponents whose talents are more theatrical if essentially less effective. That is exactly, and regrettably, what happened on Monday night.

In the case of the score card presented by José Juan (Jo Jo) Guerra, the Mexican judge who made Leonard a winner by 118–110 or ten rounds to two, Hagler was so outrageously wronged that professional boxing's claims that it can measure performances in the ring with something approaching consistent accuracy and fairness were made to appear laughable. If the relative effectiveness of two competing fighters is so difficult to calibrate, or so open to blindly subjective interpretations, that Guerra could score as he did while his fellow judge, Lou Filippo from Los Angeles, made Hagler the winner by seven rounds to five, what we are dealing with is simply not a legitimate form of contest.

Leonard was given a split decision because the third judge involved, Dave Moretti of Nevada, scored the fight seven rounds to five (115–113) in his favour. If Moretti had awarded Leonard one round fewer, and Hagler one more, the result would have been a draw and the champion would have kept his title.

Ray Leonard's real accomplishment lay in pulling off an epic con-trick, one that was a testament to the mischievous richness of his intelligence and the flawlessness of his nerve. The natural priority of most fighters is to seek to dominate their opponents but throughout the thirty-six minutes of this match Leonard was far less concerned with impressing Hagler than with manipulating the minds of the judges.

His plan was to catch their attention with isolated but carefully timed flurries of flashy punches, relying on these superficially dramatic though rarely telling flourishes to blur the officials' appreciation of how much time he was spending in retreat (and occasionally headlong flight) from the relentlessly chasing Hagler. Enough hand speed and mastery of deceptive lateral movement had survived from those days when he was one of the greatest welterweights the game has known to enable him to apply that policy of 'stealing' rounds early in the fight.

But Hagler, characteristically, refused to be discouraged and once he had abandoned a foolish initial commitment to leading with his left hand and was moving in behind the right jab he began to make Leonard less and less comfortable in the role of grand illusionist. Scoring at ringside, I could not make Hagler come out any worse than a winner by seven rounds to five and that view hardened to a firm conviction after a couple of hours closeted alone with the film of the fight in the New York studios of HBO Television last Thursday.

A long and tough career has aged him beyond the thirty-two years shown on his birth certificate, and he is unquestionably a fading talent. Hands that were never the most explosively quick in boxing are now frequently almost ponderous and his aggression does not generate the devouring intensity of old. But he did press through Leonard's elaborate ruses persistently enough to register a conspicuously greater volume of *worthwhile* blows, especially to the body.

There would have been nothing unjust about giving him two of the first six rounds, since he took the fifth in a big way and was in such close contention for the third and fourth that either might have been scored for him. And if Leonard, who admits to being fatigued halfway through and 'exhausted' before the end, won a single round out of the last six that was surely his maximum. So how could Hagler lose?

The answer is straightforward. Two of the judges, like most of the crowd, were so amazed by Sugar Ray Leonard's capabilities last Monday night that they imagined they saw him do much more than he actually did. Conversely, having expected extreme destructiveness from Hagler, they declined to give him credit for the quiet beating he administered. It was all unnecessarily cruel on the loser, considering that Leonard could have felt triumphant without the gift of the decision.

Already there have been serious discussions about a rematch. No doubt Marvin Hagler is prepared to give the Fates of the fight game another chance to treat him fairly. That certainly won't involve letting Jo Jo Guerra in on the act.

ROUND 15
'Bright Lights, Fat City'

For a world heavyweight champion to attract lots of media attention is only what you might expect. Like the beautiful women, the flashy cars and all the other trappings of success, it goes with the territory.

Recently, however, Mike Tyson has all but disappeared under a welter of bad press. An unprecedented deluge of press hysteria threatens to obscure the fact that, after all, his main business is conducted in the ring. Can he weather the storm? Can any young man cope with a series of misfortunes, misjudgements and downright hostility to his every move; or are we witnessing yet another classic case of too much too soon?

Yet assuming that the trouble does blow over and that Iron Mike can resume his destructive career, one other more important question remains. Is Mike Tyson a great champion, or merely a terrifying one? Does he have real heart or is he currently just the toughest kid on the block? In this chapter, Tom Callahan takes an in-depth look at the phenomenon that is Michael Gerald Tyson.

Iron Mike and the Allure of the 'Manly Art'

Tom Callahan

An explanation for boxing, at least an excuse, has never been harder to summon or easier to see than it is now, simmering in the eyes of Mike Tyson. Muhammad Ali's face, when his was the face of boxing, at least had a note of humour, a hint of remorse, even the possibility of compassion, though he gave no guarantees. Tyson does: brutal, bitter ones.

The usual case for boxing as art or science is rougher to make in the face of this face. Valour can be redeeming; so can grace, poise, bearing, even cunning. But this is a nightmare. The monster that men have worried was at the heart of their indefinable passion, of their indefensible sport, has come out in the flesh to be the champion of the world. Next Monday night, be will he served Michael Spinks.

Perhaps it is anachronistic to mention only men. Maybe boxing is an anachronism: the manly art of self-defence. Take it like a man. Be a man. In Archibald MacLeish's play *J.B.*, Job told the Comforter, 'I can bear anything a man can bear – if I can be one.' But nobody talks about being a man any more. When it comes to blood lust, female gills pant up and down too. In the matter of boxing's fascination for writers, gender has certainly not been disqualifying. Still, the suspicion persists that males secrete some kind of archetypal fluid that makes it easier for them to understand what's at work here.

As a fictional character, Tyson would be an offence to everyone, a stereotype wrung out past infinity to obscenity. He is the black Brooklyn street thug from reform school, adopted by the white benevolent old character from the country who could only imagine the terrible violence done to the boy from the terrible violence the boy can do to others. 'I'll break Spinks,' Tyson says. 'None of them has a chance. I'll break them all.' Other sports trade on mayhem, but boxing is condemned for just this: intent.

It is not a sport to Tyson. 'I don't like sports; they're social events.,' he says, though he holds individual athletes in casual esteem. The basketball star Michael Jordan, for one ('Anyone who can fly deserves respect'), or the baseball and football player Bo Jackson. Tyson says of Jackson, 'I love that he's able to do both, but I heard him say that he doesn't like the pain of football. That makes me wonder about him. Football is a hurting business.'

If objections to a blood sport were simply medical and not moral, the outsize linemen who blindside diminutive quarterbacks would inspire grim alarms from the American Medical Association instead of cheery press-box bulletins about 'mild concussions'. The fact of boxing, not the fate of boxers, bothers people. Naturally, the pugilistic brain syndrome of Ali is saddening. And when Gaetan Hart and Cleveland Denny were breaking the ice for the first match of Leonard–Duran, it was regrettable that nearly no one at ringside so much as bothered to look up or today can even very easily recollect which one of them died. Regrettable, but not precisely regretted.

Only the most expendable men are boxers. All of the fighters who ever died – nearly 500 since 1918, when the Ring book started to keep tabs – haven't the political constituency of a solitary suburban child who falls off a trampoline. Observers who draw near enough to fights and fighters to think that they see something of value, something pure and honest, are sure to mention the desperate background and paradoxical gentleness, which even Tyson has in some supply. 'I guess it's pretty cool,' he says, to be the natural heir to John L. Sullivan, to hold an office of such immense stature and myth, to he able to drum a knuckle on the countertop and lick any man in the house. 'If you say so.'

Beyond the power and slam, the appeal of boxing may just be its simplicity. It is so basic and bare. In a square ring or vicious circle, stripped to the waist and bone, punchers and boxers counteract. Tyson is already the first, and potentially the second, so the eternal match-up of gore and guile doesn't just occupy him outwardly, it swirls inside him as well. Modern movie-makers are good at capturing the choreography of fights – they understand the Apache dance. But in their Dolby deafness they overdo the supersonic bashing and skip one of the crucial attractions: the missing. Making a man miss is the art. Fundamentally, boxers are elusive. They vanish one moment, reappear the next, rolling around the ring like the smoke in the light.

If the allure of boxing is hazy, the awe of the champion is clear. Regional vain-glories like the World Cup or the World Series only aspire to the global importance of the heavyweight champion. Sullivan, Jack Dempsey, Joe Louis and Ali truly possessed the world – countries that couldn't have picked Jimmy Carter out of a line-up recognised Ali at a distance – to the extent that, in a recurring delusion, the world had trouble picturing boxing beyond him. When Dempsey went, he was taking boxing with him. If Louis surrendered, the game would be up. Without Ali, it was dead. Wiser heads, usually balanced like towels on the shoulders of old trainers, always smiled and said, 'Someone will come along.' Tyson's place in the line is undetermined, but he is certainly the one who came along.

In what is now a two-barge industry, Spinks will also have something to say about lineage. The fight is in Atlantic City instead of Las Vegas, which might be called the ageing champion of fight towns if the challenger were not so decrepit. Atlantic City forces its smiles through neon casinos that, like gold crowns, only emphasise the surrounding decay. Similarly, Tyson is the younger party involved, but it hardly seems so. The boardwalk age guessers would be lucky to pick his century. He is twenty-one.

All over Tyson's walls at the Ocean Club Hotel are the old sepia photographs out of which he has stepped, going back to Mike Donovan, Jack Blackburn and Joe Jeannette, who in 1909 fought a forty-nine-rounder that featured thirty-eight knockdowns. Louis, Rocky Marciano and Ali are there, but Jack Johnson, Jim Jeffries and Stanley Ketchel are more prominent. (John Lardner told Ketchel's 1910 fate in a pretty good sentence: 'Stanley Ketchel was twenty-four years old when he was fatally shot in the back by the common law husband of the lady who was cooking his breakfast.') The repeaters in Tyson's gallery are Joe Gans and Battling Nelson. In a seventy-nine-year-old picture, Nelson is posing after a knockout with his gloves balanced defiantly on his hips. Tyson struck that same attitude five months ago over the horizontal remains of Larry Holmes.

'I like them all,' says the curator from Brownsville and Bedford-Stuyvesant, completing his tour, 'but Nelson and Gans are special. Both of them great fighters [lightweights] and fellow opponents near their peak at the same time. That's always special.'

In this at least, Michael Spinks can concur. Though ten years older than Tyson, he has managed to register three fewer professional bouts – thirty-one to thirty-four – and only four of those against heavyweights. All told, the two men share sixty-five victories and uneven parts of the mystical championship. While Tyson owns the various belts, Floyd Patterson says, 'Spinks has the real title, my old title, the one handed down from person to person.' Spinks was first to get to Holmes (whom he outpointed twice), the acknowledged champion for seven years. Patterson forgets, though, that Holmes's branch of the title originated when Michael's older brother Leon skipped a mandatory defence in order to preserve a lucrative re-match with Ali. Holmes won his championship from Ken Norton, who won it from no one. He was assigned the vacated title on the strength of a slender decision over Jimmy Young that may have represented a backlash against the creaking mobster Blinky Palermo. Boxing is a dazzling business.

Cus D'Amato, the manager who stood up to the fight mob in the 1950s, who defied the murderous Frankie Carbo and helped break the monopolist Jim Norris, died in 1985 at seventy-seven and left Tyson in his will. 'More than me or Patterson,' says D'Amato's other old champion, the light heavyweight José Torres, 'Tyson is a clone of Cus's dream. Cus changed both of us, but he made Mike from scratch.' In Brooklyn, Tyson had drawn the absent father and saintly mother, the standard neighbourhood issue. 'You fought to keep what you took,' he says, 'not what you bought.' His literary pedigree is by Charles Dickens out of Budd Schulberg. When Tyson wasn't mugging and robbing, he actually raised pigeons, like Terry Malloy. A tough amateur boxer named Bobby Stewart discovered Tyson in the 'bad cottage' of a mountain reformatory and steered him to D'Amato's informal halfway house at Catskill, NY.

Torres recalls the very sight of Tyson at thirteen: 'Very short, very shy and very wide.' D'Amato pegged him for a champion straight off, though the resident welterweight Kevin Rooney was dubious. 'He looked like a big liar to me; he looked old.' Hearing that he was destined to be champ, Tyson shrugged laconically. But before long, everyone in the stable began to see him out of Cus's one good eye. 'If he keeps listening,' Rooney thought, 'he's got a chance.' The fighters' gym has a fascination of its own: the timeless loft, the faded posters, the dark and smelly world of the primeval man.

To D'Amato, the punching and ducking were rudimentary. Hands up, chin down. Accepting discipline was harder, and controlling emotion was hardest of all. 'Fear is like fire,' he never tired of saying. 'It can cook for you. It can heat your house. Or it can burn it down.' D'Amato's neck-bridging exercises enlarged Tyson's naturally thick stem· to nearly twenty inches, and the rest of him filled out in concrete blocks. Like every old trainer, D'Amato tried to instill a courtliness at the same time as he was installing the heavy machinery. 'My opponent was game and gutsy,' the seventeen-year-old Tyson remarked after dusting a Princeton man during the Olympic trials of 1984. 'What round did I stop the gentleman in, anyway?'

But in two tries Tyson could not quite best the eventual gold-medal winner, Henry Tillman, who fought him backing up (Spinks's style, incidentally). When the second decision was handed down, Tyson stepped outside the arena and began to weep, actually to bawl, a cold kind of crying that carried for a distance. He was a primitive again. As the US boxing team trooped through the airport after the trials, a woman mistakenly directed her good wishes to the alternate, Tyson. 'She must mean good luck on the flight,' said the super heavyweight Tyrell Biggs, a future Tyson opponent who would rue his joke.

Turning pro in 1985, Tyson knocked out eighteen men for a start, twelve of them within three minutes, six of those within sixty seconds. He did not jab them; he mauled them with both hands. They fell in sections. His first couple of fights were in Albany, on the undercard of the welterweight Rooney, at an incubator suitably titled 'the Egg'. Rooney worked Tyson's corner and then fought the main events. Knowing time was short, D'Amato thought to leave a trainer too. 'We were fighters together first,' says Rooney, thirty-two, who has not warred in three years (his delicate face is practically healed) but never officially retired. 'That's my advantage as Mike's trainer, knowing how a fighter thinks. We're a legacy: he's the fighter; I'm the trainer. We're not in Cus's league, but we're close enough.' At any mention of D'Amato, Tyson is capable of tears.

For a time, boxing people questioned whether Tyson was tall enough, scarcely 5 feet 11 inches. 'My whole life has been filled with disadvantages,' he replied in a voice incongruously high and tender. Tyson's provocative description of himself as a small child is 'almost effeminate-shy'. But no one doubted the man was hard enough. He wanted to drive Jesse Ferguson's 'nose bone into his brain'. Civilised fighters like Bonecrusher Smith might choose to hang on in hopes of a miracle, but Tyson wearily informs every opponent, 'There are no miracles here.' When the circle finally came round to Biggs, the Olympic jester, Tyson 'made him pay with his health. I could have knocked him out in the third round [rather than the seventh], but I wanted to do it slowly so he could remember this a long time.'

Even for boxing, what this depicts is stark. But Tyson doesn't wince; he shrugs. 'Basically I don't care what people think of me. I would never go out of my way to change someone's mind about me. I'm not in the communications business.' This was made particularly clear to a wire-service reporter whose hand proffered in greeting was met with the chilling response, 'One of your trucks ran over my dog.' Tyson had confused UPI with UPS.

In contrast, Michael Spinks cares how he is perceived. He keeps a dictionary handy, and privately speaks it into a tape recorder, since the time he was embarrassed by an unfamiliar word. As for communications, he is willing even to puzzle out cryptograms. From across the ring before Spinks's first Holmes fight, he studied the vacant figure of Ali, trundled in for ceremonial purposes. Ali's hands were at his sides and the fingers of one of them were jumping around in a pathetic way that even Spinks took for palsy. 'Then I realised what he was doing. He was telling me, "Stick, stick, stick, side to side, stick, feint, move." I nodded my head, yes.' Do softer sports have sweeter stories?

The little brother of Leon Spinks was obliged to be a fighter, since hand-me-down grudges were the uniforms of their neighbourhood, the fiercest project in St Louis. 'What was it meant for me to do in this life?' Michael often wondered. 'I was one hell of a paper salesman: the *Post-Dispatch*. Didn't win awards but made a lot of money, at least what we considered a lot. An honest dollar, my mother kept saying, and I liked it. I was seventeen, still working at papers – tall too. "What are you doing?" the guys would ask. "Uh, I'm just helping my brother." I was one of the best dishwashers, then one of the best potwashers, you ever set your eyes on.' But he never figured out what was meant for him to do in this life.

Following his 165-pounds victory in the 1976 Olympics, Spinks resisted the pros instinctively. 'It's a strange business, where the guy who takes all the licks ends up with the least. Eventually, though, I decided I might as well try to cash in on the gold medal. Being it was such a dirty business, I had this idea that, together, Leon and I could fight the promoters and maybe come out of it with something.' In 1978, Leon won and lost the heavyweight championship quicker than anyone ever had, and began tooling the wrong way up one-way streets with his teeth out. 'Leon went haywire,' Michael says kindly. 'It was a circus. It was a jungle. Leon was Tarzan and everyone was after him.'

A younger brother cannot decently talk to an older brother like a father, so Michael could only watch and sigh. He loves Leon, who was still losing thirty-three-second fights as recently as last month. By 1981, Michael had quietly won one of the several light heavyweight championships from Eddie Mustafa Muhammad, and within another two years he consolidated all of the titles in a fifteen-round decision over Dwight Muhammad Qawi. Ten weeks before the Qawi fight, Spinks's common law wife, the mother of their two-year-old daughter, was killed in an automobile accident. Spinks cried almost all the way to the ring. The old trainer Eddie Futch despaired. But the moment Spinks arrived he seemed different. Leon was sitting at ringside in a cockeyed Stetson. 'Straighten your hat, Lee,' Michael said coldly.

Futch, a bouncy little man of seventy-seven, was a Golden Gloves team mate of Joe Louis's in 1934. Though only 140 pounds, he often sparred with Louis. 'Always, on the last day before a fight, he wanted to be with me,' Futch says happily. 'I was difficult to hit.' Eddie trained Joe Frazier, who was easy to hit. 'The pressure Frazier exerted wore men down and made them make mistakes. He was perpetually in motion, always moving, bobbing and weaving. Tyson will go along and then explode. He probably hits as hard as Joe, though.'

Norton, another Futch fighter, was as unorthodox as Spinks but less adaptable. 'Most heavyweights are locked into a habit,' says the sparring partner Qawi, co-champion no more. 'But Michael can adjust.' Even when Spinks is shadow-boxing, Futch says, 'I can see he's thinking, working out his plan, and changing it, and changing that.' Spinks pledges, 'I'll take something in with me, but I'll react to what I find in there.'

Showing a modest manner uncommon among the unbeaten,

Spinks explains, 'I decided to become a heavyweight when I realised there was no money in being a light heavyweight.' The fight is promising his side $13.5 million. The new bulk of 208 pounds becomes Spinks as well as his old 175, but he concedes, 'I've been hit harder by the bigger men and have found no pleasure in it.' (He will spot Tyson maybe ten pounds; Tyson will return four inches in height and five inches in reach.) On the chance that history was right about light heavyweights never being able to step up, Spinks had left his daughter home from the first Holmes fight. 'The second is the one she shouldn't have seen,' he says, acknowledging a near-loss. In boxing, this qualifies as breathtaking honesty.

Spinks's fellow Olympian, Sugar Ray Leonard, laughs at that. 'He always seems so cynical and pessimistic,' Leonard says. 'First doom, then gloom, and finally he prevails. At the Olympics, I remember Michael Spinks as a guy who did things that worked, though they happened to be wrong. He'd step right, step left, cross his feet and hit you. He'd always set you up for the punch he wouldn't throw. And he seemed forever to be looking for something.'

Not Tyson, surely. 'He's a very powerful young man,' whistles Spinks through an air-conditioned smile. 'The majority of the guys he's fought have worried about getting hit – I worry about it too. He's got such an advantage; he's so strong. But he does things that are mistakes that he might have to pay for.' Is Spinks afraid? 'Sure, I've got to have my fear,' he says. 'I refuse to go into the ring without it.' But he also says, 'I have a nice grip on my pride: I boss it around. I wear it when I should. I throw it in the corner when I don't need it.' He'll need it sometime Monday night.

'This is the first time Tyson is going to meet some talent; Spinks is a thinking fighter,' says the venerable trainer Ray Arcel, eighty-nine, who carted thirteen opponents to Louis before beating him with Ezzard Charles. ('And you know something? As happy as I was for my guy, that's how sad I was for Joe.') Nothing can touch boxing for beautiful old men. 'Tyson is learning how to think too,' Arcel says. 'He's picked up a lot from those old films he studies, including a little Jack Dempsey.' He first saw Dempsey in 1916 in New York City, against John L. Johnson.

'John *Lester* Johnson,' Tyson yawns. 'No decision. Just ten rounds, I think. Dempsey wasn't a long-fight guy. He would break you up.' A puzzlement curls his eyebrows. 'When you're a historian, you know things, and you don't even know why you know them.' Preparing for the day's sparring, greasing himself like a Channel swimmer and admiring the reflection in a long mirror, he sounds almost bookish, until Rooney turns up a copy of Plutarch's *Lives* and Tyson inquires archly, 'Who wrote that? Rembrandt?'

In his own field, he is erudite. 'Howard Davis was middle class, wasn't he?' Tyson muses idly, referring to another Olympian on Spinks's team. 'Davis was a real good boxer. You can come from a middle-class background and be a real good boxer. But you have to know struggle to be the champ.' Without socks, robe or orchestra, wearing headgear as spare as a First World War aviator's, Tyson hurries out to demonstrate his point against an unsteady corps of clay pigeons with perfect names like Michael ('the Bounty') Hunter and Rufus ('Hurricane') Hadley. The slippery leather thuds reverberate through the hall.

Not much like Rembrandt, Tyson fights by the numbers. 'Seven-eight,' Rooney calls the tune, signalling for combinations. 'Feint, two-one. Pick it up, six-one. There you go, seven-one. Now make it a six.' The savage sight of Tyson advancing on his sparring partners recalls the classic moan of an early matchmaker: 'He fights you like you stole something from him.' Uppercuts are especially urgent. 'If you move away too much,' says Oliver McCall, the best gym fighter of the nine revolving lawn sprinklers, 'he'll punch your hipbone and paralyse you in place.' Hurricane comes out of the ring still spinning. 'He hit me on the top of my head,' he whines. 'It burns.'

In training-camp workouts and at ringside on fight night, the cauliflower reunions fill in another piece of the picture. They are bitter-sweet delights. Few of the usual suspects favour Spinks. Jake LaMotta thinks Tyson 'is gonna go down as one of the greatest fighters of all times, and he's gonna break all records, and he's gonna be around a long, long time, and he's gonna make over $100 million. I could be wrong, but that's my opinion.' Billy Conn, the patron saint of overblown light heavyweights, says, 'I think Tyson will fix him up in a couple of rounds.' Ali likes Spinks, but then Ali liked Trevor Berbick, whom Tyson knocked down three times with one punch. 'I don't think Tyson will even be able to hit Spinks,' Ali says. 'He's like rubber.'

Nobody speaks it with huge conviction, but the most promising theory on behalf of Spinks holds that the real world has recently descended on Tyson in the forms of a famous wife, a flamboyant mother-in-law, a $4.5 million mansion in Bernardsville, NJ, a parade of luxury cars (including a dinged one worth $180,000 that he tried to give away to the investigating officers) and a custody battle that pits the well-cologned manager Bill Cayton against the understated promoter Don King. Last August, once Tyson had all the belts, King threw a coronation for history's youngest heavyweight champion. The melancholy scene recalled King Kong crusted with what the promoter called 'baubles, rubies and fabulous other doodads'. Beholding the dull eyes and meek surprise under the lopsided crown and chinchilla cloak, King said he was reminded 'of Homer's Odysseus returning to Ithaca to gather his dissembled fiefdoms.' Sighs Tyson: 'It's tough being the youngest anything.'

According to Patterson, 'When you have millions of dollars, you have millions of friends.' The Tyson camp's slice of this fight is $22 million, bringing his bundle so far to more than $40 million. 'I originally picked him, and I still do,' Patterson allows, 'but now I give Spinks a chance.' Torres looks at it the other way: 'Who knows? It could be good. After all, doesn't he come from turmoil?' A little overwhelmed, Tyson says, 'When I'm out of boxing, I'm going to tell everyone I'm bankrupt.' In a sepia mood again, he adds that 'Damon Runyon never wrote about fighters beating up their wife or getting into car accidents.'

Before Tyson arranged to meet Robin Givens, twenty-three, the television actress (Head of the Class) who took him for a husband in February, he once said, 'I look in the mirror every day. I know I'm not Clark Gable. I wish I could find a girl who knew me when I was broke and thought I was a nice guy.' Following the wedding ceremony, auditors and lawyers started to arrive. In Givens's estimation, 'he's strong and sensitive and gentle. I feel protected, but he's so gentle that sometimes I think I have to protect him.' Among her previous heart-throbs were Michael Jordan and the comedian Eddie Murphy. Tyson likes to say, 'I suaved her.' But he mentions, 'It's no joke, I'll tell you. If you're not grown up and you want to grow up real quick, get married.' In a slightly different context, but only slightly, he says, 'So many fighters have been called invincible. Nobody's invincible.'

Almost alone among boxers, Tyson has no entourage. It seems to be the only cliché he has avoided. He does his pre-dawn roadwork by himself on the boardwalk, grateful for the solitude. 'I don't have any friends. I get paranoid around a lot of people. I can't relax.' Besides Rooney and Cutman Matt Baranski, only Steve Lott is admitted to the inner sanctum. 'I'm the spit-bucket man,' Lott says with shining eyes. 'I would give my life for that.' He was a handball buddy of Jimmy Jacobs's, an honoured player who died at fifty-eight last March, reportedly of leukaemia. Jacobs and his business partner Cayton, keepers of the most extensive film archives in boxing, were long-time benefactors of D'Amato's teacherage and co-managed Tyson. Lott is essentially a public relations liasion, but is as devoted as Tyson to the flickering images of history, and seems astounded that they suddenly include him.

'To be in the corner!' Lott exclaims. 'To be in the dressing-room! In that room before the fight, just the four of us, our heartbeats are deafening. When it gets really quiet, it's almost a despair. I don't know what it is. Maybe we don't want it to be over.' Coming to life on the subject, Tyson says, 'That's my favourite time, just before. I'm so calm. The work is over. You fight and you go home. Before or after, I don't respect any of them more than another. What they look like doesn't really matter. I never dwell on what's to be done or what's been done. I just don't think of stuff like that. In my heart, I know what to do.'

He is referring to horror, and a good many people do not want it done. In the regular processes of human cruelty, nobody is arguing against competition or any of the subtler forms of combat. It's just that using brains to extinguish brains seems a little direct. Developing balance to knock somebody off balance, honing eyesight to administer shiners, marshalling memory and ingenuity and audacity and dexterity – and co-ordinating all of them against themselves, and against co-ordination – seems self-destructive to a society.

Speaking in Japan some time ago, José Torres was asked why Puerto Rico had so many boxing champions and Japan so few. 'You can't have champions in a society that is content,' he answered. 'My kids can't be champions. I spoiled them.' Ken Norton's son has become a pro football player. 'You have to know struggle,' Tyson says.

Of course, those who would take boxing away from the strugglers offer no plan to replace it. And no one wants to acknowledge that it may be irreplaceable. The high-minded view is that boxing will exist only as long as whatever it reflects in mankind exists, although picturing Spinks slaughtering Tyson is easier than imagining a world without men who ball their fists for pleasure or prizes. The big fight doesn't come along so often any more, defined as the kind that can get in people's stomachs and occasionally have trouble staying there. But here it is again, for twelve rounds or less.

Perhaps the true horror is that there has always been a class poor enough for this, and maybe that's why so many people avert their eyes. Why others have to watch is a perplexity, and why some have to cheer is personal.

EPILOGUE

The Lion in Winter

Muhammad Ali and his Entourage

Gary Smith

Around Muhammad Ali, all was decay. Mildewed tongues of insulation poked through gaps in the ceiling; flaking cankers pocked the painted walls. On the floor lay rotting scraps of carpet.

He was cloaked in black. Black street shoes, black socks, black pants, black short-sleeved shirt. He threw a punch, and in the small town's abandoned boxing gym, the rusting chain between the heavy bag and the ceiling rocked and creaked.

Slowly, at first, his feet began to dance around the bag. His left hand flicked a pair of jabs, and then a right cross and a left hook, too, recalled the ritual of butterfly and bee. The dance quickened. Black sunglasses flew from his pocket as he gathered speed, black shirt-tail flapped free, black heavy bag rocked and creaked. Black street shoes scuffed faster and faster across black mouldering tiles: *Yeah, Lawd, Champ can still float, Champ can still sting!* He whirled, jabbed, feinted, let his feet fly into a shuffle. 'How's that for a sick man?' he shouted.

He did it for a second three-minute round, then a third. 'Time!' I shouted at the end of each one as the second hand swept past the 12 on the wristwatch he had handed to me. And then, gradually, his shoulders began to slump, his hands to drop. The tap and thud of leather soles and leather gloves began to miss a quarter-beat . . . half-beat . . . whole. Ali stopped and sucked air. The dance was over.

He undid the gloves, tucked in the black shirt, reached reflexively for the black comb. On stiff legs he walked towards the door. Outside, under the sun, the afternoon stopped. Every movement he made now was infinitely patient and slow. Feeling . . . in . . . his . . . pocket . . . for . . . his . . . key . . . Slipping . . . it . . . into . . . the . . . car . . . lock . . . Bending . . . and . . . sliding . . . behind . . . the . . . wheel . . . Turning . . . on . . . the . . . ignition . . . and . . . shifting . . . into . . . gear . . . Three months had passed, he said, since he had last taken the medicine the doctor told him to take four times a day.

One hand lightly touched the bottom of the wheel as he drove; his clouded eyes narrowed to a squint. He head tilted back, and the warm sunlight trickled down his puffy cheeks. Ahead, trees smudged against sky and farmland; the glinting asphalt dipped and curved, a black ribbon of molasses.

He entered the long driveway of his farm, parked and left the car. He led me into a barn. On the floor, leaning against the walls, were paintings and photographs of him in his prime, eyes keen, arms thrust up in triumph, surrounded by the cluster of people he took around the world with him.

He looked closer and noticed it. Across his face in every picture, streaks of bird dung. He glanced up towards the pigeons in the rafters. No malice, no emotion at all flickered in his eyes. Silently, one by one, he turned the pictures to the wall.

Outside, he stood motionless and moved his eyes across his farm. He spoke from his throat, without moving his lips. I had to ask him to repeat it. 'I had the world,' he said, 'and it wasn't nothin'.' He paused and pointed. 'Look now . . .'

Black blobs of cows slumbering in the pasture, trees swishing slowly, as if under water rather than sky. Merry-go-rounds, sliding boards and swings near the house, but no giggles, no squeals, no children.

'What happened to the circus?' I asked.

He was staring at the slowly swishing trees, listening to the breeze sift leaves and make a lulling sound like water running over the rocks of a distant stream. He didn't seem to hear.

And I said again, 'What happened to the circus?'

The Doctor

A man of infinite variety. Medical doctor, jazz connoisseur, sports figure, confidant of the great.

(*Excerpt from Ferdie Pacheco's publicity brochure*)

This is a painting of myself when I was thirty and living alone and messing around with a German woman who loved it when there was sweat and paint all over me . . . and this is a screenplay that I've just cut down from 185 pages to 135 . . . and this one here is a 750-page epic novel, a very serious look at the immigrant experience in Tampa . . . and this is a painting I did of Sherman's March – that stream of blue is the Union soldiers . . . and that one is a screenplay I just finished about two Cubans who steal a Russian torpedo boat, and a crazy Jewish lawyer – Jerry Lewis is going to play the part and direct it – picks them up in a boat . . .'

In one way, Ferdie Pacheco was just like his former patient Muhammad Ali: he needed laughter and applause. He led people to each of his paintings, lithographs, cartoons and manuscripts the way Ali once led them to continents to watch him talk and fight. Both worked on canvas: Ali, when his was not near to dance on, used parlour magic tricks to make eyes go bright and wide; Pacheco, when his was not near to dab on, told long tales and jokes, dominating a dinner party, from escargots to espresso, with his worldliness and wit.

In another way, they were not alike at all. Ali lived for the moment and acted as he felt, with disregard for the cord between action and consequence. This allured the doctor, whose mind teemed with consequence before he chose his action. 'In an overcomplicated society,' he says, 'Ali was a simple, happy man.'

Twenty-five years ago Pacheco was a ghetto doctor in Miami. Today he can be found in his home, white shorts and paint-smeared white smock covering his torso, blue Civil War infantryman's cap atop his head, stereo blaring Big Band jazz, telephone ringing with calls from agents, reporters and television executives as he barefoots back and forth, brushing blue on three different canvases and discoursing, for anyone who will listen, upon the plot twist he has just hatched for chapter sixteen of his latest novel. He receives a six-figure salary from NBC for commenting on fights, has quit medicine, has become a painter whose works sell for as much as $40,000, and has completed 600 pen-and-ink drawings converted into lithographs (17,000 of which sold on the first mail-out order), six books (two of which have been published, including *Fight Doctor*), eight screenplays (four of which have sold), and a play that may soon be performed in London. He has also formed a Florida-based film production company and appeared across the country as a speaker. 'But on my tombstone,' he says, 'it will say "Muhammad Ali's doctor". It's like being gynaecologist to the Queen.'

In our time, will we see another comet that burns so long and streaks so fast, and whose tail has room for so many riders? 'The entourage' some called the unusual collection of passengers who took the ride; the travelling circus, the hangers-on, others called it. 'These people are like a little town for Ali,' his manager, Herbert Muhammad, once said. 'He is the sheriff, the judge, the mayor and the treasurer.' Most were street people, thrown together on a lonely mountaintop in Pennsylvania where Ali built his training camp, until they burst upon the big cities for his fights. They bickered with each other over who would do what task for Ali, fist-fought with each other at his instigation – two of them once even drew guns. And they hugged and danced with each other, sat for hours talking around the long wooden dinner table, played cards and made midnight raids on the refrigerator together. 'That's right,' said Herbert Muhammad. 'A family.'

Because they were there for Ali, he never had to worry about dirty underwear or water bills or grocery shopping; he could remain an innocent. Because Ali was there for them, they could be mothers and fathers to the earth's most extraordinary child.

For a decade and a half he held them together, took them to the Philippines, Malaysia, Zaïre, Europe and the Orient, their lives accelerating as his did, slowing when his did, too. But among them one was different, the one who obeyed the law of consequence. Ferdie Pacheco ejected while the comet still had momentum, and made a missile of himself.

'I had an overwhelming urge to create,' he says. And an ego that kept telling him there was nothing he couldn't do. 'On napkins, tablecloths, anywhere, he'd draw,' says his wife, Luisita. 'I shouted "Help me!" when I was delivering our child. He said, "Not now" – he was busy drawing me in stirrups.'

Few knew him in the early Ali days: what reason was there to consult the doctor when Ali was young, physically unflawed and all-but-unhittable? Pacheco was the son of Spanish immigrants, a first-generation American, who had established a general practice in Miami's black Overtown district and become a regular at Miami Beach boxing matches, where he met corner-man Angelo Dundee and began to treat Dundee's boxers for free. One day, a patient named Cassius Clay came to him. And Pacheco became part of the entourage.

'It satisfied my Iberian sense of tragedy and drama,' he says, 'my need to be in the middle of a situation where life and death are in the balance, and part of it is in your hands. Most people go out of their way to explain that they don't need the spotlight. I see nothing wrong with it.

'Medicine – you do it so long, it's not a high-wire act without a net any more. At big Ali fights, you got the feeling you had on a first date with a beauty queen. I'd scream like a banshee. It was like taking a vacation from life.'

The first signal of decline was in Ali's hands. Pacheco began injecting them with novocaine before fights, and the ride went on. Then the reflexes slowed, the beatings began, the media started to question the doctor. And the world began to learn how much the doctor loved to talk. Style, poise and communication skills had become the weaponry in the land that Ali conquered: a member of the king's court who could verbalise – not in street verse, as several members could, but in the tongue the mass markets cried for – and foresee consequence as well, could share Ali's opportunities without sharing his fate. The slower Ali spoke, the more frequently spoke the doctor.

Ali reached his mid-thirties stealing decisions but taking more and more punishment; Pacheco and his patient reached a juncture. The doctor looked ahead and listened, heard the crowd's roar fading, the espresso conversation sobering. His recommendation that Ali quit met deaf ears. The same trait that drew him to Ali began to push him away.

He mulled his dilemma. Leave and risk being called a traitor? Or stay and chance partial responsibility for lifelong damage to a patient who ignored his advice?

Pacheco followed his logic. He wrote Ali a letter explaining that cells in Ali's kidneys were disintegrating, then parted ways with him and created laughter and applause on his own. Ali followed his feelings and went down a different path.

Today the ex-fighter turns dung-streaked canvases to the wall, the ex-doctor covers his wall with new canvases. In his studio, Pacheco shakes his head. 'I feel sorry for Ali, he says, 'but I'm fatalistic. If he hadn't had a chance to get out, I'd feel incredibly sad. But he had his chance. He chose to go on. When I see him at fights now, there's no grudge. He says, "Doc, I made you famous." And I say, "Muhammad, you're absolutely right.'"

The Facilitator

What if a demon crept after you one day or night in your loneliest solitude and said to you: 'This life as you live it now and have lived it, you will have to live again and again, time without number; and there will be nothing new in it, but every pain and every joy and every thought and sigh and all the unspeakably small and great in your life must return to you. . . . The eternal hourglass of existence will be turned again and again – and you with it, you dust of dust!' Would you not throw yourself down and gnash your teeth and curse the demon who thus spoke?

Friedrich Nietzsche

Warm Vegas night air washed through the 1976 Cadillac convertible. 'We had fun, mister,' said the driver. 'We *lived,* mister. Every day was history. Millionaires would've paid to do what I did. To be near *him.'*

He fell silent for a few blocks. The lunacy of lightbulbs glinted off his glasses and his diamond-studded heavyweight championship ring. 'When I was a little boy, I used to watch airplanes in the sky until they became a dot, and then until you couldn't even see the dot. I wanted to go everywhere, do everything. Well, I *did.* Europe, Africa, the Far East. I saw it all. He was pilot, I was navigating. Hell, yes. The most exciting days of my life. Every day, I think about them. We were kids together, having fun. He was my best friend. I think I might have been his.'

The car stopped at an intersection. A woman, thick in the thighs and heavy with makeup, walked across the beam of his headlights. His eyes didn't flicker. Frantically, hopelessly, the blinking lightbulbs chased each other around and around the borders of the casino marquees.

'You could feel it all around you, the energy flow,' he said. His foot pressed the accelerator, his shoulders rested back against the seat. 'When you're with someone dynamic, goddam, it reflects on you. You felt: let's go *do* it. I met presidents and emperors and kings and queens and killers, travelling with him. Super Bowls, World Series, hockey, basketball championships I saw. I was big in the discos, Xenon, Studio 54. There was myself, Wilt Chamberlain and Joe Namath: the major league of bachelors.'

Quiet again. The traffic light pooled red upon the long white hood. Dead of summer, down season in Vegas. The click of the turn signal filled the car. Then the click-click-click of a cocktail waitress, high-heeled and late for work. He peered into the neon-shattered night. 'What could I find out there tonight?' he asked. 'A girl more beautiful than I've been with? A girl more caring than I've been with? What would she tell me I haven't heard before? What's left that could impress me? What's left I haven't done or seen? It burnt me out, I tell you. It burnt me out for life . . .'

Gene Kilroy had no title. Everyone just knew: he was the Facilitator. When Ali wanted a new Rolls-Royce, Kilroy facilitated it. When he wanted to buy land to build a training camp, Kilroy facilitated it. When a pipe burst in the training camp or a hose burst in the Rolls, when Marlon Brando or Liza Minnelli wanted to meet Ali, or Ali wanted to donate $100,000 to save an old-folks' home, Kilroy facilitated it.

At hotels he usually stayed in a bedroom that was part of Ali's suite. As soon as they entered a city, he collected a list of the best doctors, in case of an emergency. He reached for the ever-ringing phone, decided who was worthy of a visit to the throne room. He worried himself into a ten-Maalox-a-day habit, facilitating. 'Ulcer,' he said. 'You love someone, you worry. Watching him get hit during the Holmes fight, I bled like a pig – I was throwing it up in the dressing-room. And all the problems before a fight. It was like having a show horse you had to protect, and all the people wanted to hitch him to a buggy for a ride through Central Park.'

The trouble with facilitating was that it left no mark, no KILROY WAS HERE. He has covered the walls of his rec room with fifty Ali photos. He reminisces every day. He watches videos of old Ali interviews he helped facilitate, and sometimes tears fill his eyes. 'I wish I had a kid I could tell,' he said. And then, his voice going from soft to gruff. 'I'll get married when I find a woman who greets me at the door the way my dogs do.'

The Vegas casinos, they knew what Kilroy might be worth. All those contacts around the world, all those celebrities who had slipped into the dressing-room on a nod from the Facilitator: perfect qualifications for a casino host. First the Dunes hired him, then the Tropicana and now the Golden Nugget.

Each day he weaves between blackjack tables and roulette wheels, past slot machines and craps tables, nodding to dealers, smiling at bouncers, slapping regulars on the back, dispensing complimentary dinners and rooms to high-rollers and 'How are ya, hon?' to cocktail waitresses. He no longer gambles: all the lust for action is gone. All that remains is the love of arranging a favour, of helping other members of Ali's old 'family' when they hit hard times, of facilitating someone else's wants now that his are gone.

'As you know, I was all over the world with Ali,' he said, leading a multi-millionaire into one of the Golden Nugget's suites. 'I got the royal gold-carpet treatment everywhere. But this' – he swept his arm across the room – 'solidifies the epitome of luxury. *Look.* Your jacuzzi. Your sauna.' Again and again his beeper would sound, and he would be connected with another wealthy client. 'Sure, I'll have our limo pick you up at the airport . . . Your line of credit is all set, $100,000.'

Whenever Ali comes to Vegas to see a fight, he will mix with high-rollers at Kilroy's request or sign a couple of dozen boxing gloves, a stack of a hundred photographs, mementos Kilroy passes out to favoured clients. In his world, Ali souvenirs are currency. 'One man was so proud of the things I'd given him,' he said, 'that when he died, he was buried with his Ali picture and boxing gloves. I can give people their dreams.'

When Ali is near, Kilroy looks at him and remembers what the two of them once were. Sometimes he feels helpless. How can he facilitate away Ali's great fatigue with life – when he, too, feels sated and weary? 'I remember one day not long ago when he was signing autographs, and I was standing next to him. We heard someone say, "Look at Ali, he's a junkie." Muhammad's eyes get kind of glassy sometimes now, you know. I wanted to choke the guy. But Ali nudged me and kind of smiled. God, I hope he wins this last fight . . .'

The Motivator

The scene: a small motel room in downtown Los Angeles that costs, at monthly rates, $5.83 a night. A little bit of afternoon light makes it through the curtains, falling on a tablecloth etched with the words GOD – MOTHER – SON. On top of the television stands a small statue of Buddha, its head hidden by a man's cap. Four packs of playing cards and a Bible lie on the head of the bed; tin dinner plates are set on a small table. Affixed to a mirror are a photograph of a young Muhammad Ali and a leaflet for a play entitled *Muhammad Ali Forever*.

On the bed, propped against a pillow, is a fifty-seven-year-old black man, slightly chubby, with black woolly hair on the sides of his head and, on the top, a big bald spot with a tiny tuft of hair growing at the very front. As he talks, his eyes go wide and wild . . . then far away . . . then wet with tears.

His name is Drew (Bundini) Brown, the ghetto poet who motivated Ali and maddened him, who invented the phrase, 'Float like a butterfly, sting like a bee' and who played bit parts in *The Color Purple* and *Shaft;* who licked Ali's mouthpiece before sliding it in but never said a yes to him he didn't mean; who could engage the champion in long discussions of nature and God and man, then lie in the hotel pool before a fight and have his white woman, Easy, drop cherries into his mouth; who, when he felt good, charged two $300 bottles of wine at dinner to Ali's expense account and then made Ali laugh it off; and who, when he felt bad, drank rum and shot bullets into the night sky at the mountain training camp in Pennsylvania – a man stretched taut and twanging between the fact that he was an animal and the fact that he was a spirit.

Oh, yes. A visitor sits in a chair near the window of the motel room, but often Bundini Brown talks as if he is ranting to a crowd on a street corner – or as if he is completely alone:

> The old master painter from the faraway hills,
> Who painted the violets and the daffodils,
> Said the next champ gonna come from Louisville.

I made that up 'fore we was even champion. Things just exploded in my head back then. Guess that's why Ali loved me. I could help him create new things. See, he never did talk that much. People didn't know that about him, 'less'n they slept overnight and caught him wakin' up. All that talkin' was just for the cameras and writers, to build a crowd. He was quiet as can be, same as now. But now people think he's not talkin' 'cause of the Parkinson's, which is a lie.

I remember when he fought Jerry Quarry, after that long layoff. Going from the locker-room to the ring, my feet wasn't even touchin' the ground. I looked down and tried to touch, but I couldn't get 'em to. Like I was walkin' into my past. Me and the champ was so close, I'd think, 'Get off the ropes'– and he'd get off the ropes! Man, it made chill bumps run up my legs. We were in Manila, fightin' Frazier. The champ came back to the corner crossin' his legs. Tenth or eleventh round, I forget. Angelo said, 'Our boy is through.' I said, 'You're goddam wrong, my baby ain't through!' I was deeply in love with him. Ali tried to fire me every day, but how he gonna fire me when God gave me my job? So I stood on the apron of the ring, and I said out loud, 'God! If Joe Frazier wins, his mother wins, his father wins, his kids win. Nobody else! But if Muhammad lose – God! – we *all* lose. Little boys, men, women, black and white. Muhammad lose, the world lose!'

And you know what? The nigger got up fresh as a daisy. Everybody seen it! Got up fresh, man, *fresh!* And beat up on Frazier so bad Frazier couldn't come out after the fourteenth round! God put us together for a reason, and we shook up the world!

(*He picks at a thread on the bedspread.*) People'd see us back then and say, 'It's so nice seein' yall together.' We made a lot of people happy. I was a soldier. (*His hands are shaking. He reaches down to the floor, pours a glass of rum as his eyes begin to fill with tears.*) I was happy then. It'd be good for Muhammad if I could be with him again. Be good for me, too. Then I wouldn't drink as much. By me being alone I drink a lot. Always did say I could motivate him out of this sickness, if me and the champ was together. He needs the medical thing, too, but he needs someone who truly loves him. If we were together again, more of the God would come out of me. (*His voice is almost inaudible.*) Things used to explode in my head . . . I'm kind of runnin' out now . . .

He asked me to go stay on the farm with him. (*His eyes flare, he starts to shout.*) What you goin' to do, put me to pasture? I ain't no horse! I don't want no handouts! I got plans! Big things gonna happen for me! I gotta get me a job, make some money, take care of my own family 'fore I go with him. If I don't love my own babies, how in hell I gonna love somebody else's?

First thing I'd do if I had some money, I'd go to the Bahamas and see my baby. King Solomon Brown's his name. Made him at Ali's last fight, with a woman I met down there. He was born on the seventh day of the seventh month. There's seven archangels and seven colours in the rainbow, you know.

I brought him to America and lived with him until he was one. Then he went back to the Bahamas with his mother. Didn't see him for a year and a half, then I went back. Wanted to see if he'd remember me. I said, 'A-B-C-D-E-F-G – dock-dock' (*he makes a sound with his tongue and the roof of his mouth*) – that's what I always used to teach him – and he *remembered!* He ran and leapt into my arms – I mean, jumped! – and we hugged, and it wasn't like I was huggin' somebody else, we was one body, we was one! (*He wraps his arms around himself and closes his eyes.*) I'll never forget that hug. Couldn't bring him back to America, I had no house for him to come back to. Stayed eight weeks and went broke. Came back and after that I'd see kids on the street and think of my kid and I'd start to cry . . . Why don't you get up and leave now? Put two eggs in your shoes and beat it. You stirrin' up things, you know. (*The visitor starts to stand.*)

I'll make some money. I'll get a home he can come to, and put him in school. Got two grandchildren, too, and I wanna be near 'em. They're by my son, Drew, he's a jet pilot in the Persian Gulf. And I have another son, Ronnie, here in Los Angeles. One son black, one son white, born a day apart. And then Solomon. I'm a boymaker. Don't see my kids like I want to. Can't go back to my babies till I got somethin' to give 'em. Right now, I'm broke. I said, *broke,* not poor, there's a difference. (*He glances across the room and speaks softly.*) I know one thing. You get used to good food and a clean bed, hard to get used to somethin' else. Why don't you leave now? Please?

(*He rises and goes to the door, shredding a piece of bread and tossing it outside to the pigeons.*) People don't know it, but feedin' the birds is like paintin' a picture . . . Some people think Muhammad's broke, too. He ain't broke. He's broken-hearted. He hasn't found himself in what he really want to do. Maybe he just be in the freezer for a few years. Maybe he's going through this so he has time to think. Last time I was with him, his fifteen-year-old son said to him, 'Daddy, Bundini is your only friend, the only one that doesn't give up on you.' Muhammad looked at me, and we started cryin'. But this is not the end for Ali. Somethin' good gonna happen for him. Maybe not while he's still alive on this earth, but Ali gonna *live* for a long time, if you know what I mean. Like my kids, even when I'm gone, I'm gonna be livin' in 'em . . . if I can be around 'em enough to put my spirit into 'em. Go fishin' with 'em. There you go again, you got me talkin' about it. Didn't I ask you to leave? *(The visitor reaches for his shoulder bag.)*

It ain't nothin' for me to get up and walk down the street and have fifteen people yell, 'Hey, Bundini, where's the champ?' That one reason I stay in my room. *(He pauses and looks at the visitor.)* You think I'm alone, don't you? Soon as you leave, God's gonna sit in that chair. I call him Shorty. Ha-ha, you like that, don't you? By callin' him that, means I ain't got no prejudice about religions. I was born on a doorstep with a note 'cross my chest. It read, 'Do the best you can for him, world.' I had to suck the first nipple come along. I didn't run away from home – I been runnin' *to* home. I'm runnin' to God. And the nearest I can find to God is people. And all around me people are fightin' for money. And I'm tryin' to find out what makes apples and peaches and lemons, what makes the sun shine. What is the act of life? We all just trancin' through? Why can't we care for one another? There's a lady that come out of church the other day and got shot in the head. I want to know what the hell is goin' on. God, take me home if you ain't gonna give me no answer. Take me home now. If you're ready to die, you're ready to live. Best thing you can do is live every day like it's the last day. Kiss your family each day like you're not comin' back. I want to keep my dimples deep as long as I'm here. I want to see people smile like you just did.

(His lips smile, but his eyes are wet and shining.) The smarter you get, the lonelier you get. Why is it? When you learn how to live, it's time to die. That's kind of peculiar. When you learn how to drive, they take away the car. I've finally realised you need to be near your kids,

that you need to help 'em live better'n you did, that you can live on by feedin' your spirit into your babies. But now I ain't got no money and I can't be near 'em. Back when I was with the champ, I could fly to 'em anytime. See, I was in the Navy when I was thirteen and the Merchant Marine when I was fifteen, and they was the happiest days of my life, 'cause I was alone and didn't have no one to worry about. But now I'm alone and it brings me misery . . . C'mon now, get on up and leave. Talkin' to you is like talkin' to myself . . .

See this bald spot on my head? Looks like a footprint, don't it? That come from me walkin' on my head. Don't you think I know I'm my own worst enemy? I suffer a lot. If my kids only knew how I hurt. But I can't let 'em know, it might come out in anger. And 'fore I see 'em, I gotta have somethin' to give to 'em. I owe $9,000 'fore I can get my stuff out of storage. (*He bites his lip and looks away.*) One storage place already done auctioned off all the pictures of Ali an' me, all my trophies and memories from back then. Strangers have 'em all. . . . (*A long silence passes.*) Now the other storage place, the one that has all Ali's robes from every fight we ever fought, every pair of trunks we fought in, lot of jockstraps, too, enough stuff to fill a museum – I owe that place $9,000, and I'm talkin' to 'em nice so they won't auction that off, too, but I don't think they'll wait much longer. Sure I know how much that stuff's worth, but I can't sell it. That's not right. I want that stuff to be in my babies' dens some day. That's what I'm gonna give my babies. I can't just sell it . . . (*His head drops, he looks up from under his brow.*) You know somebody'll pay now?

(*He rubs his face and stares at the TV set.*) You stirrin' it up again. Go on, now. You know if you just keep sittin' there, I'll keep talkin'. Pretty please? (*He gets to his feet.*) You can come back and visit me. We friends now. I can't go out, I gotta stay by the phone. I'm waitin' on somethin' real big, and I ain't gonna get caught offguard. Somethin' big gonna happen, you wait and see . . .

A few days later, Bundini Brown fell in his motel room and was found paralysed from the neck down by a cleaning woman. And then he died.

Seven years ago, when the group broke camp at Deer Lake for the final time, everyone contributed money for a plaque that would include all their names. They left the task to Bundini Brown and departed.

Today the camp is a home for unwed mothers. Infront of the log-cabin gym, where babies squeal and crawl, stands a tall slab of grey granite, chiselled with sixteen names and surrounded by flowers. Bundini Brown had bought a tombstone.

AFTERWORD

A Champ Like No Other

Gilbert Rogin

I'm going to tell you about Bundini giving me the shirt off his back, about the feel of the wind, how age brings you down off your toes, and a bunch of other stuff. Ali and I go back to when he was Cassius Clay and there was no entourage. But I'm getting ahead of myself, being a front-to-back man, because before I met Ali, I met Slim Jim Robinson, only I didn't know it at the time. 7 February 1961. I was in the lobby of Convention Hall in Miami Beach, where Ali was to have his fourth pro fight. A skinny guy carrying a little AWOL bag caught my eye since he was walking like he had a train to catch. Next time I saw him he was getting into the ring to fight Ali, so in a sense he introduced me to him. He wasn't wearing a robe. Either he couldn't afford one or didn't own a bigger bag. And the reason he had been in such a hurry was he was late for the fight. (He should've slowed some, for in this case it turned out to be better never than late.) Slim Jim Robinson. When the bell rang he took this stance: right foot as far back as it could go and turned almost the other way around, so if, as he suspected, he found out he didn't belong in the same ring with Ali, he would be halfway home. He was right. TKO 1.

Ingemar Johansson was another story. The *Ring Record Book* doesn't list an Ali–Johansson fight, but it happened. I was there. The fight took place that same month. Ingemar was in Palm Beach training for the third Patterson fight, and someone thought it would be a great idea if he came down to Miami Beach to spar with Ali. Someone was wrong.

They were to go three rounds. Ingemar quit before the end of two. Ali didn't put a licking on him. He hardly hit him. But then he didn't try. He just came to dance. What happened was Ingemar couldn't hit Ali. And, oh, how he tried. He tried to jab him in the first round, and Ali's head wasn't there. Ingemar was steamed, so in the second round he tried to knock Ali out with his big right hand. What he nearly did was throw out his back because all he was hitting was air. So he climbed out of the ring.

I'd never seen anything like it. Still haven't. Never will. The kid –
Ali was nineteen – undressed the man. I knew right then he was
going to be heavyweight champ. What I didn't know was that I'd
seen his best fight.

November 1962. We were in a hotel in LA, where Ali was to meet
Archie Moore – just me, Ali, Angelo Dundee, who trained him, and
his brother, Rudy. He and Rudy, in bed sheets, popping out of closets
to scare Ang, stuffing burning rags under his door, reaching out their
window with broomsticks to rattle his blinds, Ali reciting his poems
on street corners. Once I saw Ang slip a note under Ali's door. 'I help
him with his poetry,' he said. TKO 4.

But as Moore said afterwards, 'When you fight a man, he's past his
prime . . . One thing – if Cassius live, he certainly got to grow older.'

One day before he did, Ali said, 'Sometimes I wonder when a big
fist comes crashing by and at the last minute I move my head the
smallest bit and the punch comes so close I can feel the wind, but it
misses me. How do I know to move just enough? How do I know
which way to move?'

Then he no longer did. Then came the entourage, the great
clamorous mob. When he fought George Chuvalo on 29 March
1966, in Toronto, Bundini was history for having hocked Ali's
championship belt. But before he was canned, I asked if I could have
one of his FLOAT LIKE A BUTTERFLY, STING LIKE A BEE T-shirts.
He told me he only had six, but if I put him in the story, he would
make do with five. How could I leave him out? Man was a quote
machine.

After the fight, in Ali's room, crowded with Moslems, a voice said,
'What's he doing here? He don't belong.' To which Ali said, 'He
stays.' I asked who'd spoken. Minister Louis, I was told, sings
calypso. What's he sing? 'The White Man's Heaven is the Black Man's
Hell.'

Minister Louis, who became Louis Farrakhan, was right about me.
I didn't belong. The music had stopped, Ali had come down off his
toes, the entourage swanned and squabbled. I went on to other
things; Ali, too – the Rumble, the Thrilla, great flat-footed fights. But
once in a movie-house in Greenwich Village, since razed, after a
boxing match on theatre TV, I heard a familiar voice boom out, 'Giiil
Rogin, world's greatest spoatswritah!' The Champ.

In the ensuing years I told that story to other writers who covered him, and each one said Ali had said the same thing to him. Ali was right. There were a lot of us greatest. But there was only one of him, never be another. On his toes, dancing, hands held lightly at his sides, wicked smile, feeling nothing but the wind.

BIBLIOGRAPHY

The editors wish to gratefully acknowledge and give special thanks for permission to use the following extracts in this collection:

Joe Louis: Black Hero in White Charles Scribner's Sons 1985
Farewell to Sport Alfred Knopf 1936
The Fight Little Brown 1976
Sting Like a Bee José Torres, Bert Randolph Sugar 1971
Sugar Ray Leonard and Other Noble Warriors Simon and Schuster 1987
Only the Ring was Square Prentice-Hall 1981
Gerry Cooney: He Coulda Been a Contendah! New York Post 1987
McIlvanney on Boxing Stanley Paul 1982
Don Dunphy at Ringside Henry Holt Inc. 1988
The Fight Game (The World's Work (1913) Ltd) Frank Butler 1951
Still Fighting Old Wars (*Sports Illustrated*) Gary Smith 1988
Muhammad Ali's Entourage (*Sports Illustrated*) Gary Smith 1988
On the Waterfront Budd Shulberg 1956, W H Allen 1988
The Good, the Bad and the Ugly: The Story of Boxing Stanley Paul 1986
The Weary Champion and *I Swear Joe Louis was Licked* Mirror Group Newspapers Ltd
On Boxing Dolphin/Doubleday 1987
The Sweet Science Viking/Penguin Inc. 1956 (originally published in *The New Yorker*)
In This Corner Peter Heller, Simon and Schuster 1973
Benny: The Life and Times of a Fighting Legend Mainstream Publishing (Edinburgh) Ltd 1982
Leonard/Hagler; the Fight and its Aftermath Boxing Illustrated 1987
Iron Mike and the Allure of Boxing Time/Life Inc. 1988
Leave the Fighting to McGuigan – The Official Biography of Barry

McGuigan Viking/Penguin 1985
How Hagler Won the Fight The Observer 1987
Quinn's Book Hodder and Stoughton 1988
Fifty Grand from *Men Without Women* Jonathan Cape 1928, William Collins 1988
A Champ Like No Other Sports Illustrated 1988
An Appreciation of Cassius Clay Partisan Review
Greatest Crawford Reprinted (from Boxing Illustrated 1987) Jerry Izenberg